Latin America

E. Bradford Burns

A Concise Interpretive History

Latin America

a
concise
interpretive
history

Latin America

a

concise

interpretive

history

E. Bradford Burns

University of California at Los Angeles

WITHDRAWN

PRENTICE-HALL, INC., ENGLEWOOD CLIFFS, NEW JERSEY

ISBN: P 0–13–524298–3
       C 0–13–524306–8

Library of Congress Catalog Card Number: 71–170031

PRINTED IN THE UNITED STATES OF AMERICA

10 9 8 7 6 5 4 3

PRENTICE-HALL INTERNATIONAL, INC., *London*
PRENTICE-HALL OF AUSTRALIA, PTY. LTD., *Sydney*
PRENTICE-HALL OF CANADA, LTD., *Toronto*
PRENTICE-HALL OF JAPAN, INC., *Tokyo*
PRENTICE-HALL OF INDIA, PRIVATE LIMITED, *New Delhi*

I dedicate this book to my students of History 8,
Reform and Revolution in Latin America, at UCLA,
in order to thank them—at least partially—
for their patience, understanding,
cooperation, help, and good humor.

Contents

Preface   *xi*

Acknowledgments   *xv*

1. *The Origins of a Multiracial Society*   *1*

THE LAND   3
THE INDIAN   6
THE EUROPEAN   11
CONFRONTATION AND CONQUEST   14
THE AFRICAN   20

2. *The Institutions of Empire*   *25*

LAND AND LABOR   29
THE STATE   41
THE CHURCH   58

3. *Independence*   *65*

A CHANGING MENTALITY
BEGETS NEW ATTITUDES AND ACTION   67

THE SLAVES
DECLARE HAITI'S INDEPENDENCE   77

AN UNSUCCESSFUL
POPULAR REVOLUTION IN MEXICO   78

ELITIST REVOLTS   80

4. *National Consolidation*   *85*

THE TRANSFER
AND LEGITIMIZATION OF POWER   89

THE TENSE SOCIETIES   97

ECONOMIC STAGNATION   107

5. *The Emergence of the Modern State*   *117*

POLITICAL STABILITY   120

MODERNIZATION   125

ECONOMIC PROSPERITY   131

THE SOCIAL MILIEU   136

CONTINUITY AND CHANGE   141

THE PRESENCE OF THE UNITED STATES   143

6. *The Past Repudiated*   *149*

THE MIDDLE SECTORS IN POLITICS   152

MEXICO'S VIOLENT RESPONSE TO THE PAST   159

NATIONALISM AS A FORCE FOR CHANGE   168

CHANGING RACIAL ATTITUDES   175

7. *Development, Democracy, and Disillusionment*   *185*

THE ROCKY ROAD TO DEVELOPMENT   188

A FLIRTATION WITH DEMOCRACY   207

THE REVOLUTIONARY OPTION   214

DISILLUSIONMENT   229

Statistical Tables   *237*

Glossary   *245*

A Guide to the Paperback Literature in English   *251*

Index   *261*

List of Maps

LATIN AMERICA:
THE OUTSTANDING GEOGRAPHIC FEATURES   4

THE VICEROYALITIES IN LATIN AMERICA
AT THE END OF THE EIGHTEENTH CENTURY   28

A POLITICAL MAP
OF CONTEMPORARY LATIN AMERICA   88

Preface

Latin America is a huge region in the process of change from a traditional to a more modern society. At some times and in some places the pace of that change has been nearly imperceptible. Yet, at other times and in other places the change has taken place at a dizzying speed. Though change has been erratic, sometimes ineffectual, often spotty, and occasionally reversed, it is nonetheless the most salient characteristic of Latin America in the twentieth century.

Certainly by the standards of the United States and Western Europe, Latin America is underdeveloped. The majority of the Latin Americans are undernourished, underemployed, undereducated, and underpaid. Paradoxically they live in poverty in a region which holds great promise of wealth. Becoming more fully aware of that promise, they want to take advantage of it, to tap their own resources for their own improvement and enrichment. In short, they yearn to raise their standards of living. Seemingly one of the major obstructions in their pursuit of improvement is a complex of institutions, patterns, and attitudes fastened on Latin America during the decades in which the Iberians were discovering, conquering, and settling the vast area in the sixteenth century. Many of those institutions, patterns, and attitudes contained vestiges from the Middle Ages, a period already well on the wane in the Iberian peninsula.

But in the New World those seeds from the past took root and flourished. Europe also transferred some aspects of its developing capitalism—commercial agriculture and mercantilism, for example—to the New World setting. The huge estate, monoculture, rigid class structures, and other such inheritances from the sixteenth century have long since proved their resiliency and revealed their injustices and iniquities—and not least of all their inefficiency—but still they continue to exist, today often hidden beneath a deceiving veneer of modernity. Those dominating characteristics from the past are precisely what a growing majority of Latin Americans want to alter. To fully modernize, to bring the Latin American nations into the twentieth century, it is necessary to substitute newer institutions for those discredited inheritances of the colonial past. To build a new society in which the Latin Americans are masters of their own destiny, most of the peoples of Latin America now seek to dismantle those neofeudalistic institutions in order to replace them with others more compatible with the goals of modernization and progress. Certainly the prospect of social revolution constitutes one of the major and most conspicuous aspects of change. Greater numbers of people from an ever more complex society seek to express their opinions. They want at least some voice in the exercise of power. They also want to insure that there is sufficient mobility for them to improve their positions.

This desire for change engenders tension, stress, ferment, and violence in twentieth-century Latin America. The unrest promises to persist until the change from archaic to modern institutions is made, until Latin America is wrested from the past and propelled into the twentieth century.

The struggle for change, then, is the leitmotiv of contemporary Latin America. No one can hope to understand the complexity of Latin America without appreciating this powerful drive for change. Dr. C. P. Snow, the well-known British scientist and novelist, emphasized the importance of the force for change in the twentieth century in his *The Two Cultures and the Scientific Revolution*. After pointing out that the gap between the industrialized and the nonindustrialized nations widens daily, he warned, "This disparity between the rich and the poor has been noticed, most acutely and not unnaturally, by the poor. Just because they have noticed it, it won't last for long. Whatever else in the world we know survives to the year 2,000 that won't. Once the trick of getting rich is known, as it now is, the world can't survive half rich and half poor." One wonders then for how long will the Latin America we know today survive, since less than 10 percent of the population control most of the wealth, while the other 90 percent of the population eke out a miserable existence.

Starting with the Mexican Revolution of 1910, the Latin Americans began to try to bridge that yawning gap between the wealthy few and the impoverished many and in the process to reduce the control foreigners customarily have exercised over their national economies. With each decade, the struggle intensified. Those few who benefited from the neocolonial system resisted change; those who felt they might benefit by restructuring institutions waved the banner of change. The titanic struggle between the changeless and the changing has made, is making, and will continue to make Latin America the scene of considerable violence in the twentieth century.

Preoccupation with the problems and goals of the United States has clouded our vision of Latin America's struggle for justice and development. Tending to interpret Latin America's struggles and problems from our own quite different experiences and perspective, we have misread the meaning of events in Latin America to such an extent that we have made it nearly impossible to understand fully either what is occurring there or its long-range significance for ourselves, our country, and our future. This has become so true that we have unjustly cast Latin America's struggle for change and development into the context of our own Cold War conflicts with the USSR without perceiving that Latin America's struggle is much less a duel between the ideologies of capitalism and communism than it is a conflict between reformers and counterreformers. Confusing a struggle for change as a conflict between communism and capitalism, a dangerous misreading of events, the United States government has committed a series of unfortunate errors which have alienated many of the important forces favoring genuine reform in Latin America. The United States, which considers itself a paragon of democratic government, has actively and generously supported every type of repressive dictatorship in this hemisphere. Apparently the only criterion for United States support is a firm denunciation of communism. Consequently Washington has embraced Rafael Trujillo, Anastasio Somoza, Alfredo Stroessner, to name but three of the most blatantly repressive military dictatorships of recent decades, all governments which have tended to preserve, indeed to strengthen, those iniquitous institutions from the past which hobble Latin America's progress. To the disappointment of many, the United States has not become the champion of the change and reform a majority of Latin Americans want. Eduardo Frei, elected president of Chile on the Christian Democratic Party platform, pointedly informed the United States government in 1964:

It seems to me that you North Americans have not tried to understand why communism progresses in underdeveloped countries. I have the impression that you believe that the communists gain ground because we do not have sufficient repressive laws and apparatus. That is not true. The communists become stronger in poor countries because they frequently are the only ones who speak out in favor of a radical change of the archaic structure.

Then President Frei went on to warn, "The biggest threat, as I see it, is that Latin America will try to stop communism by stopping reform and progress, and there is nothing better prepared to open the door to communism than such action. We need to champion and lead reform. Then we have nothing to fear." A paranoid obsession with communism rather than a firm commitment to support the reforms necessary to eradicate or lessen the miserable conditions upon which radical extremism can so easily feed has characterized United States policies and attitudes toward Latin America. Instead of serving as the democratic mentor of the hemisphere, the United States has become the dreaded policeman, a repressive agent, a force willy-nilly associated with the preservation of the past.

The communists have no monopoly over the desire for change and reform in Latin America. They simply have been astute enough to understand its broad appeal. Wisely they have identified themselves with it and with those national elements favoring the use of reform, local resources, and technical advances to raise the standard of living and to increase the wealth of the community. For the United States to divorce itself from those elements in Latin American society which advocate change is to run the distinct risk of alienating ourselves from future popular governments. The intention of this concise history is to emphasize the growing desire for change in Latin America and the reasons for it in the hope of persuading the educated public that that desire merits our support and encouragement.

Acknowledgments

My interests in Latin American history range widely; teaching the introductory course in that subject for the past decade at four universities and to students varying from freshmen to graduates permitted me to indulge those broad interests. This concise, interpretive history reflects those interests as well as my approach to the challenging study of the many and diverse nations with which we share this hemisphere. My reading, research, and travels provided the background information for this book, while the questions and enthusiasm of my students certainly helped to shape its presentation. My own ideas concerning Latin American history have changed considerably over the past decade. I suppose—indeed, I hope—they will continue to do so. This book mirrors my present views and interpretations. I owe a debt of gratitude to many people, here, on the Iberian Peninsula, and in Latin America, who generously shared with me their insights and knowledge. I especially want to single out Dauril Alden, Thomas M. Bader, Henry Bruman, and Collin MacLachlan, who read the manuscript and offered wise suggestions for its improvement. However, I bear the responsibility for the content, the interpretations, and any errors.

E. BRADFORD BURNS

Hollywood Hills
January 1, 1972

one

The Origins

of a

Multiracial Society

The Mayan Temple of Kukulcan at Chichen Itzá, Yucatán, Mexico

The New World provided a vast and varied stage upon which met men of three diverse and distant continents: Asia, Europe, and Africa. Representative of the three races, they arrived at different times and for different reasons. They mixed, mingled, and miscegenated. Together they contributed the ingredients which confected the unique Latin American civilization.

THE LAND

Contemporary Latin America, a huge region of a continent and a half, stretching 7,000 miles southward from the Rio Grande to Cape Horn, varies widely in its geographic and human composition. Geopolitically the region encompasses 18 Spanish-speaking republics, French-speaking Haiti, and Portuguese-speaking Brazil, a total of approximately 8 million square miles and a rapidly growing population exceeding 270 million. That population increases at the rate of nearly 3 percent a year. Still, Latin America is relatively underpopulated, although at least the two smallest states, Haiti and El Salvador, do suffer the effects of an over-

3

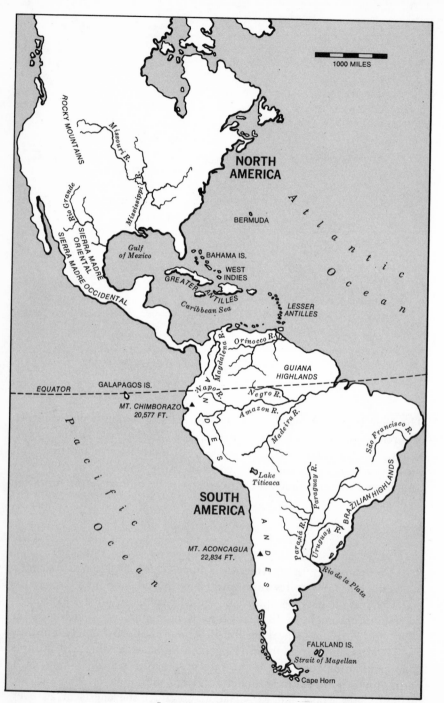

ROCKY MOUNTAINS

Missouri R.

NORTH AMERICA

Rio Grande

SIERRA MADRE ORIENTAL

SIERRA MADRE OCCIDENTAL

Mississippi

BERMUDA

Gulf of Mexico

BAHAMA IS.

WEST INDIES

GREATER ANTILLES

Caribbean Sea

LESSER ANTILLES

A t l a n t i c   O c e a n

Orinocco R.

Magdalena R.

GUIANA HIGHLANDS

EQUATOR

GALAPAGOS IS.

Napo R.

Negro R.

MT. CHIMBORAZO 20,577 FT.

Amazon R.

Madeira R.

A N D E S

São Francisco R.

Lake Titicaca

SOUTH AMERICA

BRAZILIAN HIGHLANDS

Paraguay R.

P a c i f i c   O c e a n

MT. ACONCAGUA 22,834 FT.

Paraná R.

Uruguay R.

A N D E S

Rio de la Plata

FALKLAND IS.

Strait of Magellan

Cape Horn

1000 MILES

Latin America: The Outstanding Geographical Features

crowded population. The area is roughly twice the size of Europe with one-third of Europe's population. It occupies 19 percent of the world's land but contains only 7 percent of the world's population.

Most of that area lies within the tropics. In fact, only one country, Uruguay, has no territory in the tropics. South America reaches its widest point, 3,200 miles, just a few degrees south of the equator, unlike North America which narrows rapidly as it approaches the equator. The concept of an enervating climate is a false one. The cold Pacific Ocean currents refresh much of the west coast of Latin America, and the altitudes of the mountains and highlands offer a wide range of temperatures which belie the latitude. For centuries, and certainly long before the Europeans arrived, many of the region's most advanced civilizations flourished in the mountain plateaus and valleys. Today many of Latin America's largest cities are in the mountains or on mountain plateaus: Mexico City, Guatemala City, Bogotá, Quito, La Paz, and São Paulo, to mention only a few. Much of Latin America's population, particularly in Middle America and along the west coast of South America, concentrates in the highland areas.

In Mexico and Central America, the highlands create a rugged backbone which runs through the center of most of the countries leaving coastal plains on either side. Part of that mountain system emerges in the Greater Antilles to shape the geography of the major Caribbean islands. In South America, to the contrary of Middle America, the mountains closely rim the Pacific coast, while the highlands skirt much of the Atlantic coast, making penetration into the flatter interior of the continent difficult. The Andes predominate. The world's longest continuous mountain barrier, it runs 4,000 miles down the west coast and fluctuates in width between 100 and 400 miles. Aconcagua, the highest mountain in the hemisphere, rises to a majestic 23,000 feet along the Chilean-Argentine frontier. The formidable Andes have been a severe obstacle to exploration and settlement of the South American interior from the West. Along the east coast, the older Guiana and Brazilian Highlands average 2,600 feet in altitude and rarely reach 9,000 feet. Running southward from the Caribbean and frequently fronting on the ocean, they disappear in the extreme south of Brazil. Like the Andes, they too have inhibited penetration of the interior. The largest cities on the Atlantic side are all on the coast or like São Paulo within a very short distance of the ocean. In contrast to the west coast, the east boasts of some extraordinary natural harbors of which Todos os Santos Bay and Guanabara Bay, on which are located respectively the cities of Salvador and Rio de Janeiro, are excellent examples.

Four major river networks, the Magdalena, Orinoco, Amazon, and La Plata, flow into the Caribbean or Atlantic, providing an access into the interior missing on the west coast. The Amazon ranks as one of the world's most impressive river systems. Aptly referred to in Portuguese as the "river-sea," it is the largest river in volume in the world. Its volume exceeds that of the Mississippi 14 times. In places it is impossible to see from shore to shore and over a good part of its course the river averages 100 feet in depth. Running eastward from its source 18,000 feet up in the Andes, it is joined from both the north and south by more than 200 tributaries. Together this imposing river and its tributaries provide 25,000 miles of navigable water. The magnitude of the river always has excited the imaginations of the men who traveled on it. William Lewis Herndon, who sailed down the river in the mid-nineteenth century, marveled, as many had before and would after: "The march of the great river in its silent grandeur was sublime, but in the untamed might of its turbid waters, as they cut away its bands and tore down the gigantic denizens of the forest it was awful. I was reminded of our Mississippi at its topmost flood."

Farther to the south, the Plata network flows through some of the world's richest soil, the Pampas, a vast flat area shared by Argentina, Uruguay, and Brazil. The river system includes the Uruguay, Paraguay, and Paraná Rivers but it gets its name from the Río de la Plata, a 180-mile-long estuary separating Uruguay and the Argentine province of Buenos Aires. The system drains a basin of over 1.5 million square miles. Shallow in depth, it still provides a vital communication and transportation link between the Atlantic coast and the southern interior of the continent.

No single country better illustrates the kaleidoscopic variety of Latin American geography than Chile, that long, lean land clinging to the Pacific shore for 2,600 miles. One of the world's bleakest and most forbidding deserts in the North gives way to rugged mountains with forests and alpine pastures. The Central Valley combines a Mediterranean climate with fertile plains, the heartland of Chile's agriculture and population. Moving southward, the traveler encounters dense mixed forests, heavy rainfall, and a cold climate, a warning of the glaciers and rugged coasts which lie beyond. Snow remains permanent in most of Tierra del Fuego.

THE INDIAN

The continents of Asia, Europe, and Africa contributed to the peopling of the Western Hemisphere, and, as one result, a greater racial mixing has resulted than in any other part of the world. From Asia came the first migrants in various waves between 20,000 and 40,000 years ago. Anthropologists generally believe that they crossed from one continent to the other at the Bering Strait in pursuit of game animals. They slowly moved southward and dispersed throughout North and South America. Over the millennia, at an uneven rate, some advanced through hunting and fishing cultures to take up agriculture. At the same time they fragmented into myriad linguistic (estimates range up to 2,200 different languages) and cultural groups, although they maintained certain general physical features in common: straight black hair, dark eyes, a copper-colored skin, and a short stature.

Varied as the early American cultures were, a majority of them shared enough traits in common to permit a few generalizations. The family or clan units served as the basic social organization. All displayed a profound faith in supernatural forces which they believed shaped, influenced, and guided their lives. For that reason, the *shamans*, men intimate with the supernatural, played important roles in the indigenous societies. They provided the contact between the mortal and the immortal, between man and the spirit. In most rituals and celebrations, the participants danced, sang, beat a drum, shook a rattle, and possibly played a flute. Common to the oral literature of most of the groups were stories of the cultural hero, the ancestor who taught the early members of the tribe their way of life, and the prankster whose exploits aroused both mirth and admiration. None of the early Americans possessed a sense of private ownership of land. Like the air he breathed, the land he used belonged to all. He revered the earth as sacred, not to be destroyed or mutilated but to be preserved for the use of future generations. Many artifacts, instruments, and implements were similar from Alaska to Cape Horn. For example, spears, bows and arrows, and clubs were the common weapons of warfare or for the hunt. Although these similarities are significant, the differences between the many cultures were enormous and impressive. By the end of the fifteenth century, there were between 15 million and 100 million inhabitants of the Western Hemisphere. Scholars still heatedly debate the figures, and one can find forceful arguments favoring each extreme.

Mistaking the New World for Asia in 1492, Christopher Columbus called the inhabitants he met "Indians," a name which has remained to cause endless confusion. Exploration later indicated that the "Indians" of the New World belonged to a large number of cultural groups of which the most important were the Aztecs and Mayas of Mexico and Central America, the Carib of the Caribbean area, the Chibcha of Colombia, the Inca of Ecuador, Peru, and Bolivia, the Araucanian of Chile, the Guarani of Paraguay, and the Tupí of Brazil. Of those, the Aztec, Maya, and Inca exemplify the most complex cultural achievements.

Two distinct periods, the Classic and the Late, mark the history of the Mayas. During the Classic period, from the fourth to the tenth centuries A.D., the Mayas lived in Guatemala, and then they suddenly migrated to Yucatan, beginning the Late period in their civilization which lasted until the Spanish conquest. The exodus baffles anthropologists who most often suggest that the exhaustion of the soil in Guatemala limited the corn harvests and forced the Mayas to move in order to survive. Corn provided the basis for the Mayan civilization. All human activity, all religion centered on the planting, growing, and harvesting of corn. Efficient agricultural methods produced corn surpluses and hence the leisure for a large priestly class to dedicate its talents to religion and to scientific study. Extraordinary intellectual achievements resulted. The Mayas progressed from the pictograph to the ideograph and thus invented a type of writing, the only Indians in the hemisphere to do so. Sophisticated in mathematics, they discovered the zero and devised numeration by position. Astute observers of the heavens, they applied their mathematical skills to astronomy. Their careful studies of the heavens enabled them to predict eclipses, follow the path of the planet Venus, and prepare a calendar more accurate than the one used in Europe. As the ruins of Copán, Tikal, Palenque, Chichen Itzá, Mayapán, and Uxmal testify, the Mayas built magnificent temples. One of the most striking features of that architecture is the extremely elaborate carving and sculpture.

To the west of the Mayas, another native civilization, the Aztecs, was expanding and flourishing in the fifteenth century. The Aztecs had migrated from the north in the early thirteenth century into the central valley of Mexico where they encountered and conquered some prosperous and highly advanced city-states. In 1325, they founded Tenochtitlán, their beautiful capital, and from that religious and political capital they radiated outward to absorb other cultures until they controlled all of Central Mexico. The constant conquests gave prominence to the warriors and not surprisingly among the multiple divinities Huitzilopochtli, the god of war and the sun, predominated. To propitiate him, as well as other gods, required human sacrifices, increasingly on a grander scale. The Aztecs devised an elaborate and effective system of government, the pictograph, an accurate calendar, and an impressive architecture.

Largest, oldest, and best organized of the Indian civilizations was the Incan which flowered in the harsh environment of the Andes. By conquest, the empire extended in all directions from Cuzco, regarded as the center of the universe. It stretched nearly 3,000 miles from Ecuador into Chile and its maximum width measured 400 miles. Few empires have been more rigidly regimented or more highly centralized, a real miracle when one realizes that it was run without the benefit—or hindrance—of written accounts or records. The only accounting system was the *quipu*, cords upon which knots were made to indicate specific mathematical units, although some scholars now claim the Incas wove some sort of code into the threads. The highly effective government rapidly assimilated newly conquered peoples into the empire. Entire populations were moved around the empire when security suggested that such relocations would be wise. Every subject was required to speak Quechua, the language of the court. In weaving, pottery, medicine, and agriculture, the achievements of the Incans were magnificent. They particularly excelled in agriculture. Challenged by a stingy soil, they developed systems of drainage, terracing, and irrigation and learned the value of fertilizing their fields.

Many differences separated those three high Indian civilizations, but at the same time some impressive similarities existed. Society was highly structured. The hierarchy of nobles, priests, warriors, artisans, farmers, and slaves was inflexible, although occasionally some mobility, the exception rather than the rule, did occur. At the pinnacle of that hierarchy stood the omnipotent emperor encased in the greatest respect and veneration. The sixteenth-century chronicler Cieza de León, in his own charming style, illustrated the awe in which the people held the Inca: "Thus the kings were so feared that, when they traveled over the provinces, and permitted a piece of the cloth to be raised which hung round their litter, so as to allow their vassals to behold them, there was such an outcry that the birds fell from the upper air where they were flying, insomuch that they could be caught in men's hands. All men so feared the king, that they did not dare to speak evil of his shadow." Little or no distinction existed between civil and religious authority so that for all intents and purposes church and state were one. The Incan and Aztec emperors were both regarded as representatives of the sun on earth and thus as dieties, a position probably held by the rulers of the Mayan city-states as well.

Royal judges impartially administered the laws of the empires and apparently enjoyed a reputation for their fairness. The sixteenth-century chroniclers who saw the judicial systems functioning invariably praised them. Cieza de León, for one, noted, "It was felt to be certain that those who did evil would receive punishment without fail and that neither prayers nor bribes would avert it." These civilizations rested on a firm rural base. Cities were rare, although a few existed with populations exceeding 100,000. They were centers of commerce, government, and religion. Eyewitness accounts as well as the ruins which still remain leave no doubt that some of the cities were well organized and contained splendid examples of impressive architecture. The sixteenth-century chronicles reveal that some of the cities astonished the first Spaniards who saw them. Bernal Díaz del Castillo, who accompanied Hernán Cortés into Tenochtitlán in 1519, gasped, "And when we saw all those cities and villages built in the water, and other great towns on dry land, and that straight and level causeway leading to Mexico [City], we were astounded. These great towns and cues and buildings rising from the water, all made of stone, seemed like an enchanted vision from the tale of Amadis. Indeed, some of our soldiers asked whether it was not a dream!" But the vast majority of the population engaged in agriculture and were not urban dwellers. The productivity of the land made possible an opulent court life and complex religious ceremonies. The farmers cultivated corn, beans, squash, pumpkins, manioc root, potatoes, as well as other crops. None of the Indian societies recognized individual ownership of land. Communal lands, the famed *ejido* of Mexico and the *ayllu* of Peru, were worked for the benefit of the state, religion, and community. The state thoroughly organized and directed the rural labor force. Advanced as those Indian civilizations were, however, not one learned the use of iron or discovered the wheel.

The spectacular achievements of these advanced farming cultures contrast sharply with the more elementary evolution of the hunting, gathering, and fishing cultures and the intermediate farming cultures among the Latin American Indians. The Tupí tribes, the single most important native element contributing to the early formation of Brazil, illustrate the status of the intermediate farming cultures.

The Tupí tribes tended to be very loosely organized. The small and temporary villages, often surrounded by a crude wooden stockade, were, when possible, located along a river bank. The Indians lived communally in large thatched huts in which they strung their hammocks in extended family or lineage groups of as many as 100 persons. Most of the tribes had at least a nominal chief, although some seemed to recognize a leader only in time of war and a few seemed to have no concept of a leader. More often than not, the *shaman* or medicine man was the most important and powerful tribal figure. He communed with the spirits, proffered advice, and prescribed medicines. The elementary religions abounded with good and evil spirits.

The men spent considerable time preparing for and participating in tribal wars. They hunted monkeys, tapirs, armadillos, and birds. They also fished, trapping the fish with funnel-shaped baskets, poisoning the water and collecting the fish, or shooting the fish with arrows. They cleared away the forest to plant crops. Nearly every year during the dry season, the men cut down trees, bushes, and vines, waited until they had dried, and then burned them, a method used throughout Latin America, then as well as now. The burning destroyed the thin humus and the soil was quickly exhausted. Hence, it was necessary constantly to clear new land and eventually the village moved in order to be near virgin soil. In general, although not exclusively, the women took charge of planting and harvesting crops and of collecting and preparing the food. Manioc was the principal cultivated crop. Maize, beans, yams, peppers, squash, sweet potatoes, tobacco, pineapples, and occasionally cotton were the other cultivated crops. Forest fruits were collected.

To the first Europeans who observed them, those Indians seemed to live an idyllic life. The tropics required little or no clothing. Generally nude, the Tupí developed the art of body ornamentation and painted elaborate and ornate geometric designs on themselves. Into their noses, lips, and ears, they inserted stone and wooden artifacts. Feathers from the colorful forest birds provided an additional decorative touch. Their gay nude appearance prompted the Europeans to think of them as innocent children of nature. The first chronicler of Brazil, Pero Vaz de Caminha, marveled to the king of Portugal, "Sire, the innocence of Adam himself was not greater than these people's." In the beginning, the Europeans overlooked the grim affinity of the Indians for fighting and cannibalism to emphasize their inclinations to dance and sing. More extensive contact with the Indians caused later chroniclers to tell quite a different tale in which the Indians emerged as wicked villains, brutes who desperately needed the civilizing hand of Europe.

The Tupí, like many similar or simpler cultures, never achieved more than a rudimentary civilization, in no way comparable to the remarkable civilizations of their contemporaries, the Aztecs, Mayas, or the Incas. They possessed no well-established tribal organization; their agriculture was primitive; they did not know how to use stone to build; they lacked any animal for transportation; they had no written means of communication. On the other hand, they had adapted well to their tropical environment, and they had much to teach the European invaders in the utilization of the land, its rivers, and their products.

THE EUROPEAN

As the sixteenth century approached the European invader was not far off. Europe, on the eve of a commercial revolution, searched for new trade and new lands. Merchants dreamed of breaking the Arab and Italian monopolies of trade with Asia, thereby sharing the lucrative profits from spices, precious stones, pearls, dyes, silks, tapestries, porcelains, and rugs coveted by wealthy Europeans. Portugal led the quest for those new trade routes.

Like the neighboring kingdoms in Spain, Portugal had been the crossroads of many peoples—Iberians, Celts, Phoenicians, Greeks, Carthaginians, Romans, Visigoths, and Moslems—and had blended together their cultures. The last of the many invaders of the peninsula, the Moslems, had begun their conquest of Iberia in 711. The Christians initiated their crusade to reconquer the peninsula in 732 at the Battle of Tours and intermittently continued it until Granada fell in 1492.

Portugal, to assert its independence, had to free itself both of Moslem control and Castilian claims. In 1139, Afonso Henriques of the House of Burgundy used for the first time the title "King of Portugal," a title officially recognized in 1179 by the Pope, then arbiter of such matters. The new state struggled to expel the Moslems and finally succeeded in driving their remaining armies from the Algarve, the far south, in 1250. Neighboring Castile, deeply involved in its own campaign against the Moors reluctantly recognized the existence of Portugal. The task of consolidating the new state fell to King Denis, whose long reign, 1279–1325, marked the emergence of Europe's first modern national state.

Portugal became for a time Europe's foremost sea power. Its location, perched on the westernmost tip of continental Europe, was well suited for that role. Most of the sparse population, less than a million in the fifteenth century, inhabited the coastal area. They faced the great, grey, open sea and nearby Africa. At peace at home and with no imminent foreign threats to prepare for, Portugal could turn its attention outward. In a society dominated by the Church, religious motives for expansion played at least a superficially important role. The Lusitanians hoped to defeat the enemies of their faith in Africa and to carry the word of God to that continent. They sought to circumvent Moorish domains in order to attack their enemy from the rear. They also wanted to make contact with a potential ally, the oft-mentioned Prester John, sovereign of a Christian kingdom somewhere in Africa. Thus it was in heretical Africa the Portuguese initiated their overseas expansion in 1415 with the conquest of strategic Ceuta, guardian of the opening to the Mediterranean. However, the commercial reasons for expansion were probably more compelling than the religious ones. Lisbon as the entrepôt of Asian merchandise created a vision of wealth which dazzled men of all classes.

The first to appreciate fully that the ocean was not a barrier but a vast highway of commerce was Prince Henry (1394–1460), known as "the Navigator" to English writers although he was a confirmed landlubber. That provident prince, significant as the symbol of Portuguese maritime expansion, surrounded himself with navigators, cosmographers, and scholars at his residence on Sagres Peninsula, the westernmost tip of Portugal. Listening to the expert advice of his day, he defined Portugal's policy of exploration: systematic voyages outward, each based on the intelligence collected from the former voyager and each traveling beyond its predecessor. The improvements in geographic, astronomical, and navigational knowledge which characterized a century of accelerating seaborne activity facilitated the task of the men of Sagres. In a moment of great maritime triumph, the Portuguese launched the caravel, a ship which could tack, and, thus, sail against the wind. As a direct consequence of those improvements and with the encouragement of Prince Henry, the Lusitanians sailed farther and farther out to sea and away from their base. They reached the Madeira Islands by 1418 or 1420, the Azores between 1427 and 1432, Cape Bojador by 1434, and at the time of the death of the prince were sailing the Gulf of Guinea, some 3,000 miles down the African coast. Then, three decades later, in 1488, Bartolomeu Dias rounded the Cape of Good Hope and pointed the way to a water route to India.

News from Christopher Columbus that he had reached India by sailing west in 1492 momentarily disturbed the Portuguese who were on the verge of reaching the Orient by circumnavigating Africa. Unlike Portugal, Spain had earned little reputation for maritime prowess. In the last quarter of the fifteenth century, some Spanish expeditions plied the African coast, one of which laid Spanish claims to the Canary Islands. Most Spanish energy, however, had been expended internally on the struggle against the Moors and on the effort of unification. The marriage of Isabel of Castile to Ferdinand of Aragon in 1469 forged the major link in Spanish unity. Thereafter, first the external and then the internal policies of Castile and Aragon harmonized. Those two monarchs increased the power of the crown by humbling both the nobility and the municipal governments. They equated religious with political unification and expelled those Jews and Moors who refused to embrace the Roman Catholic faith. The infamous inquisition sternly enforced religious conformity. When Isabel died in 1504, Ferdinand ruled as king of Aragon and regent of Castile.

At the same time as the two monarchs were unifying Spain, they accelerated the struggle to expel the Moors. In 1492, Granada, the last Moorish domain on the Iberian Peninsula, fell. Providentially, in that same year, Columbus opened a new horizon for the Spaniards. The energy, talent, and drive which previously had gone into the reconquest, that holy and political campaign allying cross and sword for eight centuries, were invested immediately in overseas expansion. The Spaniards carried with them many of the ideas—religious intolerance and fervor, suspicion of foreigners, more prestige for the soldier than the farmer— as well as many of the institutions—viceroyalty, captaincy-general, the posts of *visitador* and *adelantado*—developed during the long reconquest.

The return of Columbus from his first voyage intensified rivalry between Spain and Portugal, both of which sought to guard their own sea lanes and prohibit the incursion of the other. War threatened until diplomacy triumphed. At Tordesillas in 1494, representatives of the two monarchs agreed to divide the world. An imaginary line running pole to pole 370 leagues west of the Cape Verde Islands gave Portugal everything discovered for 180 degrees east and Spain everything for 180 degrees west. With the exception of an interest in the Philippines, Spain concentrated its attention on the Western Hemisphere. Within the half of the world reserved for Portugal, Vasco da Gama discovered the long-sought water route to India. His protracted voyage in 1497–99 joined East and West by sea for the first time. Subsequent voyages by Columbus in 1493–96, 1498–1500, and 1502–4, suggested the extent of the lands he had discovered but proved that in fact he had not reached India. Portugal, at least for the moment, monopolized the only sea lanes to India, and that monopoly promised to enrich the realm. The cargo Vasco de Gama brought back to Lisbon repaid 60 times over the original cost of the expedition. For the time being, the Portuguese maritime routes were proving to be far more lucrative than those of the Spaniards. The kings of Portugal became rich merchants and the Portuguese turned to the sea as never before. Pedro Alvares Cabral received command of the fleet being prepared to follow up the exploit of da Gama. While sailing to India in 1500, the fleet veered off course and Cabral discovered and claimed Brazil, which later was found to fall within the half of the world the Tordesillas treaty allocated to Portugal. Along the coasts of South America, Africa, and Asia, the Portuguese eagerly established their commercial—not colonial—empire. The Chief Cosmographer of the Realm boasted, "The Portuguese discovered new islands, new lands, new seas, new people; and what is more, new sky and new stars." It was a glorious age for Portugal, and one of the great epic poets of all times, Luís de Camões, composed *The Lusiads* to commemorate the achievements.

The discovery of the Americas was an accident, the unforeseen by-product of an Iberian search for new maritime routes and desire for direct trade with the East. At first, the discovery did not seem particularly rewarding. The Western Hemisphere loomed up as an undesirable barrier to a direct water route to Asia. Furthermore, the native inhabitants displayed scant interest in trading with the Iberian merchants.

CONFRONTATION AND CONQUEST

The discoveries of Columbus and Cabral brought the Iberians face to face with the Indians of the New World. The confrontation puzzled each side and awoke a great deal of mutual curiosity. The Iberians referred back to Biblical and classical literature in an effort to explain to themselves who the Indians were; for their part, at least one group of Indians identified the Europeans with prophetic utterances that a bearded white man would emerge one day from the ocean.

Since commerce had motivated those oceanic explorations which resulted in the discoveries, the Iberians hoped to trade with the inhabitants they encountered. The peoples of the simple societies of the Caribbean and along the coast of eastern South America showed scant inclination for such commercial intercourse. In fact, they had little to offer the Iberians and required even less from them. The Portuguese soon found along the coast rich stands of brazilwood, a wood which gave the newly discovered land its name and furnished an excellent red dye much in demand by the new European textile industries. The crown established a monopoly over its exploitation and eagerly sold its rights to merchants. Fernão de Noronha was the first to buy the contract, and in 1503 he dispatched ships to fetch the dyewood. The ship captains bartered with the Indians, exchanging trinkets for the brazilwood they cut. A lucrative trade in the wood developed during the sixteenth century. In addition to its limited economic role, Brazil served strategically for many decades as the guardian of the western flank of the prized trade route to the Orient. So long as Portugal held a monopoly over that seaborne trade, Brazil received only minimal attention.

On the other hand, for three decades after Columbus's discovery, Spain searched the eastern coast of the New World for a westward passage, a route other European states began to seek as well. Columbus made three long voyages touching the largest Caribbean islands and coasting along the shores of Northern South America and Central America. In 1513, Juan Ponce de León reconnoitered the coast of Florida and that same year Vasco Núñez de Balboa marching across Panama came upon the Pacific Ocean which he promptly claimed for his monarch. The desire to get to that ocean by some water route intensified. In 1516, Juan Díaz de Solís discovered the mouth of the Río de la Plata, while in the following two years Francisco Hernández de Córdoba and Juan de Grijalva sailed along the coast of Yucatán.

At the same time the Spaniards began to settle some of the major Caribbean islands. On his second voyage Columbus transported men and supplies to establish the first such colony. On the northern coast of Hispaniola, he marked out a grid pattern for a town, set up a municipal government, divided up the land among the colonists, and assigned Indians to each settler to work their land. He thereby established a pattern of colonization faithfully imitated in the succeeding decades wherever the Spaniards went in the New World. Many of the new arrivals searched hopefully for gold, but the islands yielded little. Others turned to agriculture. The monarchs encouraged the migration of artisans and farmers to the New World. In his instructions to one governor departing for the Indies in 1513, the Spanish king ordered him to take "farmers so that they may attempt to plant the soil." Similar orders were repeated frequently. Sugar cane was planted as early as 1493. By 1520, it was a profitable industry with at least 28 sugar mills operating on Hispaniola. Domestic animals imported onto the islands multiplied rapidly. Ships returning to Spain carried sugar and hides. The monarch and merchants of Spain sought to encourage such trade. In 1503, Ferdinand sanctioned the establishment of the Casa de Contratación in Seville to oversee the commerce between Spain and the New World. Nonetheless, much of the agricultural production in Spanish America, at least during the first century and a half, went to feed the colonists and to provide supplies for conquest, expansion, and further settlement.

The Spanish pattern of exploration and settlement changed after 1521, a year marking the circumnavigation of the globe by Ferdinand Magellan and the conquest of central Mexico by Hernán Cortés. The long voyage begun by Magellan in 1519 but concluded by Juan Sebastián del Cano in 1521, after Magellan was killed by natives in the Philippine Islands, proved—at last—that it was indeed possible to reach Asia by sailing west. His expedition had found the way around the barrier of North and South America but it had proven also that the westward passage was longer and more difficult than the African route used by the Portuguese. At the same time Spain realized it did not need the route to India. Conquered Mexico revealed that the New World held far more wealth in the form of the coveted gold and silver than the Spaniards could hope to reap from trade with Asia. Spanish opinion changed from deprecating the New World as an obstacle to the East to considering it as a rich treasure chest. No longer considered simply a way station on the route to Asia, America became the center of Spanish attention.

History provides few epics of conquest more remarkable than Cortés's sweep through Mexico. His capture of the opulent Aztec empire initiated a period of conquest during which Spain defeated the major Indian nations and made their inhabitants subject to the Castilian monarch. Generally those conquests were private undertakings, the result of a contract, known as a *capitulación*, signed between the monarch and the aspiring conquistador who was given the title of *adelantado*. The adelantados invested their own money into their enterprises, and like any investor they expected a handsome return on their money. Diverse other motives propelled them as well. By subjugating new peoples to the crown, they hoped to win royal titles, preferments, and positions. By introducing heathens to Christianity they sought to assure God's favor now as well as guarantee for themselves a fitting place in the life hereafter. The adelantados by no means wandered around the Americas unchecked by the monarchs. Royal officials accompanied all the private expeditions to insure respect for the crown's interests and fulfillment of the capitulación.

The conquest of large empires by a relatively few Spaniards proved to be surprisingly easy. Gunpowder and the horse, both of which startled the Indians, were tremendous tactical advantages, at least initially. Furthermore, the Spaniards found the Indians divided among themselves. In Mexico, the tribes subjugated by the Aztecs were only too happy to join with the Spaniards to defeat their Indian enemies. In the Incan empire, rivalry between two claimants to the crown already had split the empire. The introduction of European diseases decimated the ranks of the Indians who lacked immunity to them. For those reasons, Spanish conquest spread rapidly after Cortés's victory. Central America fell to the Spaniards by 1525. Yucatán, after putting up a bitter resistance, surrendered to the invaders in 1545. Between 1513 and 1543, the Spaniards explored and claimed the territory in North America between the Carolinas and Oregon. In fact, two-thirds of the territory of the continental United States was at one time claimed by Spain. By the time George Washington was inaugurated as President, Spain had colonized a far greater area, ranging from San Francisco to Santa Fé to San Antonio to St. Augustine, than that encompassed by the original 13 states.

Spain's expansion into South America was equally prodigious. Once again the adelantados knew little or nothing of the lands they invaded. Yet they were ready to face anything, and they triumphed over everything. Inspired by the success of Cortés and excited by rumors of a wealthy kingdom along the west coast of South America, Francisco Pizarro sailed south from Panama to initiate Spanish conquest of that continent. Only on his third attempt, in 1531–32, did he succeed in penetrating the Incan heartland, but it was still not until 1535 that Pizarro completed his conquest of the Incan empire. The wealth he encountered surpassed that which Cortés had found in Mexico. From Peru, other expeditions fanned out into South America: Sebastián de Benalcázar seized Ecuador in 1533, Pedro de Valdivia conquered the central valley of Chile in 1540–41, and Gonzalo Pizarro crossed the Andes to explore the upper Amazon in 1539. From that expedition Francisco de Orellana and a small band of men floated down the Amazon, reaching the Atlantic Ocean in 1542.

Spanish attention in South America focused on Peru and most of the other explorations, conquests, and settlements of South America radiated from that center. Two exceptions were the Caribbean coast and the Plata region. Settlement of the northern coast began from the Caribbean. Charles V granted a large section of the Venezuelan coast to the Welsers of Augsburg in 1528 in return for financial aid, but that banking house failed to colonize it successfully and in 1546 the grant was rescinded. Several small settlements were made along the Colombian coast, and in 1536 Gonzalo Jiménez de Quesada set out to conquer the Chibcha Indians in the mountainous interior and he brought that highly civilized Indian kingdom within the Spanish pale of empire. The Río de la Plata attracted some interest first as a possible westward passage to the Orient and later as a possible route to the mines of Peru. Pedro de Mendoza searched in 1535–36 to open such a route and the early settlements in the Platine basin date from his efforts.

Spanish dominion of the New World expanded with amazing rapidity. Within half a century after Columbus' discovery, Spanish adelantados had explored and conquered or claimed the territory from approximately 40 degrees north—Oregon, Colorado, and the Carolinas—to 40 degrees south—mid-Chile and Argentina—with the exception of the Brazilian coast. Spanish settlers had colonized in scattered nuclei an impressive share of that territory. Reflecting the Spanish preference for urban living, those settlers already had founded many of Latin America's major cities: Havana, 1519; Mexico City, 1521; Quito, 1534; Lima, 1535; Buenos Aires, 1536 (refounded in 1580); Asunción, 1537; Bogotá, 1538; and Santiago, 1541. The Spaniards built Mexico City and Bogotá where Indian cities had long existed, not an uncommon practice. The rich silver and gold mines of Mexico and Peru stimulated the economy, but the economy enjoyed a sounder base than that. Gold and silver were preferred exports; agriculture provided the basis for exploration and expansion. Wherever the Spaniards settled they introduced domesticated animals and new crops. Stock raising turned once unproductive lands into profitable grazing areas, and the introduction of the plow made it possible to exploit land unmanageable under the hoe culture of the Indians. The crown encouraged agriculture by sending seeds, plants, animals, tools, and technical experts to the New World.

Immediately visible was the European influence on the New World and its inhabitants. The Europeans transplanted their social, economic, and political institutions across the ocean. They required the Indians to swear allegiance to a new king, worship a new God, speak a new language, and alter their work habits. In the process of exploiting the Indians, the Europeans also deculturated and disorganized them, forcing them into the role of European peasants. Their labor they were forced to give but their loyalty they held in reserve. The gulf between the master and the peasant has seldom been bridged in Latin America.

In the confrontation of the New and Old Worlds, the Americas also influenced the course of events in Europe. The abundance of gold and silver shipped from Mexico, Peru, and Brazil caused prices to rise in Europe and helped to finance industrialization. Introduced into Europe were new products: tobacco, rubber, cacao, and cotton (today's commercial cottons derive principally from those cultivated by the American Indians); new plants: potatoes and corn, two of the four most important food crops of the world; and drugs: quinine, coca used in cocaine and novocaine, curare used in anesthetics, datura used in pain relievers, and cascara used in laxatives. The Americas forced upon European scholars new geographic, botanical, and zoological information, much of which contradicted the classical writers. As one result, scholars questioned hoary concepts. Those contradictions came at about the same time Copernicus published his heliocentric theory (1543) and thus helped to usher in an age of modern science. The vast extension of empire in the New World strengthened the European monarchs, who derived wealth and thus independence from their overseas domains and generally exercised greater power overseas than at home. Such great empires required innovation and revision of governmental institutions. The struggles over boundaries in the New World agitated the European courts and more than once threw European diplomacy into a crisis. Art, music, and literature sooner or later expressed Indian themes. It has been estimated that nearly 50,000 Indian words were incorporated into Spanish, Portuguese, English, and French. The New World was not simply the passive recipient of European civilization; rather it modified and changed Europe's civilization and contributed to the development of the Old World.

To adapt to their new environment, the European settlers depended heavily on the Indians and were not reticent to learn from the conquered. Initially, only Iberian males arrived. The female was noticeably rare during the first half-century of conquest. Her scarcity conferred a sexual license on the virile conquerors, who promptly took up with Indian women. As a result there appeared almost at once a "new race," the mestizo, a blend of European and Indian well adapted physically and psychologically to the land. Borrowing the essential from the diverse cultures of both parents, the mestizos accelerated the amalgamation of two cultures. However, the Indians provided more than sexual gratification. They showed the Europeans the best methods to hunt and fish, the value of the drugs the forests offered, the quickest way to clear the lands, and how to cultivate the crops of the New World. When necessary, the Europeans adopted the light boats skillfully navigated by the Indians on the inland waters and copied the methods used by the Indians to build simple, serviceable structures. As a concession to the tropics, the Europeans adopted the Indian hammock—as did the navies of the world. One early arrival to Brazil noted his delight with the hammock in these words: "Would you believe that a man could sleep suspended in a net in the air like a bunch of hanging grapes? Here this is the common thing. I slept on a mattress but my doctor advised me to sleep in a net. I tried it, and I will never again be able to sleep in a bed, so comfortable is the rest one gets in the net." In truth, the Europeans depended heavily on the Indians during the early decades of settlement in order to accommodate to the novel conditions. Thomas Turner, an Englishman who lived in Brazil for two years at the end of the sixteenth century, summed up that dependence in his observation, "The Indian is a fish in the sea and a fox in the woods, and without them a Christian is neither for pleasure or profit fit for life or living."

The Indian at first was the principal source of labor. Reluctant to engage in manual work, the conquerors and the settlers who followed them persisted in coercing others to do it for them. The Europeans forced the natives to paddle their canoes; to guide them through the interior; to plant, tend, and harvest their sugar, wheat, tobacco, and cotton; to guard their cattle and sheep; to mine their gold and silver; and to wait upon them in their homes. In short, the Indians were the instruments by which wealth was created in the new colonies and as such were indispensable to the Europeans.

When the Indian proved inadequate or where his numbers were insufficient, particularly in the Caribbean and Brazil, the colonists began to look elsewhere for their labor supply. Soon their attention focused on Africa as the most likely source for labor. At that moment the black was introduced into the New World.

THE AFRICAN

Africa, the second largest continent, offers extremes of contrasts: mountains and savannas, deserts and jungles. Three impressive river networks, the Nile, Congo, and Zambesi, add to the variety. The relatively small population contributes further to the diversity. Divided into hundreds of tribes, their cultures range from the primitive through the sophisticated. The improving quality and greater quantity of studies of the African past reveal that many groups developed highly complex societies. The base of the social structure was the family. Many of the societies were rigidly hierarchical. Kings ruled the tribes, and in the larger and more complex societies did so through chiefs and subchiefs. The economy was agricultural but many artistic and mechanical skills were well developed: woodcarving, bronzework, basketry, gold smithing, weaving, and iron-working. One European visitor to the Gambia Coast marvelled, "The blacksmiths make all sorts of tools and instruments for tillage, etc. as also weapons and armour, being indifferent skillful at hardening of iron, and whetting it on common stones." Trade was carried on in organized markets. Indeed, commerce was well developed on local and regional levels and in some instances reached transcontinental proportions.

Repeated invasions by the Phoenicians, Greeks, Romans, and Arabs brought foreigners to Africa as early as 1100 B.C. The fall of Ceuta in 1415 heralded new European incursions. The commercial potential—

gold, ivory, cotton, and spices—attracted the Europeans who soon enough discovered that the black man himself was the continent's most valuable export. Between 1441 and 1443, the Portuguese began to transport the blacks to Europe for sale. It was only by such force that the blacks left their continent.

From the very beginning, some blacks from the Iberian peninsula participated in the explorations and conquests of the Americas. It is believed that the first African slaves reached the New World as early as 1502. Later, the slave trade, carried on with the sanction of the Iberian monarchs, brought large numbers of blacks directly from Africa to the New World. Probably the first shipments of slaves arrived in Cuba in 1512 and in Brazil in 1538, and they continued until Brazil abolished its slave trade in 1850 and Spain finally terminated the slave trade to Cuba in 1866. A majority of the three million slaves sold into Spanish America and five million into Brazil over a period of approximately three centuries came from the west coast of Africa between the Ivory Coast and South Africa. Blacks could be found in all parts of Latin America and formed a large part of the population. They quickly became and remained the major work force in the Caribbean and in Brazil. Their presence dominated the plantations which they worked and their influence spread quickly to the "big house" where the African women served as cooks, wet nurses, and companions of the lady of the house, while the black children romped with white children. African influence also permeated the cities where the blacks worked as domestic servants, peddlers, mechanics, and artisans. In the sixteenth century, blacks outnumbered whites in Lima, Mexico City, and Salvador da Bahia, the three principal cities of the Western Hemisphere.

Handicapped by the removal of all their possessions when taken into slavery, the Africans, uprooted and brutalized, still were able to contribute handsomely to the formation of a unique civilization in the New World. First and foremost was the black himself: his strength, his skill, and his intelligence. He utilized his former skills and his intelligence permitted him to master new ones quickly. In fact, he soon exercised—and in some cases perfected—all the trades and crafts of the Europeans. Visitors to the Caribbean and Brazil remarked on the diversity of skills mastered and practiced by the blacks. They were masons, carpenters, smithies, lithographers, sculptors, artists, locksmiths, cabinetmakers, jewelers, and cobblers. Around the plantations and in the cities, those black craftsmen, artisans, and mechanics became an indispensable ingredient in the New World society.

Herdsmen in Africa, the blacks mounted horses to become cowboys in the New World. They followed the cattle into the Brazilian hinterlands and helped to occupy the rich platine pampas. In these, as well as other ways, they participated in the conquest and settlement of the interior. In Brazil after the discovery of gold, the blacks were transported into Minas Gerais to mine the gold which created the Luso-Brazilian prosperity of the eighteenth century. In fact, they allegedly introduced the wooden pan into the gold-washing process to improve it. From the plantations and mines, they helped to transport the raw products of the land to the ports where other blacks loaded the wealth of Latin America onto ships which carried it to the markets of Europe. The blacks were even expected to defend the system which exploited them. In doing so, they sacrificed their blood to protect the Luso-Spanish empires at Havana, San Juan, Cartagena, Recife, Salvador, Rio de Janeiro, and elsewhere.

The blacks possessed a leadership talent which the slave system never fully tapped. It became evident when the runaway slaves organized their own communities, known variously as *palenques* or *cumbes* in Spanish America and *quilombos* in Brazil, or when slaves revolted against their masters. The extent of those slave rebellions is still unknown and awaits the careful investigation of future scholars. An authority on the blacks in Mexico points out that black slave revolts occurred there in 1537, 1546, 1570, 1608, 1609, 1611, 1612, and 1670. One viceroy informed his monarch that the blacks in New Spain sought "to buy their liberty with the lives of their masters." According to our present knowledge, most of the slave revolts in Brazil took place in the early nineteenth century. Between 1807 and 1835, there were nine revolts or attempted revolts. Brilliant black leadership directed the slaves to freedom in Haiti, a story considered later along with the other independence movements.

Mixing with both European and Indian, the Africans contributed their blood to the accelerating racial mixture of the New World. Mulattoes, the cross of white and black, sambos, the cross of Indian and black, and myriad other interracial types resulting from the combination of the mixed descendants of white, black, and Indian appeared immediately after the introduction of the African slaves. Illustrative of the extent of the mixture of white and black was the population of Salvador da Bahia at the end of the colonial period. In 1803, the city boasted of a population of approximately 100,000, of which 40,000 were black, 30,000 white, and another 30,000 mulatto. The Brazilian social historian Gilberto Freyre once remarked, "Every Brazilian, even the fairest blond, bears in his soul, if not in both his soul and body—for there are many in Brazil whose whiteness hides a tint of black dye—the shadow, or at least the imprint, of the Negro."

It would be difficult to think of any activity concerned with the formation and development of society in Latin America in which the blacks did not participate. Few institutions were more fundamental to or stronger in Latin American society than the Church, which proved not to be immune to African influences. The blacks helped to smooth away some of the asceticism of churchgoing by enlivening some of the religious festivals. They drew them out into the streets and enhanced them with folkplays, dances, and music. Much of the contribution was rooted in syncretism by which they sought to fuse their own beliefs with those of the Roman Catholic Church. They did, in fact, develop a syncretized religion, still very visible in Cuba, Haiti, and Brazil. Wherever the Africans went in the New World, they modified the culinary and dietary habits of those around them. Many of the rice and bean dishes so common in Latin America have African origins. Yams, okras, cola nuts, and palm oil are but a few of the contributions of the African cooks. They also employed new utensils in the kitchen, such as the wooden spoon and the mortar and pestle. The Africans introduced thousands of words into the Spanish and Portuguese languages and helped to soften the pronunciation of both. Their proverbs, riddles, tales, and myths mixed with those of Europeans and Indians to form the richly varied folklore of Latin America. The music, whether classical or popular, bears the imprint of African melodies. The blacks continued to sing the songs they remembered from their homelands and to accompany themselves they introduced a wide range of percussion instruments. With the music went dances. The samba, frevo, and merengue descend from African imports.

With the forced migration of the blacks to the New World, the racial tryptich—Mongoloid, Caucasian, and Negroid—was complete. Each contributed to the formation of a unique civilization representing a blend of the three. Overlaying that civilization were some powerful institutions imported unchanged from the Iberian Peninsula.

Monastery of San Francisco and Market, Quito, Ecuador

two

The

Institutions

of Empire

The American domains of the Iberian crowns furnished increasingly greater amounts of wealth. Brazil proved that a distant plantation economy could be lucrative. Sugar profits more than made up for high transportation costs. The rapid discovery of fabulous deposits of gold and silver in Spanish America was the exact reward the crown coveted. The potential and then realization of wealth conferred a new importance on the New World for the Iberians. To administer the lands and to promote their wealth, the crowns extended their governments across the Atlantic. The cross as well as the scepter swayed over western continents. The Church busied itself converting the heathen and in the process helped to implant Iberian civilization. From the imperial point of view, the Iberians succeeded brilliantly. They converted millions of Indians to Christianity and incorporated most of them within the two empires; they explored, conquered, and settled millions of square miles; they produced an incalculable wealth; they constructed architectural gems and founded flourishing cities; and what was truly impressive, they ruled an area many times the size of the motherlands for over three centuries.

The Viceroyalties in Latin America at the End of the Eighteenth Century

To understand the land and labor systems which developed in the New World, it is necessary to remember that the Iberians set out on their voyages of discovery primarily to increase their trade and hence their wealth and only secondarily to expand their empire or to Christianize the heathen. Consequently, the Americas, at first anyway, frustrated the Iberians. The Indians of the Caribbean and the Brazilian coast showed no inclination for or interest in transoceanic trade. The Portuguese contented themselves for three decades with brazilwood they found growing along the shore. The Spaniards did not even have that to stimulate commerce. With minimal trade and little readily visible wealth, the disappointed adelantados could only hope to extract what tribute they could from the bewildered Indians—golden trinkets, tobacco, corn, etc.—or to use the Indians to create some form of wealth.

Seeing their conquest of the New World as a kind of continuation of their reconquest of the Iberian peninsula, the Spaniards transferred intact many institutions which they had used during the peninsular crusade. One such institution was the *encomienda,* literally "the entrustment," which made its appearance in the Caribbean soon after discovery. Once used for the Moors, the adelantados and their lieutenants employed it in the Americas as a means to both Christianize and exploit the Indians. The institution required the Spanish *encomendero* to instruct the Indians entrusted to him in the Christian religion and the elements of European civilization and to defend and protect them. In return he could demand tribute and labor from the Indians.

The crown hesitated to approve the transfer of the encomienda to the Caribbean. After all, the monarchs had just unified Spain and were in the process of strengthening their powers in the peninsula. They were reluctant therefore to nourish in the New World a class of encomenderos who could impose their will between the monarchs and their new Indian subjects. It smacked too much of feudalism for royal tastes. In accordance with her desires to centralize authority in the crown, Isabel ordered in 1501 that the governor of the Indies free the Indians from the encomiendas. When that experiment resulted in the flight of all Indians from the plantations and their refusal to work for the Spaniards, the queen changed her mind. By royal *cédula,* or edict, in 1503 she in effect legalized and institutionalized the encomienda in the New World:

> As we are informed that because of the excessive liberty enjoyed by the Indians they avoid contact and community with the Spaniards to such an

extent that they will not even work for wages, but wander about idle, and cannot be had by the Christians to convert to the Holy Catholic faith . . . I order you, our Governor, that beginning from the day you receive my letter you will compel and force the Indians to associate with the Christians of the island and to work on their buildings, and to gather and mine the gold and other metals, and to till the fields and produce food for the Christian inhabitants and dwellers of the island.

That cédula, like those which preceded and followed it, expressed sincere concern over the welfare of the Indian subjects and admonished the Spaniards to treat them well, but it also sanctioned a labor system which would permit many abuses. The colonists also widely misapplied royal authorization to enslave Indians who made "unjust" wars on the Europeans. They so frequently explained their enslaved Indians to royal officials as captives in "just" war that the crown eventually had to forbid enslavement for any cause.

The encomienda system spread rapidly across the West Indies and contributed significantly to the mounting death rate of the natives. Not so much by its overwork and mistreatment as by concentrating the Indians, it facilitated the spread of European diseases, smallpox, typhus, measles, and influenza, which proved lethal to the indigenous populations who had built up no immunity to them. It is estimated that between 1519 and 1650 about six-sevenths of the Indian population of Middle America were wiped out. Other areas of the Americas suffered proportional decreases. The accelerating deaths, the abuses, and the enslavement enraged the churchmen, particularly the Dominicans, who forcefully reminded the king of his obligations.

The papal approval of Iberian territorial claims made it clear that the monarchs must Christianize, civilize, and protect the Indians, a responsibility the kings took very seriously. At great expense, the monarchs dispatched missionaries to preach to the heathens and to convert them. The lot of the early missionaries was extremely difficult. Not only did they have to master the Indian languages, win the Indians' confidence, and persuade them to embrace Catholicism, but they had to fight against the planters and miners who feared the interferences of the religious with their labor system. They had every cause for that fear. Alarmed by the declining numbers of their charges, the churchmen raised their voices in defense of their neophytes to protest the practices of the colonists and to prod the royal conscience. In their anger and concern, they took the Indians' case directly to the monarchs to whom they vividly reported the mistreatment and enslavement of their American subjects.

Those prods to the king's conscience coupled with his own political misgivings about the increasing power of the encomendero class prompted Ferdinand to take action to control the encomiendas. In 1512, he promulgated the Laws of Burgos, the first general code for the government and instruction of the Indians. Its purpose was to regulate Spanish-Indian relations and insure the fair, humane treatment of the Indians. By so doing, the crown would limit and supervise the power of the encomenderos over the Indians. The theory as pronounced in Madrid sounded fine—it amply demonstrated the noble intention of the king to protect his Indian subjects—but the royal officers in the Indies found it difficult if not impossible to translate theory into practice. They faced the protests, threats, and power of the angry encomenderos.

Cortés immediately and successfully transplanted the institution to Mexico where he liberally divided up the Indians among his followers. For himself, he alloted an encomienda of 100,000 Indians. The others were considerably smaller. Although royal officials in Santo Domingo approved his action, the crown by 1519 was reluctant to see the encomienda spread. In fact, in 1520, Charles V abolished the institution. By then, it was too firmly entrenched in the New World to be so summarily eradicated. The encomenderos refused to acknowledge the abolition, and the royal officials did not enforce the law. As is evident, the crown in Spain, and the royal officials in the New World did not always act in harmony.

The encomenderos were not reticent to press their case before the monarch. They dispatched their own representatives to Madrid who emphasized the barbarian nature of the Indians, their indolence and ignorance. Without force, they emphasized, the Indians simply would not work. Their labors here on earth, the argument ran, were but small compensation for the eternal salvation offered by the Roman Catholic faith to which the Europeans introduced them. Further, they pointed out, the civilizing hand of Europe taught the natives how to better care for and feed themselves. In the final analysis, those encomenderos regarded their charges as a just reward for their participation in conquest or for some service rendered the crown. They adamantly refused to do the menial labor themselves; the encomienda provided the means to get work done. Their powerful lobby at court persuaded Charles to modify his position.

Still, the king's mind would not rest; he realized that in the encomenderos he had a strong rival for power in the New World. The conquest of highly disciplined, sedentary Indian empires in the highlands of Middle and South America increased the strength of the encomenderos who controlled those Indians. The growing potential of a challenge from the encomendero class determined the monarch to take action. As in the past, the king's jealousy of his power in the New World coincided with religious concern over the welfare of the Indians.

Religious pressures had been mounting again. The strongest voice to be raised in defense of the Indians was that of Bartolomé de las Casas, a Dominican missionary and later bishop. Indignant, he returned to Spain from the Caribbean in 1515 to plead before Ferdinand the cause of the Indians. For the next half-century he pressed their case. Las Casas sternly reminded the monarch that the Pope had granted him territory in the New World solely for the purpose of converting the heathen. Thus, he argued, Spain had no right to use the natives for secular goals. He requested that all Spaniards except the missionaries be recalled. Foremost among those who opposed Las Casas was Juan Ginés de Sepúlveda who relied heavily on Aristotelian theory for his arguments. Because of the intellectual superiority of the Europeans, Sepúlveda reasoned, the Indians should be subjected to them in a kind of natural servitude which would permit the Indians to improve themselves by observing a better example of virtue, devotion, and industry. Las Casas won the debates. Pope Paul III indicated his support of the cause of Las Casas by a bull in 1537 declaring that the Indians were fully capable of receiving the faith of Christ, that is that they possessed souls, and should not be deprived of their liberty and property.

In response to both his fear and conscience, Charles promulgated the New Laws in 1542. They forbade the enslavement of the Indians, their compulsory personal service, the granting of new encomiendas, and the inheritance of encomiendas. More positively they declared the Indians to be free persons, vassals of the crown, and possessed of their own free will. The colonists protested vehemently. Rebellion threatened in Mexico, but in Peru encomenderos rose up to defy the law. Once again under extreme pressure, the monarch modified some of the laws and revoked others. Still, although the encomienda would continue for some time in parts of the sprawling American empire, the king had checked it. After the mid-sixteenth century the institution waned. The state exerted even greater control over the declining Indian population.

Replacing the encomienda as the major labor institution in Spanish America was the *repartimiento*, the temporary allotment of Indian workers for a given task. Significantly, under this institution royal authorities controlled and parceled out the Indians. The Spanish colonist in need of laborers applied to a royal official explaining both the work to be done and the time it would take and requesting a specific number of Indians to do it. In theory, the crown officials looked after the welfare of the Indians to insure that the payment was fair and the working conditions satisfactory; in practice, the abuses of the repartimiento system abounded. The planters and miners constantly badgered the royal officials to bend the system to better fit local needs. The institution flourished in the last half of the sixteenth century and in the first half of the seventeenth, and in fact some vestige of the institution probably has never died out in those areas where the Indian populations are still heaviest. A traveler to Guatemala in the mid-nineteenth century described the operation of the repartimiento in the northern province of Verapaz in words which could have been written three centuries earlier. In the twentieth century, the government of Jorge Ubico (1931–44) imposed a work law on the Guatemalan Indians all too reminiscent of the aims of the repartimiento.

In addition to furnishing an agricultural labor force, the repartimiento system also provided the major share of the workers for the mines in Spanish America. The State paid close attention to the labor situation in the mines, which furnished the single most important source of its income. While gold mines were few in number, silver mines proved to be relatively plentiful and rich. The major silver strike was made at Potosí in 1545. To work that fabulous lode, the Spaniards devised the burdensome *mita* of Potosí, a special type of repartimiento. All adult male Indians of the Peruvian Andes were subject to serve in the mita for one year out of every seven. Far from his home, the Indian miner worked under the most dangerous conditions and earned a wage which did not suffice for half of his own and his family's expenses. Members of the family had to work in order to make up the difference.

As in Spanish America, the landowners in Brazil relied in part, at least in the sixteenth century along the coast and for several more centuries in the interior and in the north, on the Indians as a source of labor. Some employed Indian labor from the *aldeias*, the villages. The crown and the religious orders working together did their best to concentrate the nomadic Indians into villages, first organized and administered by the orders but after 1757 administered by the crown. Protected within the village, the Indians were introduced to Christianity and European civilization. In return, they gave a portion of their labor to the Church and state. That part of the aldeia system resembled the encomienda. In addition, planters could apply to the aldeia administrators for paid Indian workers to perform a specific task for a specified period of time. In that respect, the aldeia system approximated the repartimiento. The aldeia system included only a small percentage of the Brazilian Indians. The rest the planters hunted to enslave, always explaining to questioning churchmen or crown officials that they had captured their Indian slaves in a "just" war.

After their arrival in 1549, the Jesuits spoke out to protect the Indians. In the sixteenth and seventeenth centuries, three notable Jesuits, Manuel da Nóbrega, José de Anchieta, and Antônio Vieira, who had influence both in Brazil and at court, vigorously defended the Indians. They reminded the Portuguese monarch of his obligations. On the other hand, the planters sent their own representatives to court to present their point of view. Domingos Jorge Velho tersely summarized the planters' point of view to the crown in 1694:

> And if we subsequently use them [the Indians] for our tillage and husbandry, we do them no injustice; for this is done as much to support them and their children as to support us and ours. This is so different from enslaving them that it is rather doing them a priceless service, since we teach them to till, to sow, to reap, and to work for their keep—something which they did not know how to do before the whites taught them.

The debate over the role and place of the Indian within the empire, much like the one already under way in Spain, raged for several centuries.

The monarchs sympathized with the Jesuits' case. As early as 1511, King Manuel I had ruled that no one was to harm his Indian subjects upon pain of the same punishment as if he had injured a European. In his instructions to the first governor-general of Brazil, John III called for tolerance, understanding, and forgiveness toward the Indians. Relations with them were to be above all else peaceful so they might more easily be Christianized. Finally, in 1605 and again in 1609, King Philip III declared that all Indians, whether Christian or heathen, were by nature free, could not be forced to work, and must be paid for their work when they volunteered it. Strong pressure from the planters, including riots in Brazil, induced him to modify his position in 1611 in order to permit once again the enslavement of Indians taken in "just" warfare, a concession much abused. Repeated attempts were made to regulate the relations between Europeans and the Indians. The conflicts between the Jesuits and planters over such regulations on occasion became violent. The high death rate among the Indians exposed to European demands and diseases, their retreat into the interior, their amalgamation into the new Brazilian society through miscegenation, and the increasing importation of Africans to supply the growing labor needs of the colony did more to solve the complex question of Indian-European relations than did all the altruistic but impractical or ignored legislation of the Portuguese kings.

Already by the mid-sixteenth century there were virtually no Indians left in the West Indies with the result that the importation of African slaves rose markedly and the work force in the Caribbean became almost totally black. In Brazil, too, the diminishing number of Indians caused the planters to seek even larger numbers of African slaves, who by the end of the sixteenth century furnished the most productive labor in Brazil. In the highland areas of Spanish America, the blacks never replaced the Indians.

The continued decline of the Indian population in the seventeenth century intensified the competition among the landowners for the diminishing supply and prompted them to devise a new method to ensure a more dependable labor system: they contracted the Indians as wage laborers. The crown approved the development as a progressive step, the creation of a large wage-earning class. To the monarch it seemed to verify that the Indians had been assimilated at last into the empire, that they had been in effect Europeanized. However, the system proved to be one more device of the landowners to exploit the labor of the Indians. Contract wage labor became debt peonage. It tied the Indians and their descendants, the peasants in the agricultural society of the New World, to the landowner by debt. The hacendados made deceptively friendly loans to the Indians, loans which were to be repaid with labor. The wages paid for such labor never sufficed to liquidate the debt. Fathers passed the debts on to sons and through that system, which lasts in much of Latin America today, the landowners assured themselves of a ready labor supply.

It is obvious that the search for a viable labor system in Latin America was long and convoluted. In the Caribbean and in Brazil the Indians were enslaved or held in encomiendas and aldeias. Their numbers declined rapidly. The Brazilian and Caribbean planters eventually solved their labor shortages by importing African slaves. In the highland regions of Spanish America, the effort to solve the labor problem evolved through three stages: encomienda, repartimiento, and debt peonage. The three systems often overlapped. In parts of the vast Spanish American empire they existed simultaneously. But the general trend was for a gradual progression through the three systems.

After an initial adjustment to the New World, the Iberians coveted the land as much as they did the Indians. Ownership of land became a basis for wealth and prestige. From the beginning the adelantados had distributed land among their followers as a reward for services rendered. The officers separately received large shares of land as well as grants of Indians. The common soldiers received appropriate quantities of land but usually were not granted any Indians. It will be recalled that on his second voyage Columbus parceled out both the land and Indians among the colonists he left behind.

In 1532, Martim Afonso, when he founded the first permanent settlement in Brazil at São Vicente, near the present-day Santos, distributed the land with a lavish hand to his followers. In his generosity he established a pattern of land distribution quite contrary to the prevailing custom in Portugal. Since 1375, the Portuguese kings had sparingly parceled out the *sesmarias*, the traditional land grants, so that no one person received more than he could effectively cultivate. Martim Afonso ignored such a precaution. As a consequence, the good coastal land was quickly divided into immense sugar plantations and not many more decades elapsed before the huge sesmarias in the interior for cattle ranches put much of the backlands under claims as well.

Over the generations many of the original grants of land grew to gigantic proportions. The more astute landowners bought out their neighbors or simply encroached upon other lands. The declining Indian population freed more and more land which the Iberians rapidly grabbed up as their awareness of its value increased. A series of legal devices confused the Indian and favored the Spaniard in acquiring land: the *congregación, denuncia*, and *composición*. The congregación concentrated the Indians in villages and thereby opened land for seizure; the denuncia required the Indians to show legal claim and title to their property—a legality for which their ancient laws had not prepared them—and failure to do so meant that the land could be seized; the composición was a means of claiming land through legal surveys, a concept once again for which the Indians had little preparation. By these, as well as other means, the Spanish landowners steadily pushed the remaining Indians, whom they had not incorporated into their estates as peons, up the mountainsides and onto arid soils, in short, into the marginal lands. Coupled with the many ways the Spaniards had of acquiring land were the entailment and primogeniture laws which protected the land and prohibited its division. The Spanish crown tolerated if it did not encourage the large landholdings in its American possessions.

On the other hand, the Portuguese monarchs, critical of the inefficiency of the large fazendas most of whose land lay fallow and hence unproductive, belatedly tried to reverse the course well underway in Brazil. Repeatedly, promulgated decrees—in 1695, single sesmarias were limited to four by one leagues in size; in 1697, they were reduced to three by one; in 1699, all land not under cultivation was to be expropriated, and so on throughout the eighteenth century—sought vainly to limit the size of the estates. One of the viceroys late in the eighteenth century, the Marquis of Lavradio, complained bitterly that those huge estates, poorly managed and often only partially cultivated, retarded the development of Brazil. He pointed to the unused fields held by their owners as symbols of prestige, while at the same time he noted that farmers petitioned him for land to till. Some of the regions had to import food they were perfectly capable of producing themselves. Nonetheless, the latifundia which originated at the birth of the colony remained as a dominant characteristic of Brazil as it did of Spanish America.

Some of the haciendas and fazendas achieved immense proportions. There were instances of haciendas in Mexico exceeding one million acres. In Brazil the unmeasurable ranch of Diaz d'Avila by all accounts surpassed most European states in size. Begun in the late sixteenth century in northern Bahia, it centered on the São Francisco River and extended endlessly into the interior. The huge estates were worlds in themselves.

The Luso-Brazilians quickly developed the prototype of the plantation economy, thanks to the ready and profitable market they found in Europe for sugar, a crop which grew exceedingly well along the coast from Maranhão to São Vicente. By 1550, Pernambuco, the richest and most important of the sixteenth-century captaincies, produced enough sugar in its 50 mills to load annually 40 or 50 ships for Europe. The Brazilian sugar plantations flourished during the last half of the sixteenth and first half of the seventeenth centuries, as the mills busily ground the cane into sugar. for the international market. The economic pattern of a single crop for international trade was early fastened onto Brazil. In Spanish America, for a long time the haciendas produced for local markets. One of their chief responsibilities was to feed the mining towns. Only as the eighteenth century neared did those haciendas enter into international trade on a scale comparable to that of the Brazilian plantations.

The type of life exemplified by the hacienda or fazenda often has been termed "feudal," a term which carries a strong emotional overtone connoting exploitation. Certainly the classical feudalism of medieval society did not appear in the New World. Weak though his power might have been in some of the remoter areas, the king never relinquished the prerogatives of sovereignty to the landlords. Royal law prevailed. Nor does the self-sufficient manorial system properly describe the large estates because for all their self-sufficiency they were closely tied by their one major cash crop to the capitalistic economy. Perhaps the patrimonialism defined by Max Weber comes closest to describing the system. Under patrimonialism, the landowner exerts authority over his followers as one aspect of his property ownership. Those who live on his land fall under his control. He could use armed force arbitrarily to enforce his authority within the bounds of his estate. With such authority, he administers his estate in a highly personal manner according to his own whims and without any set table of organization. Finally he controls all trade between his estate and the outside world. Patrimonialism seems best to describe the hacienda and fazenda systems as they developed in colonial Latin America.

The plantations, ranches, and mines provided a rich and varied source of income for the Iberian monarchs, capitalists, and merchants. Sugar, tobacco, cacao, indigo, woods, cotton, gold, silver, diamonds, and hides were some of the natural products the American colonies offered to the Old World. Agriculture was the principal source of wealth, while mining, more glamorous and prized perhaps, was only a secondary producer of wealth. Both Lisbon and Madrid relied heavily on the raw products of their American colonies for their foreign trade. For example, during many years the products of Brazil constituted approximately two-thirds of Portugal's export trade. Indeed, in the seventeenth century, the Iberian Peninsula depended on the New World for its prosperity.

An abundance of economic possibilities may well have been more a curse than a blessing since it permitted, indeed, encouraged, an economic dilettantism which handicapped orderly development. Despite a dazzling potential, the regional economies of colonial Latin America never diversified. They relied for their well-being on a single natural product whose sale abroad dictated the course of colonial prosperity. If a particular product sold well, an entire region prospered; if not, stagnation and misery engulfed that region. External demand dictated the colonial well-being, a dependence exaggerated by stubborn reliance on one export. The colonies had no control over their own economic destiny. Nor did the Iberians ever achieve much notable efficiency in the exploitation of those natural products with which a generous nature endowed them. More often than not, haphazard, old-fashioned, and inefficient methods characterized their exploitation. The case of sugar is an excellent example. The Portuguese held almost a monopoly on the production of that lucrative export for well over a century. Between 1650 and 1715, the Dutch, English, and French increased production of sugar in the Caribbean, employing efficient organization, new equipment, their extensive financial resources and enjoying a favorable geographic position closer to the European markets than Brazil and many of the Spanish-American producers. The result was that the sugar economies of the three European rivals of Portugal prospered, while the economies of the traditional producer languished. In mining, the Spaniards made an effort to introduce new methods and to establish schools of mining, but in general even in that vital economic activity they were slow to modernize. For their part, the Luso-Brazilians possessed scant mining knowledge and lagged far behind the Spaniards in mining techniques. The prospectors in Brazil sought out the alluvial gold in riverbeds or, secondarily, they worked the river banks and shallow deposits in the neighboring hillsides. Contrary to Spanish America, there was little subterranean mining. With the rising price of slaves, the principal source of labor in the gold fields, the miners had little excess capital for mining equipment and would not have known how to use it had they been able to buy it. Although the government in Lisbon enacted a mining code in 1702, it failed to recruit and dispatch any mining experts to the interior of Brazil to bring a modicum of order and efficiency to the careless miners. However, the government was not so tardy about collecting the "royal fifth," a tax of 20 percent of the gold mined that had to be paid to the crown in both

Portuguese and Spanish America. With quick and large profits as its goal, the economy of Latin America was largely speculative and hence subject to wide variations. The patrimonial system of land and labor contributed to those fluctuations. In sum, the economy of Latin America was not geared to its own best interests but to the making of immediate profits for the Iberian metropolises.

The momentary success of the economic dilettantism lulled the Iberians into a false sense of prosperity and satisfaction. Content with the patterns of the past, more given to the medieval than the modern, they evinced little inclination for change. On the other hand, in the seventeenth century, England began to industrialize, to experiment with commercial innovations, and to expand its trade. The English were pioneering a new path to economic prosperity which the Iberians showed slight interest in following.

With varying degrees of success, Spain and Portugal implemented mercantilist policies. They hoped to use their overseas domains to supply themselves with a variety of products which could not be produced at home and to sell the surpluses to other European nations. The object, of course, was to maintain exports in excess of imports, the desired "commercial balance." The possession of bullion supposedly marked a successful mercantilist program, but the discovery of great quantities of silver in Mexico and Peru and gold in Colombia and Brazil in reality disguised the weaknesses in Iberian mercantilist policies. The precious metals enriched Iberian coffers only momentarily. Much of that wealth ultimately flowed into northern Europe to pay for manufactured goods. Disinclined to industrialize, the Iberians furnished through their purchases part of the capital which spurred the industrialization of northern Europe. Not exclusively as a supplier of bullion but in all ways, the Americas were expected to be a source of wealth to the motherlands. Royal officials tended to look upon them as a great "milch cow," which could be exploited for the benefit of the crown, the metropolis, and—not least of all—the bureaucrats sent to the New World. The brilliant Brazilian satirical poet of the seventeenth century, Gregório de Matos, noted:

Que os Brasileiros são bestas	The Brazilians are beasts,
E estão sempre a trabalhar	Hard at work their lives long
Toda a vida por manter	In order to support
Maganos de Portugal	Portuguese knaves

Spain went farther than Portugal in controlling the trade of the New World. Only Spaniards were to traffic with the overseas domains. All commerce between the New World and Spain fell under the direction of the Casa de Contratación, aided by the *consulados*, merchant guilds, at home and overseas. The Casa authorized only Cadíz and Seville as the ports to trade with Spanish America and Vera Cruz and Porto Bello were designated their counterparts in the Americas. Under the protective guns of the royal navy, two fleets sailed each year, one to Vera Cruz, the other to Porto Bello. Those two fleets returned bearing the products of Spanish Middle and South America. Carefully as the restrictions on trade were enforced, contraband still flourished to which the slow but constant growth of Buenos Aires, after it was reestablished in 1580, testified. The English, French, and Dutch were only too eager to enter the markets of the New World, and from time to time European wars and diplomacy forced the Spaniards to legalize one or another aspect of that contraband trade. A later device to eliminate contraband trade as well as to encourage the development of neglected regions was the formation in Spain of monopolistic companies with exclusive rights in the New World. The most important of the monopolistic companies were the Honduras Company, founded in 1714; the Caracas or Guipúzcoa Company, 1728; the Havana Company, 1740; and the Santo Domingo Company, 1757. All of these companies, with the exception of the Guipúzcoa failed to turn a profit. The crown itself exercised many monopolies including salt, pepper, quicksilver, gunpowder, and stamped paper.

Portuguese mercantilism was never as effective as that of its neighbor, particularly before 1750. Attempts were made sporadically to organize annual fleets to and from Brazil protected by men-of-war, but the highly decentralized Portuguese trade patterns and a shortage of the merchant and war ships caused innumerable difficulties. Between the mid-seventeeth and mid-eighteenth centuries the crown partially succeeded in instituting a fleet system for the protection of Brazilian shipping. Still it never functioned as well as the Spanish convoys. Economic companies fared little better. The crown licensed four: the Brazil Company, 1649; the Maranhão Company, 1678; the General Pará and Maranhão Company, 1755; and the Pernambuco and Paraíba Company, 1759. In general the companies were unpopular with the residents of Brazil and the merchants, both in Portugal and Brazil. The Brazilians criticized them for abusing their monopolies and raising prices with impunity. The merchants disapproved of the monopolies which eliminated them from much trade and accused the companies of charging outlandish freight rates. All sides bombarded the companies with charges of inefficiency. The only one which seemed to have achieved some degree of success was the General Pará and Maranhão Company which brought both capital and labor to a region chronically short of both and significantly increased both rice and cotton production there.

Monopolies flourished. Brazilwood, salt, tobacco, slaves, diamonds, to mention a few, felt at one time or another the lethargic hand of monopolistic bureaucracy.

Fearful that the colonies might relax their efforts to produce the raw products most in demand in Europe, royal officials kept a sharp eye peeled for unnecessary diversification of the economy. They forbad Brazil or Spanish America to produce anything which the Iberian nations already produced or could furnish. For example, in 1590, the crown prohibited grape cultivation in Brazil because Portugal already produced a surplus of wines. With few exceptions the colonies were not encouraged to manufacture. The motherlands wanted to supply all the needed manufactured goods and earn for themselves the profits for doing so. Fear that an incipient industry might develop to the detriment of its mercantilist goals prompted the Portuguese monarch to promulgate a long series of decrees, from that of 1578 forbidding the blacksmith Bartolomeu Fernandes of São Vicente to teach his profession to that of 1785 prohibiting all manufacturing in Portuguese America. Spain was less inclined to enforce its restrictions. A healthy textile industry developed which provided cotton and woolen cloth for the lower classes. Flourishing artisans produced furniture, glassware, shoes, tiles, and tools.

Not all the mercantilist policy was negative. Within the confines of the policy, the two crowns tried to encourage the production of new crops which would find a ready market in the metropolises or in Europe. Though meeting with frequent frustrations, the Marquis of Lavradio diversified the Brazilian economy by promoting the production of indigo, rice, and wheat. Captain General Matías de Gálvez with the full encouragement of the Bourbon monarchy did all he could to increase Central America's indigo exports. Lack of imagination on the part of the two governments, the merchants—both in the Americas and in Europe—and the local farmers probably did more to hinder economic diversification and growth than did stern mercantile decrees.

THE STATE

For more than three centuries, Spain and Portugal ruled their American empires, a remarkable longevity which places them among the great imperial powers of all time. Both can rightly claim considerable political success for maintaining such vast empires for such a long period of time. They owed that success to quite different concepts of imperial organization. The Spanish colonial administration was relatively well organized, the hierarchical ranks rather well defined, the chain of command reasonably easily recognized. Not so in the Portuguese empire.

It was loosely organized, the institutions less well defined and more transitory. Although the overlapping of duties on the one hand and the failure to assign responsibility on the other characterized some of the Spanish imperial administration, it was a much more pronounced characteristic of the Portuguese government. In the eighteenth century, the Portuguese began to regularize and better define their imperial administration.

The concept of government markedly differed from our present one. Few of the political subtleties we must reckon with today had yet developed. There was neither division of power, nor any distinction between branches of government. Church and state were practically one, and although secular and ecclesiastical officials bickered and squabbled among themselves, the two institutions buttressed each other, together preserving order and stability in the empires for centuries. All power rested in the hands of the monarch who was the state. He made, executed, and judged the laws. On the one hand, he formulated the general concepts which governed the empires, and, on the other, he decreed a staggering array of minutely detailed laws such as the setting of prices in the marketplaces or ordering the type of clothing the Indians would wear. He protected and governed the Church within his vast domains. Indeed, he ruled by divine right. The king was the unquestioned authority in whom all power was vested and from whom all power emanated. That power was great, and yet tradition as well as natural and divine law imposed some limitations on its exercise. Still, the mystique and tradition of the monarchy gave the institution such force that no one questioned the king's right to rule or refused his loyalty to the crown. In all manners the king spoke the final word.

The monarchs proved to be very jealous of their powers. Both the Portuguese and Spanish rulers made the initial error of delegating too much authority to subordinates in the New World. We have already seen that the Spanish monarchs, regretting the grant of so much power to the adelantados and encomenderos, reversed themselves, and tried to restore that authority to the crown. The Portuguese monarch had made an identical error. In 1532–34, in order to colonize Brazil without reaching into the royal coffers, he had distributed Brazil to 12 donataries who were to enjoy broad powers in return for colonizing the American domains. By 1548, John III reversed his early decision and began to reassert his authority over the captaincies so recently bestowed with a lavish hand on court favorites. Once they had decided to assert absolute control over the American colonies, the monarchs never ceased their efforts to centralize power in their hands.

The great distances between the Iberian Peninsula and the New World and the slowness of communication and travel worked to confer considerable local autonomy on officials in the New World and to permit some irregularities. What it meant in practice was that the kings could only hope to dictate the broad outlines of policy, leaving much of the interpretation and implementation up to colonial and local officials. "Obedezco pero no cumplo" (I obey but I do not fulfill) became the accepted way for New World officials to manifest their loyalty to the crown while bending the laws to suit local situations. The philosophy of acknowledging the king's authority without enforcing his will—as common in Brazil as in Spanish America—accounts, at least in part, for the longevity of the empires. It permitted a certain flexibility in the laws which could accommodate many interests, the monarch's as well as the colonist's. The many laws and edicts emanating from Iberia represented the wishes of the crowns, but complex and powerful pressures in the New World exerted influence on the colonial administrators to take into account the diverse local desires and needs. The results were legal and governmental systems which probably pleased neither the crowns nor their representatives in the Americas, but the system which resulted from the compromises did work surprisingly well.

To keep their royal officials and their subjects in check, the Iberian monarchs had at their disposal many useful instruments. They sent out to the New World only officials of unquestioned loyalty. At best they suspected that the colonies increased in everyone "the spirit of ambition and the relaxation of virtues." For that reason they hesitated to appoint many Americans to high colonial posts. They frankly suspected their loyalty. The Portuguese monarchs were more prone to appoint Brazilians to high office than were the Spanish monarchs willing to name Americans to elevated offices in the New World. Americans, however, occupied many of the minor posts. Since so many of the officials had direct access to royal ears, there was considerable reporting and "tattling," which made all overseas personnel cautious. The kings encouraged it. Furthermore, those officials might receive at any time a *visita*, an on-the-spot investigation to which all subordinates could be subjected. At the end of all terms of office, each administrator could expect a *residencia*, a judicial inquiry into his public behavior. All those checks required an immense amount of paperwork, a characteristic abundantly evident in all Iberian bureaucracy. A multitude of lawyers, scribes, and notaries in all the major cities testified to the fascination with and importance of legal and bureaucratic matters. Thanks to that legal obsession elaborate law codes were drawn up in the Old World to govern the New. A monument to Spanish legalism was the famed Recopilación de Leyes de las Indias, which in 1681 brought together many scattered laws, enactments, and decrees governing the New World. It served as a supplementary code for Spanish law. Portugal too had its monumental law codes: the Ordenações Afonsinas, 1486–1514; the Ordenações Manuelinas, 1514–1603; and the Código Filipino, promulgated in 1603 and in full use in Brazil until 1823, although parts of it remained in use until 1916 when the Brazilian Civil Code was enacted. Frequently amended and supplemented, they uniformly governed the entire Portuguese empire regardless of their applicability or lack of it. The concern with law and legalities among the Iberians helped to make the monarchs' task of ruling far-flung empires easier.

Considering the size of the American colonies, the scant number of small and scattered garrisons, the few soldiers, and the handful of royal officials, almost all of whom resided in the most populous cities, the extent of metropolitan control over the American colonies was nothing short of remarkable. It must be concluded then that the crowns maintained their authority and control principally through the power of legitimacy. The Americans accepted the system, rarely questioned it, and seldom challenged it. When they did question or challenge the system prior to the end of the eighteenth century, they quickly and easily acceded to the forceful imposition of the royal will.

Although the power rested in the hands of the kings, no one person, regardless of how gifted he might have been, could have ruled the immense empires to which the Iberian monarchs held claim. They required administrative assistance, and in seeking it they developed the administrative machinery for their empires.

Brazil constituted only one portion, albeit an immense one, of the global Portuguese empire. Because of the profits from sugar and gold, it emerged as Portugal's most valuable overseas possession. Still, until the royal house of Braganza moved its court from Lisbon to Rio de Janeiro in 1807, Brazil was governed by no special laws or institutions which would have distinguished it as a separate, distinct, or privileged entity within the larger empire. Reviewing colonial Brazil's political evolution —its process of a continuous advance from a simple to a complex state— over the course of three centuries, two general characteristics stand out. First, governmental control over Brazil grew stronger, even though that process might have been erratic at times. By 1807, the king, his viceroy, and his governors exercised more power more effectively than at any time previously. Secondly, the political status of Brazil slowly improved throughout the course of three centuries. A central government under a governor-general began to exercise a modicum of authority in 1549 to bring some order and justice to the unhappy and generally ineffective rule of the donataries in their captaincies. In 1646, the king elevated Brazil to the status of a principality, and thereafter the heir to the throne was known as the Prince of Brazil. After 1720, all the chiefs of government of Brazil bore the title of viceroy. Although no document exists to show the exact date of its elevation, Brazil was in effect a viceroyalty thereafter. Finally, Prince-Regent John raised Brazil to a kingdom in 1815, thus, at least in theory, putting it on an equal footing with Portugal.

Portugal was well into the sixteenth century before the rulers made any distinction between home and ultramarine affairs. Never did the crown authorize a special body to handle exclusively Brazilian matters. Local administrators did become adept, however, in adapting the general imperial codes and fiats to suit the local scene. They had to. The third governor-general of Brazil, Mem de Sá, confided to the king, "This land ought not and cannot be ruled by the laws and customs of Portugal; if Your Highness was not quick to pardon it would be difficult to colonize Brazil."

The king could not rule his vast domains unaided. A variety of administrative organs, which, in the practice of the times, exercised a mélange of consultative, executive, judicial, and fiscal functions assisted him. One of the most important of those bodies was the Overseas Council (Conselho Ultramarino) created by John IV in 1642. It was the evolutionary result of considerable experience, numbering among its distinguished predecessors the India Board (Casa da India) and the Council for India and Overseas Conquests (Conselho da India e Conquistas Ultramarinas). The president, secretary, and three councilors of the Overseas Council usually had served in the colonies, and during its history the council included many who had resided in Brazil. The council divided itself into standing committees to treat the various military, administrative, judicial, and ecclesiastical matters. Its primary duty was to advise the king. Increasingly it showed greater concern for commercial matters.

Other governmental organs continued to have dual metropolitan and colonial responsibilities. A Treasury Council (Conselho da Fazenda) created in 1591 to replace the Treasury Supervisors (Vedores da Fazenda) administered public finances and the treasury. A Board of Conscience and Religious Orders (Mesa da Consciência e Ordens) established in 1532 advised the Crown on Indian matters. Finally a Casa da Suplicação served as a supreme court for many colonial judicial disputes.

A royal secretary or secretary of state, who, after 1736, bore the title of Minister of Navy and Overseas, also assisted the monarchs in their imperial rule. Those ministers became increasingly important in the last half of the eighteenth century. The ministers, as well as other close advisers to the crown, were selected because of loyal and often meritorious service and enjoyed unqualified royal confidence. They had direct access to the king's ear and were, of course, responsible to him. Together these secretaries, ministers, and organs formed the principal bureaucratic apparatus in Lisbon which enabled the monarch to rule his scattered overseas domains. Their experience and expertise made that rule more effective—at least in theory.

In Brazil, representatives of the royal government administered that colony. At the apex stood the governor-general, after 1720 called the viceroy. He was "the shadow of the king." His effectiveness depended largely on his own strengths and weaknesses. Those viceroys who were vigorous exerted considerable influence over the colony. Those who were weak found themselves almost unable to control the capital city and their powers eroded by ambitious bishops and subordinant bureaucrats. The viceroys of the eighteenth century tended to be stronger and more effective administrators than their predecessors, with, of course, many exceptions taken into account. Outstanding were the Conde de Sabugosa (1720–35), the Marquis de Lavradio (1769–79), and Luís de Vasconcelos e Sousa (1779–90). The king's chief representatives in Brazil served for an average term of six and one-half years in the sixteenth century, three and one-half years in the seventeenth century, and slightly less than six years in the eighteenth century. Most of them were professional soldiers and members of the nobility.

Salvador da Bahia served as the first seat of the central government of Brazil. A spendid port, it boasted in the early nineteenth century of a population of approximately 100,000, making it, after Lisbon, the second city of the empire. In 1763, the seat of the viceroyalty moved southward to Rio de Janeiro. A foreign challenge to the southern extreme of the colony prompted the transfer. Foreign threats to the northeastern sugar coast ended after the defeat and expulsion of the Dutch in 1654. The West Indies thereafter attracted most of the attention of the European maritime powers. However, by the end of the seventeenth century, Portuguese America faced a growing threat from the Spanish in the Platine region. In 1680, the Portuguese had founded the settlement of Colônia do Sacramento on the left bank of the Río de la Plata, across from Buenos Aires. The Spanish challenge to Portuguese claims to the region caused a century and a half of intense rivalry and frequent warfare along the Plata. The Portuguese crown felt it necessary to have the viceroy nearer the scene of military operations and so moved the capital 800 miles southward. Also, economic crises in the mining regions of the southeast suggested that it might be wise to have the viceroy closer to those vitally important economic centers. Furthermore, the shift of the capital reflected a broader population shift during the eighteenth century from the Northeast to the Southeast.

The governors-general and later the viceroys depended on a growing bureaucracy to carry out their primary functions of administering the colony, overseeing its military preparedness, dispensing the king's justice, and enforcing taxes. Of greatest importance was the High Court

(Relação), the first of which was established in Bahia in 1609 under the presidency of the governor-general. A second was established in Rio de Janeiro in 1751. Those courts primarily had judicial responsibilities: they functioned as the highest law tribunals in Brazil from which there was limited appeal to the Casa da Suplicação in Lisbon. They reviewed the conduct of all officials at the end of their terms of office. Secondarily they served as consultative and administrative organs. When the governor-general absented himself from the capital, the highest member of the court usually governed in his place. The governor-general often requested the advice of the legally trained judges on a host of judicial and administrative matters. Tax questions and the supervision of the treasury fell to the responsibility of another bureau, the Board of Revenue (Junta da Fazenda).

The nation which we know today as Brazil was divided during most of the colonial period into two states. The state of Brazil, about which we have talked thus far, was by far the more important of the two, but it should be noted that another, very impoverished colony existed in the far north, the state of Maranhão. The government of Maranhão was similiar to that of Brazil, only seemingly less well defined. Nor did the northern state ever develop the vitality of the southern one. It depended even more heavily upon Lisbon. The king appointed a governor-general and a chief justice after the state was established in 1621. A slow growth and a scanty population negated the need for a high court and none was ever authorized. In 1751, the capital was transferred from São Luís to Belém, a smaller although an increasingly more active port which for some time had been the effective center of the state. In recognition of the growing importance of the Amazon, the king created in 1755 the Captaincy of São José do Rio Negro (the present-day Amazonas), subordinate to the Captaincy of Pará.

Captaincies were the principal territorial subdivisions of the two states. Representatives and appointees of the king, the governors and captains-general of those captaincies carried out the same responsibilities on a regional level as the governor-general or viceroy did on a broader scale. The governor-general was charged with overseeing, coordinating, and harmonizing their efforts. Here, as in so many instances, theory and practice diverged. Distance, the varying effectiveness of personalities, intrigue, vagueness of the law, often meant that the governor-general was only first among equals and sometimes unable to exert any authority in the captaincies. In times of crisis, particularly those brought about by fear of a foreign attack on a coastal city or Spanish expansion into southern Brazil, the military authority of the governor-general or viceroy increased. His martial powers may well have been his strongest. However, more often than not, the lines of communication ran from the capital of each captaincy directly to the king, seldom passing through the colonial capital. In truth, the governor-general and his later successor, the viceroy, never exercised the same degree of control or authority as their counterparts in Spanish America.

Royal control over Brazil tightened during the eighteenth century. The absolutist tendencies noticeable during the long reign of John V, 1706–50, found their instrument of perfection in the person of the Marquis of Pombal, who ruled through the weak Joseph I, 1750–77. An ardent nationalist, Pombal hoped to strengthen his economically moribund country through better and fuller utilization of its colonies, the foremost of which unquestionably was Brazil. To better exploit Portuguese America, he centralized and standardized its government. He abolished the state of Maranhão in 1772, and incorporated it into the state of Brazil, creating for the first time (at least in theory) a single, unified Portuguese colony in the New World. After the unification of the two states, Pombal encouraged trade between them so that commerce would further cement political integration. An impatient enemy of the hereditary captaincies, the prime minister dissolved the remaining ones, with one minor exception, and brought them under direct royal control. As a further measure to fortify royal authority, Pombal expelled the Company of Jesus from the empire in 1759. He accused that powerful order of challenging the secular government and of interposing itself between the king and his Indian subjects. Pombal strengthened the government's hand in both the education and care for the Indians. For good or for bad, he ended the isolation enforced upon them by the church-controlled aldeias. By requiring the Indians to speak Portuguese, dress like Europeans, and adopt useful trades and crafts and by encouraging whites to intermarry with them, he attempted to bring them within the Luso-Brazilian community. Finally, he tried to restrict some of the independence of the municipal governments, and, although it is true that those local governments exercised less freedom than they had in their heyday, the seventeenth century, they still continued to be active and important nuclei of local politics.

The municipal government was the one with which most Brazilians came into contact and the only one in which they participated to any degree. Governing much more than just the town and its environs, the municipality extended out to meet equidistant the boundaries of the next. In sparsely settled Brazil, the municipalities contained hundreds, often thousands of square miles. European countries seemed dwarfs compared to some of those municipal giants.

The most important institution of local government was the *senado da câmara*, the municipal council. A restricted suffrage of the *homens bons*, which is to say the propertied class, elected two justices of the peace, three aldermen, and a procurator to office every three years. At first the presiding officer was selected by the other councilmen, but by the end of the seventeenth century, the crown was appointing a presiding officer in the most important towns and cities. The duties of the council varied. Meeting twice weekly, it meted out local justice, handled routine municipal business and local administration, and passed the necessary laws and regulations. The procurator executed those laws. In cooperation with the church, the senado helped to oversee local charities. The municipality enjoyed its own source of income: rents from city property, license fees for tradesmen, taxes on certain foodstuffs, charges for diverse services such as the verification of weights and measures, and fines. The senado of São Luís during the seventeenth century was particularly ambitious. So often did it summon the governor to appear before it that the king in 1677 ordered it to desist forthwith, reminding the councilors that the governor represented the crown and could not be ordered around. Sometimes the senados and governors engaged in power struggles. At times the senados dared to challenge the crown itself. To protect their interests, the larger cities maintained a representative at the court in Lisbon as a sort of lobbyist.

As Brazil's foremost historian of the colonial period, João Capistrano de Abreu has pointed out, the senado frequently served as an arena—the first one—for the struggles between the *mazombos*, the whites born in Brazil, and the *reinóis*, the whites born in Portugal. The Portuguese officials, occupying all levels of government except the municipal, enforced the universal law of the empire. Their point of view was global. They saw Brazil as one part of a larger empire which existed for the grandeur of Portugal. The mazombos sitting on the municipal councils cared only for the local scene; their vision was restricted. It was, in short, Brazilian. They wanted to enforce those aspects of the laws beneficial to them, to their community, and, to a lesser extent, to Brazil. Those different perspectives gave rise to repeated clashes in which the mazombos did not always give ground to the reinóis. In times of crises, the senado da câmara amplified its membership to become a *conselho geral*, a general council. On those occasions local military, judicial, and ecclesiastical authorities as well as representatives of the people met with the senado to discuss the emergency at hand.

A second institution of local government deserves mention because of its influence on subsequent Brazilian development: regional militias. In them the principal figure of prestige and power in an area, usually the largest landowner, bore the rank of *capitão-mor*, equivalent to colonel. The majority of them seem to have been born in the colony. In the absence of regularly constituted governmental officials in the hinterlands, those capitães-mor performed a variety of administrative and even judicial tasks. Obviously it was to their own interest to enforce law and order in their region and that they did to the benefit of local tranquility. Their power varied widely and as in so many cases depended mainly on their own abilities and strengths since the distant government could do little to help or hinder them. They often became the local strongmen or caudilhos, the precursors of the later *"coroneis,"* who control rural Brazil.

Stronger in organization and authority than governmental institutions were the patriarchal plantation families. Those large, cohesive family units appeared at the inception of the sugar industry, and the two grew together. The paterfamilias dominated the household and the plantation, ruling family, slaves, and tenants with unquestioned authority. He and other males of the household liberally expanded the basic family unit through their polygamous activities to include hosts of mestizo and mulatto children. In fact, it was in and around the plantation house that European, Indian, and African cultures blended together the most perfectly to create a Brazilian civilization. The traditional godparent relationship (*compadrio*) further ramified and reinforced the family structure. Profoundly Christian and emphatically patriarchal, those family units set the social tone and pattern for the entire colony. The strongest of the families formed a landed aristocracy which in the colonial period dominated the senados and later, in the imperial period, the newly independent national government.

Brazil by the close of the eighteenth century was widely if thinly settled. Its steady expansion from a narrow coastal band to subcontinental size represents one of the most dramatic and dynamic themes of the colonial period. As the colonists grew in number and strength in the sixteenth century, they gradually began to fill in the voids between São Vicente in the south and Olinda in the north. Foreign threats from the English, French, and Dutch hastened Portuguese occupation of the coast in order to defend it. Slowly the colonization moved northward from Olinda to conquer the north coast and finally the mouth of the Amazon. With the coast conquered by 1616, the Luso-Brazilians, disregarding the Tordesillas line, began to penetrate the interior with increasing boldness in search of slaves and gold. They carried the banner of Portugal to the Andes in the west and to the Plata River in the south. Daring *bandeirantes* (explorers) claimed thousands of square miles for the Portuguese crown. Too late Spain realized what had happened, and in the Treaty of Madrid (1750) the Castilian crown was forced to recognize its rival's conquest of the heartland of South America. Although the boundaries between Spanish and Portuguese America were altered slightly thereafter —particularly in the Plata area—Portugal successfully retained its claims to half of South America.

Population growth did not keep up with territorial expansion. Growing at a rate approximated at 1.9 percent annually, the population at the end of the eighteenth century numbered about two and one-third million with Minas Gerais, Bahia, Pernambuco, Rio de Janeiro, and São Paulo being the most populous captaincies in that order. The majority lived along the coast or in the rich river valleys. The trend to migrate to the interior accelerated by the discovery of gold had been stemmed, and in many cases reversed with some return of the population to the coast. Obviously hollow frontiers still characterized the settlement.

It was possible to distinguish five different regions of settlement. The far north, which included the vast Amazon valley, was scantily settled, a few villages dotting the river banks and coast. The Indian predominated. The economy depended on the extraction of forest products and cattle raising in the interior and the cultivation of sugar and coffee along the coast. The cattle lands of the *sertão,* the arid interior, stretching from Maranhão to Minas Gerais were the domain of the mestizos. The dry land and light vegetation grudgingly supported cattle, some horses, and a few sheep and goats. Ranches and hamlets scattered over that vast interior with no concentration of settlement. The lush sugar coast extending from Maranhão to São Vicente included excellent ports and the largest cities in Brazil; the black prevailed in that more concentrated settlement. The mining regions of Minas Gerais, Goiás, and Mato Grosso exported their gold and diamonds but retained enough of the wealth to create a few prosperous towns. Stock raising, sugar cane, and agriculture played a secondary economic role in the region. The far south boasted of excellent agricultural and pastoral lands. Immigrants, white European stock from the Azores, settled the coastal region. Their small family farms grew grapes, wheat, and olives. In contrast, bandeirantes migrated overland from São Paulo to colonize the interior of the south. There one encountered patriarchal cattle ranches and a profitable business in mule and horse raising.

Unlike Portugal, Spain possessed few overseas domains outside the Americas. Consequently, the colonial system the Spanish devised was to govern principally those vast territories in the New World. Two administrative bodies aided the king in his rule of Spanish America. The first created was the Casa de Contratación, and, as previously mentioned, it served to regulate and develop commerce with the New World. The second, the Council of the Indies (Consejo de las Indias), established in 1524, advised the king on all American affairs. It prepared most of the laws for governing the Americas, saw that those laws were executed, and then sat as a high court to judge cases involving the fracture or interpretation of those laws. Ecclesiastical matters fell within its jurisdiction as well. In the beginning, the king favored the appointment of clergymen as councilors; later he tended to select lawyers of noble blood for those positions. Always the council counted among its members some naval and military officers. Upon their return to Spain, successful administrators in the New World often sat on the council.

The viceroy served as the king's principal representative in the New World. Columbus bore the title of viceroy of any new lands he might discover when he left Spain in 1492. The crown appointed Antonio de Mendoza, a member of one of Spain's foremost families and a trusted diplomat of Charles V, as the first Viceroy of New Spain. Amid great pomp, he arrived in Mexico City in 1535 and immediately set about to restrict the authority of the adelantados and encomenderos while he strengthened and centralized the king's power in the New World. By the time he left Mexico in 1551, he had imposed law and order, humbled the landowning class, and exalted the royal powers. In short, he consolidated the conquest of New Spain. Peru became the second viceroyalty. The first viceroy arrived in 1543 to find chaos, rivalries, and civil war disrupting Spanish South America. Not until the able administration of the fifth viceroy, Fransisco de Toledo (1569–81), was the king's authority firmly imposed on his unruly South American subjects. During his long administration, Viceroy Toledo tried to improve the relations between the Indians and Spaniards, promote mining, and organize the administration of justice. Like Mendoza, his major achievement was the consolidation of Spanish rule and the imposition of the king's authority.

The *audiencia* was the highest royal court and consultative council in the New World. In some instances it also prepared legislation. The Spanish audiencia had much in common with the Portuguese *relação*. The first audiencias were established in Santo Domingo in 1511; Mexico City, 1527; Panama City, 1535; Lima, 1542; and Guatemala, 1543. In the eighteenth century, 14 such bodies were functioning. The number of *oidores*, or judges, sitting on the audiencia varied according to time and place. In the sixteenth century, their number fluctuated between three and four but later it expanded to as many as 15. Because the tenure of the oidores exceeded that of the viceroy and overlapped each other, they provided a continuity to royal administration which his office did not have. Over the audiencias in the viceregal capitals, the viceroy himself presided. The chief executive of the political subdivisions served as president of the audiencia located within his confines.

Presidencias and captaincies-general were the major subdivisions of the viceroyalties. Theoretically the presidents and captains-general were subordinate to the viceroys, but in practice they communicated directly with Madrid and paid only the most formal homage to the viceroys. Ranking beneath the presidents and captains-general were the governors, *corregidores*, and *alcaldes mayores* who administered the municipalities and other territorial divisions. Within their localities, those minor officials possessed executive and judicial authority as well as some limited legislative powers.

Municipal government, known as the *cabildo*, provided the major opportunity for the creole, the American-born white, to hold office and to exercise some political power. From it the creoles gained most of their political experience, however limited it might have been. Also, throughout the colonial period it remained the single self-perpetuating governmental institution in Spanish America. As in Brazil, the town council governed not only the town itself but also the surrounding countryside, thus in some instances exercising power over vast administrative areas. Some of the cabildos far removed from immediate viceregal supervision, such as Buenos Aires prior to 1776 and Asunción, exercised considerable autonomy. Property-owning citizens at first elected the *regidores*, the town councilmen, although later increasing numbers purchased or inherited the office or were appointed to it by the king. As royal power grew stronger in the eighteenth century, the cabildo grew weaker, and the tendency to tighten the centralization of the empire restricted the independence of the municipal governments. The cabildo probably exercised its greatest authority in the sixteenth century. In moments of crisis, the cabildo expanded to include all the principal citizens of the municipality, who were requested to offer their advice. That *cabildo abierto* became the agency of transition from colonial to independent government in several places in the early nineteenth century.

Spanish government floundered in a morass of inefficient and corrupt bureaucracy in the seventeenth century but revived briskly in the eighteenth. The long War of the Spanish Succession (1700–1713) brought the Bourbon Philip V to the Castilian throne and with him refreshingly new ideas. The crown reasserted its authority. With French absolutism as his model, Charles III ruled (1759–88) as one of Spain's strongest and most effective kings. The Bourbons selected their administrators less because of their birth and more because of their demonstrated ability and efficiency. With their help the reinvigorated monarchy reformed the colonial administration and in the process greatly centralized it.

The power of the Council of the Indies waned as the ministers of the king took over many of its former duties. In the eighteenth century, the chief responsibility for the government of Spanish America rested in the hands of the Minister of the Indies. The Casa de Contratación also felt the weight of Bourbon reforms. The king's ministers absorbed so many of its powers that it became useless and was abolished in 1790. As the population grew and spread and as development intensified, the crown thought it wise to redivide territorially Spanish-American government so that the king's representatives could more intensely care for the territories under their authority. Two new viceroyalties were created: New Granada in 1717 (it was abolished in 1724 only to be recreated again in 1739) and La Plata in 1776. Likewise, the crown authorized new captaincies-general: Venezuela, 1731; Louisiana, 1763; Cuba, 1777; and Chile, 1778.

The most radical innovation was the establishment of the intendency system, an administrative unit used by the Bourbons in France and copied by their relatives on the Spanish throne. It was another important measure of the Bourbons to centralize authority and thereby increase power. The intendants, royal officials of Spanish birth, with extensive judicial, administrative, and financial powers, were to supplant the numerous governors, corregidores, and alcaldes mayores in the hope that a more efficient and uniform administration would increase the king's revenue and bring an end to numerous bureaucratic abuses and corruption. In financial affairs, the intendants reported directly to the crown. In religious, judicial, and administrative matters, they were subject to the viceroy and they were to respect his military prerogatives. In 1764, Cuba became the first intendancy, and by 1790 the system extended to all the Spanish-American colonies. The new administrative system seemed to auger well, but no comprehensive judgment can be rendered since the outbreak of the Napoleonic wars in Europe followed by the struggles for independence in Latin America allowed such a short time for it to function.

As another reform measure, Charles III in the 1760s created a colonial militia with creole officers in order to shift some of the burden of the defense of his distant domains onto the Americans themselves. The soldier always had played an important role in the development of the Americas. He conquered, defended, and extended the empire. Great prestige accompanied high rank. Many, if not most, of the viceroys held exalted military rank at the time of their appointment, and their military experience enhanced their authority in the New World. The granting of military commissions to the creoles afforded them a new prestige. Usually the high ranks were reserved for—or bought by—wealthy members of the local aristocracy, and as a consequence many desired them as a means of identifying with the rich and the powerful, in short, the elite, of the colonies. Hence, a close identification developed between high military rank and the upper class. Further, the creole officers enjoyed a most practical advantage, the *fuero militar*, a special military privilege, which exempted them from civil law. In effect, it established the military as a special class above the law, the effects of which would be increasingly disruptive for Latin American society.

The Bourbon kings, in particular Charles III, infused a new and more liberal economic spirit into the empire. They hoped to strengthen

Spain by liberalizing trade, expanding agriculture, and reviving mining in the Americas. They dispatched European engineers and mining technicians to the New World to encourage the adoption of the latest mining techniques. The crown authorized the establishment of a College of Mining in Mexico, a visit to which prompted Baron von Humboldt to remark: "No city of the new continent, without excepting those of the United States, can show scientific establishments as fine or as well established as the capital of Mexico." Trade policies became more practical in the eighteenth century. Cadiz lost its old commercial monopoly when the king permitted other Spanish ports to trade with the Americas. The fleet system gradually disappeared. After 1740, Spanish ships commonly rounded Cape Horn to trade with Peru and slowly abandoned the old isthmian trade route. In the 1770s Charles lifted the restrictions on intercolonial commerce. The altered trade policies helped to bring about the previously mentioned demise of the Casa de Contratación. The crown chartered trading companies to encourage agriculture by expanding production of and commerce in certain crops, another means of developing trade. Those reforms were enacted with imperial motives in mind, for the final benefit more of the metropolis than the colonies. The Americans did not favor all of the reforms, while, on the other hand, they did not think that some of them went far enough.

Spain's empire in America at the end of the eighteenth century swept southward from California and Florida, through the Caribbean, Mexico, and Central America down the length of South America. Approximately 16 million people inhabited those Spanish-governed domains. The empire had grown by steady expansion, rapid in the sixteenth century, more slowly thereafter. From the original settlements in the Caribbean, the central valley of Mexico, and the highlands of Peru, adelantados followed by colonists had pushed into new regions. In the older colonies, agriculture continued to progress; in the newer ones it became established and advanced rapidly. The real riches of the New World were its farms, ranches, and plantations. The silver and gold mines poured forth their treasure, but despite their glitter and attraction they remained secondary to agriculture as a source of wealth. Unfortunately very few shared in the growing wealth of the Americas.

Most of America's riches flowed to Europe north of the Pyrenees, pausing only briefly in Spain. Still, enough remained in the New World to construct some monumental buildings whose presence still testifies to an opulent age. Chuch and state built lasting architectural masterpieces. Imposing public buildings, busy universities, magnificent churches, massive convents bespoke the luxury, learning, and refinement of the great cities of which Mexico City and Lima ranked foremost. The bustling ports of Veracruz, Havana, Porto Bello, La Guaira, Callao, Valparaiso, and Buenos Aires shipped the wealth of the New World aboard ever larger numbers of merchantmen to the markets of Europe and welcomed the merchandise and immigrants of the Old World.

One of the most active ports of the New World was Porto Bello, the major entrepôt for trade between South America and Spain. It teamed with commercial activity during the weeks the fleet anchored in its harbor. Two young Spanish scientists, Jorge Juan and Antonio de Ulloa, visited that Caribbean port in the mid-eighteenth century and left the following description of the movement they witnessed there:

> The ships are no sooner moored in the harbor than the first work is to erect in the square a tent made of the ship's sails for receiving its cargo at which the proprietors of the goods are present in order to find their bales by the marks which distinguish them. These bales are drawn on sledges to their proper places by the crew of every ship and the money given them is proportionally divided.
>
> While the seamen and European traders are thus employed, the shore is covered with droves of mules from Panama, each drove consisting of more than one hundred, loaded with chests of gold and silver from the merchants of Peru. Some unload them at the exchange, others in the middle of the square; yet, amid the hurry and confusion of such crowds, no theft, loss, or disturbance is ever known. He who has seen this place during the tiempo muerto, or dead time, solitary, poor, and a perpetual silence reigning everywhere, the harbor quite empty, and every place wearing a melancholy aspect, must be filled with astonishment at the sudden change, to see the bustling multitudes, every house crowded, the square and streets encumbered with bales and chests of gold and silver of all kinds, the harbor full of ships and vessels, some bringing by way of Rio de Chape [Chagres] the goods of Peru, such as cacao, quinquina or Jesuits' bark, vicuña wool, and bezoar stones; others coming from Carthagena loaded with provisions. Thus a place at all other times detested for its deleterious qualities becomes the warehouse and market of the riches of the Old and New Worlds and scene of one of the most considerable branches of commerce in the whole world.
>
> After the ships have been unloaded and the merchants of Peru together with the president of Panama have arrived, the fair is ready to begin. Representatives of the various merchants and traders then go on board one of the principal galleons in the harbor and there in the presence of the commodore of the galleons and the president of Panama, the former as the patron of the Europeans and the latter, of the Peruvians, the prices of the various goods and merchandise are settled. After three or four meetings, agreements are made, signed, and made public. In accordance with them, each sets about to make his sales and purchases. In that way all fraud is avoided. The purchases and sales, as likewise the exchange of money, are transacted by brokers both from Spain and Peru. After this, everyone begins to dispose of his goods; the Spanish brokers embarking their chests of money and those of Peru sending away the goods they have purchased.

To handle the lucrative trade, a small merchant class developed in Spanish America. Those merchants later united into the *consulados* and obtained for themselves formidable privileges and prerogatives. Together with the consulados in Seville and Cadiz they exercised a virtual monopoly over the trade and commerce of Spanish America.

Probably no area better illustrated the growth and prosperity of Spanish America in the eighteenth century than the Plata region, particularly the region around Buenos Aires. Today Argentina is the most prosperous Spanish-speaking nation in the world, but its beginnings were humble. In contrast to the faltering start of Buenos Aires, some of the interior towns, Tucumán, Mendoza, Córdoba, and Salta, had begun to prosper early. Those towns not only were surrounded by fertile land to exploit but also had Indians near at hand who could be coerced into tilling the soil. Further, close to the silver of Peru, they found a ready market among the miners for their sugar, fruits, cattle, mules, and grain. On the other hand, Buenos Aires languished after its refounding in 1580. The Lima merchants persuaded the crown not to open that Atlantic port to trade. In theory, goods from Buenos Aires made a 3,000 mile overland trip to Lima, thence by sea to Panama to be transported by mule across the isthmus, and finally by sea again on the fleets to Spain. The *porteños*, as the inhabitants of Buenos Aires are called, argued for the opening of their port and the logical direct trade with Spain that would result. Only thus, without the tremendous transportation costs of the Lima route, could their products compete in European marketplaces. Without royal sanction for the opening of the port, Buenos Aires succumbed to the temptation of contraband. The port thus provided a natural, albeit illegal, commercial outlet for Asunción, Córdoba, and Potosí. The silver which made its way down from Peru paid for slaves, sugar, textiles, and a thousand other manufactured goods demanded by the wealthy inhabitants of the interior who found it cheaper to buy them from the merchants of Buenos Aires than from Lima.

Buenos Aires grew rapidly in the eighteenth century for strategic and commerical reasons. After the Portuguese founded Colônia do Sacramento (1680), Buenos Aires assumed a new strategic importance in the Spanish empire, and the crown gave it increasing attention so that it could counter the Luso-Brazilian threat of expansion. At the same time the pampas were giving abundant evidence of their fecundity. Salted meat, hides, and wool became increasingly important exports and awakened the Spanish government to an appreciation of the natural wealth of the region. The statistics indicated the rising importance of the port: the population quadrupled in the last half of the eighteenth century from approximately 12,000 to 50,000 and royal revenue derived from import and export taxes jumped tenfold from 100,000 pesos in 1774 to one million in 1780.

After the establishment of the Viceroyalty of the Plata in 1776 with its seat in Buenos Aires, the crown gave every encouragement to trade. The presence of the viceroy accompanied by an army of bureaucrats and officials prompted the construction of new governmental buildings, the paving of streets, the laying out of parks, and in the early 1780's the opening of a theater for the amusement of the inhabitants. The change which had overtaken Buenos Aires mirrored similar changes which had taken place throughout Latin America by the end of the eighteenth century.

THE CHURCH

Significant for the formation of Latin America was the presence of the 12 friars accompanying Columbus on his second voyage to the New World and of six Jesuits in the retinue of Brazil's first governor-general, Tomé de Sousa. The Iberian monarchs thereby signified their intention to fulfill their responsibility to Christianize the heathen in the newly discovered lands. The instructions to Columbus stated that "the King and Queen, having more regard for the augmentation of the faith than for any other utility, desire nothing other than to augment the Christian religion and to bring divine worship to many simple nations." The immense task of evangelizing the Indians confronted the Church, challenging its vitality. The task involved more than simple conversion. By Christianizing the Indians, the missionaries would also be Europeanizing them: teaching the trades, manners, customs, languages, and habits of the Spanish and Portuguese.

Conversion was essential, according to Iberian thought, not only to give the aborigines the true faith and eternal salvation but also to draw them within the pale of empire, that is, to make them loyal subjects to Their Most Catholic Majesties. To be Portuguese or Spanish was to be Roman Catholic. The two were intimately intertwined, and consequently Church and state appeared as one. The populace embraced the Catholic faith unquestioningly and whether understanding its dogmas or not defended it devotedly. The Iberians were born, reared, married, and buried Catholics. The Church touched every aspect of their lives. The monarchs defended the faith within their realms in return for which the Pope conferred royal patronage upon the crown, by bulls to the Spanish monarchs in 1501 and 1508 and to the Portuguese monarchs temporarily in 1515 and permanently in 1551. Holding power in all but purely spiritual matters, the monarchs collected the tithe and decided how it should be spent, appointed (and at times recalled) the bishops, priests, and other ecclesiastical officials, authorized the construction of new churches, determined the boundaries of the bishoprics, and of great significance approved and transmitted papal messages—or refused to. The royal patronage meant, in short, that the state dominated the Church, but conversely it allowed the Church to pervade the state. If the king and his ministers had a final say in church matters, it is equally true that clerics often occupied the top administrative posts in government. Churchmen often served as ministers, captains-general, viceroys, and even regents. Cardinal Henry, after all, ruled the Portuguese empire in the sixteenth century.

To carry out its initial assignment to introduce the Indians both to Christianity and European culture the Church depended on the effectiveness of the missionaries, who belonged to the regular clergy, that is, the religious orders as contrasted with the secular clergy who served as priests in the growing number of churches. In the sixteenth century, the missionaries displayed an unflagging zeal. They were as aggressive in their spiritual conquest as the soldiers had been in their physical conquest. The regular clergy, particularly the Dominicans, Jesuits, and Franciscans, devoted their considerable energy to their neophytes. Pedro de Gante and Juan de Zumárraga in Mexico, Bartolomé de las Casas in the Caribbean, Manuel da Nóbrega and José de Anchieta in Brazil exemplified the sincere concern of the Church for the Indian's welfare, its dedication to his cause, and its love for the native American.

Conversion of the sedentary, concentrated Indian groups proved much easier and quicker than conversion of the scattered, nomadic tribes. The prelates decided that the wisest course would be to gather the nomadic natives into villages, the aldeias in Brazil and the *reducciones* in Spanish America, where they could more easily be instructed, Christianized, and protected under a watchful eye. The village system permitted the maximum use of the few regular clergy: usually one or two brothers administered each village and in that way supervised many Indians. Each village centered on a church, built of course by the indigenous converts themselves. Around it were a school, living quarters, and warehouses. The ringing of church bells awoke the neophytes each day, summoning them to mass. Afterwards, singing hymns along the way, they marched outside the village to cultivate the fields. The brothers taught reading, writing, and the mastering of useful trades to the young and able. Indian sculptors, painters, masons, carpenters, bakers, and locksmiths, among others, were soon practicing their trades. Many of the villages achieved a high degree of self-sufficiency, and most raised some commercial crops, such as tobacco, sugar, or wheat, for sale to outside markets. Also large cattle herds tended by the neophytes provided hides and meat for sale. Alexander von Humboldt, a German visitor to Latin America at the end of the colonial period, inspected some of the missions and noted that where once nomadic Indians roamed, "The road leads through plantations of sugar, indigo, cotton, and coffee. The regularity which we observed in the construction of the villages reminded us that they all owe their origin to monks and missions. The streets are straight and parallel; they cross each other at right angles; and the church is erected in the great square situated in the center." Although the brothers administered the missions through various Indians whom they appointed to office and invested with the customary symbols of that office, those churchmen in the final analysis rigidly controlled the lives of their charges. It was not a simple figure of speech when they spoke of the neophytes as "their children," for that was exactly how they regarded them. Under their guidance, the Indians contributed to the imperial economy, worshipped as Roman Catholics, dressed like Europeans, mastered European trades, and paid homage to the king in Lisbon or Madrid. Thus, those touched by the village system were brought by the determined hand of the missionaries into the empire.

Within the empires, the missions served a military function. The village system minimized Indian revolts and warfare, thereby freeing soldiers for other duties. The missions also helped to hold distant frontiers against foreign claims and intrusions. In the imperial schemes of defensive colonization they played vital roles in California, Texas, the Plata, and the Amazon.

As the missionaries enthusiastically attended to conversions, clerical organization and hierarchy were transferred from the Old World to the New where they followed perfectly the European model. The Spanish crown authorized the first bishoprics in 1511, two in Hispaniola and one in Puerto Rico. By 1600, there were five archbishoprics and 27 bishoprics in Spanish America, numbers which jumped to ten and 38 respectively before the end of the colonial period. The Portuguese crown erected the Bishopric of Brazil in 1551, and in 1676 approved the creation of the Archbishopric of Brazil with its see in Salvador. Two new bishoprics, Rio de Janeiro and Pernambuco, were established at the same time. By the end of the eighteenth century there were four others. It is interesting to note that the African bishoprics of São Tomé and Angola also were suffragan to the Archbishop of Bahia. The Church in Angola in every way depended heavily on Brazil. Serafim Leite, distinguished historian of the Jesuits in Brazil, has affirmed, "The evangelization of Angola was in the hands of the Jesuits of Portuguese America."

Of major importance to the social and religious lives of the colonists were the lay brotherhoods, voluntary associations of the faithful. They built handsome churches, merrily celebrated the feast days of patron saints, and dutifully maintained charitable institutions such as hospitals and orphanages. Indeed, works of charity, education, and social assistance composed some of the noblest chapters of the history of the Roman Catholic Church in the New World.

The Church maintained a careful vigil over its flock. Nonetheless, some examples of moral corruption among the clergy provided bawdy gossip for colonial ears. Alleged backsliders—especially Jewish converts, the New Christians—could expect to account for themselves before the Inquisition. Philip II authorized the establishment of the Holy Office in Spanish America in 1569 and it began to operate in Lima in 1570; Mexico City in 1571; and Cartagena in 1610. Significantly he exempted the Indians from the jurisdiction of the Inquisition "because of their ignorance and their weak minds." It served as much a political as a religious end in its vigilant efforts to purge and purify society in order to make it unified and loyal. The considerable power of the Inquisition lasted until the last half of the eighteenth century when the winds of the Enlightenment blew across the Iberian Peninsula, causing the flames of the Holy Tribunal to flicker. As an institution it was never established in Brazil, but it operated there through the bishops and three visitations from Inquisitors, one between 1581 and 1595, another in 1618, and a third from 1763 to 1769. In general, the hand of the Inquisition rested lightly on Brazil.

While the Church censored books and kept one ear attuned for discussions which might criticize dogma or question the divine right of kings, it also educated Americans and fostered most of the serious scholarship in the New World. In the sixteenth century, some sensitive intellectual churchmen wrote excellent studies of the very Indian cultures they were helping to eradicate. To learn of the Indian past, scholars still consult Bernardino de Sahagun for the Aztecs, Diego de Landa for the Mayas, Bernabé Cobo for the Incas, and José de Anchieta for the Brazilian Indians. In order to facilitate the mastery of the Indian tongues, and thus to speed up the process of Christianization, the friars compiled dictionaries and grammars of the many Indian languages. Their work continued and in some cases even broadened as the colonial period lengthened, and one of their major scholarly contributions of the eighteenth century was to the natural sciences. Since churchmen composed a large share of the educated of the colonies, it was from their ranks that most of the teachers came. The Church exercised a virtual monopoly over education. Monasteries housed the first schools and taught reading, writing, arithmetic, and Catholic doctrine. Contrary to the attitude of the Portuguese crown, the Spanish monarch encouraged the founding of universities in the New World, granting the first charters in 1551 to the University of Mexico and the University of San Marcos in Lima.

The clergy occupied most of the chairs. Before Harvard opened its doors in 1636, a dozen Spanish American universities were offering a wide variety of courses in law, medicine, theology, and the arts.

Foremost among the Church's scholars were the Jesuits, and they staffed some of the best colonial schools. Well organized and militant, they also displayed an industry and efficiency which made the order very powerful economically. Their success aroused the jealousy of other religious orders as well as the suspicion of the crown. Always protective of their powers, the Iberian kings disliked the ultramontane views of the Society of Jesus. That the Black Robes would appeal to the pope—or God—over the head of the king or take orders directly from Rome and bypass the channels through Madrid and Lisbon did not harmonize with growing absolutism of eighteenth-century Iberia. As was mentioned in a previous discussion, Pombal drove the Jesuits from Portuguese domains in 1759 as one means of fortifying royal authority. Approximately 600 were forced to leave Brazil. In 1767, Charles III followed suit, expelling some 2,200 Jesuits from Spanish America.

Perhaps the relations between Church and state were not always perfect examples of harmony but they were sufficiently tranquil to allow the Church to wax wealthy in the New World. Having converted (at least superficially) the Indians in the sixteenth century, the Church turned its attention to the mundane matters of organization and amassing property and riches. Tithes, the sale of papal indulgences, and parochial fees provided a small share of the Church's income. The legacy furnished the principal source of wealth. In their wills, the affluent were expected to leave at least part of their wealth to the Mother Church in whose bosom they died. As one visitor to Caracas at the opening of the nineteenth century observed, "A will that did not provide some legacy for the convents was considered an irreligious act that left many doubts about the salvation of the soul that committed this error. . . . The mania for annuities accompanied that for donations to the convents. Whoever had property and failed on dying to leave a part of it subject to an annuity left a stain on his memory." Over the decades the Church accumulated vast estates, much of which it administered wisely during the colonial period. It quickly became the largest landowner in the New World. When the Jesuits were expelled from Brazil, it was discovered that the Company was by far the largest single property owner in the colony. Financial transactions further filled ecclesiastical coffers. Banks were extremely rare and the elite possessed little liquid capital. When the landowners or merchants needed to borrow money, they usually applied to the more provident monasteries which had capital to loan for a fee and at established interest rates.

The Church wealth was by no means evenly distributed. In cities such as Lima, Salvador da Bahia, Ouro Preto, Quito, Antigua, and Mexico City, ostentatiously imposing churches crowded one another, while "shocking poverty" characterized hundreds of humble parish churches dotting the countryside. While some of the higher clergy lived on incomes surpassing those of many of the sovereign princes of Germany, impoverished clerics administered to the needs of the faithful in remote villages. Maldistributed the Church's treasure might have been but no one seriously doubted the awesome extent of it. To its collection, multiplication, and management, the Church eventually came to devote much of its time. Security and comfort supplanted the zeal and concern characteristic of the Church during the century it dedicated to the conversion of the Indians.

The wealth reinforced the conservative inclinations of the Iberian Church. After the initial phase of evangelizing, it too exploited the Indians, as well as the African slaves, to till Church lands or to erect larger and more opulent edifices. To the masses it preached resignation. If God had made them poor, a sin it would be to question why. Poverty was to have its reward in the next life. It was not from the masses that the Church drew its leadership. Generally the sons of the wealthy and/or noble became bishops and archbishops, positions in the New World dominated by the European-born. Thus, the highest ranks of the clergy, like those in the military and civil service, were associated with and filled by the aristocracy. In wealth, power, prestige, and monopoly of education, the Roman Catholic Church by the end of the eighteenth century ranked as an omnipotent institution in the Western Hemisphere. Its influence weighed heavily, not only in the social and religious life of the community, but in politics and economics as well.

three

Independence

Juan O'Gorman, "Mexican Independence Mural"

During the long colonial period, the psychology of the Latin Americans, particularly the elite, changed significantly. A feeling of inferiority before the Iberian-born gave way to a feeling of equality and then to superiority. At the same time, nativism, a devotion to one's locality, matured into feelings of nationalism, a group consciousness attributing supreme value to the land of one's birth and pledging unswerving dedication to it. Those changes intensified the Latin Americans' resentment of the authority, control, and direction of the metropolises. Inspired by the North American example and encouraged by the changes wrought in Napoleonic Europe, they declared their independence in order to realize their potential and chart their own future. In all cases, except in Haiti and during the early stages of the Mexican revolution, the creole and mazombo elites directed the movements toward independence and broke the ties with the former mother countries.

A CHANGING MENTALITY BEGETS NEW ATTITUDES AND ACTION

Reasoning, questioning, and inquiry characterized the attitude of the European intellectuals in the seventeenth and particularly in the eighteenth century. Under the influence of the Enlightenment, man became increasingly concerned with life here on earth, rather than with the metaphysics of celestial existence. As one result, he set about to study, explore, and improve his temporal life.

Before the end of the first century of Iberian colonization, the inhabitants of the New World began to reflect on themselves, their surroundings, and their relations to the rest of the world. They spoke and wrote for the first time in introspective terms. Juan de Cárdenas, although born in Spain, testified in his *Problemas y Secretas Maravillosos de las Indias* (The Marvellous Problems and Secrets of the Indies), published in 1591, that in Mexico the creole surpassed the peninsular in wit and intelligence. Evincing a strong devotion to New Spain, Bernardo de Balbuena penned his *La Grandeza Mexicana* (The Grandeur of Mexico) in 1604 in praise of all things Mexican. He implied that for beauty, interest, and charm, life in Mexico City equaled—or surpassed—that in most Spanish cities. In 1618, Ambrósio Fernandes Brandão made the first attempt to define or interpret Brazil in his *Diálogos das Grandezas do Brasil* (Dialogues of the Greatness of Brazil). In doing so, he exhibited his devotion to the colony, chiding those Portuguese who came to Brazil solely to exploit it and return wealthy to the peninsula. Poets, historians, and essayists reflected on the natural beauty of a generous nature. They took up with renewed vigor the theme extolled in the early sixteenth century that the New World was an earthly paradise. A climax of sorts was reached in the early nineteenth century when the Brazilian poet Francisco de São Carlos depicted paradise in his long poem *A Assunção* in terms which made it sound strikingly similar to Brazil. A few distinguished visitors who glimpsed the Iberian colonies spoke with awe of the beauty and potential they beheld. Exemplary of their observations was the remark of Alexander von Humboldt that "The vast kingdom of New Spain, if cultivated with care, would alone produce what the rest of the world produces, sugar, cochineal, cacao, cotton, coffee, wheat, hemp, linen, silk, oil, wine. It would supply all the metals, without excluding mercury." Physically Iberian America impressed native and foreigner alike to be a privileged region, an idea which had prompted the colonial Brazilian intellectual Sebastião da Rocha Pita to remark, "The sun now rises in the West."

Concentrating ever more earnestly on themselves and their surroundings, the elite in the New World searched for ways of improving their conditions. The intensification of that search coincided with the sweep of the Enlightenment across Latin America. As manifested in that part of the world, the Enlightenment became primarily a search for and then promotion of useful knowledge. It was a selective search. The Latin American intellectuals drew from the enlightened ideologies those practical examples which best suited their goals. Principal attention focused on science, economics, commerce, agriculture, and education. Political matters received secondary attention and religion, at least for the time being, little at all. The American intellectuals read Smith, Locke, Benito Feijóo, António Vernei, Rousseau, Diderot, Raynal, Montesquieu. Nor did they neglect ideas emanating from the United States, whose declaration of and struggle for independence and resultant federal republic fascinated the Ibero-American elite. In every region of Latin America, at least a few intellectuals had read Thomas Paine, Thomas Jefferson, or Benjamin Franklin. Copies of the Declaration of Independence, the Federalist Papers, the Constitution of 1787, and Washington's Farewell Address circulated. The Yankee merchant David Curtis DeForest, for example, active in the Platine region in the first decade of the nineteenth century propagated the ideas of Paine, presented a copy of Washington's Farewell Address to Manuel Belgrano who translated and published it, and donated copies of works by Montesquieu, Voltaire, and Rousseau to the public library of Buenos Aires. Those three French philosophers enjoyed the greatest popularity among the intellectuals of the New World. There was no doubt that French ideas predominated.

The new ideas entered Latin America with minimal difficulty. The frown of neither the Inquisitor nor the customs officer could stem the intellectual tides. A French visitor to Brazil during the waning years of the colonial period commented on the ease with which the censor's prohibitions on book imports could be evaded. One bookdealer in Minas Gerais in the mid-eighteenth century offered such efficient service that the imprint date of the European book and the arrival date of that book in Minas Gerais were sometimes only one year apart. Inventories exist of private libraries from disparate parts of the Iberian-American empire, Francisco de Miranda's in Havana, Antonio Narino's in Bogotá, Francisco de Ortega's in Buenos Aires, Luís Vieira's in Mariana, representative of the local preference for the enlightened writers and philosophers of the eighteenth century. The owners seemingly read the books in their libraries. The intellectuals delighted in quoting from European authors. The Peruvian José Baquíjano y Carillo in his *Elogio* (1781) referred to Montesquieu, Linguet, and Raynal; the Mexican José Antonio Alzate y Ramírez mentioned in his *Observaciones* (1787) Reaumur, Nollet, Monnet, and the *Encyclopédie*.

The pressures of the British and French on the Iberian monarchs for greater trade with their American empires, burgeoning European contraband in the Americas, and the more liberal commercial code promulgated by Spain in 1778 brought Latin America into close contact with Europe and with European ideas. Foreigners visited the Americas, many of them on scientific missions: Peter Loefling was in Nueva Granada, 1754–61; Nikolous von Joequin, in the West Indies and Venezuela, 1755–59; Alexander von Humboldt, in Cuba, Mexico, and South America,

1799–1804; and many others. Foreigners likewise helped to introduce the latest thought into eighteenth-century Brazil, a colony always more accessible than Spanish America. The Portuguese monarchs dispatched various and varied scientific expeditions to Brazil, many of whose members were foreigners as the names Reverend, Consfeldt, Schwebel, Galluzi, Hestcko, Rorich, Goltz, Hatton, Havelle, Brunelli, Capassi, and Landi testify. Occasionally foreign ships visited Brazilian ports. For example, in 1759, both French and English squadrons dropped anchor in Salvador.

Representatives of the American elite traveled in Europe and American students went to Iberian universities and at times beyond to French and English universities. Miranda, Simón Bolívar, Manuel Belgrano, Bernardo O'Higgins, José de San Martin, and José Bonifácio all studied and traveled in Europe. All espoused ideas of the Enlightenment, and it is probably no coincidence that together they freed South America. Those travelers made contact with foreign academies and maintained their contact through correspondence.

Once admitted, the new ideas diffused rapidly throughout the colonies. The universities of Spanish America, of which 23 existed at the opening of the nineteenth century, contributed to their spread. Professors and students alike challenged the hoary theories of Aristotle and the scholastic tradition. Lectures covered the ideas of Descartes, Newton, Leibniz, and Locke. In at least one instance, the ideas of the French naturalist Lamarck on the theory of evolution were being discussed in a New World classroom within a year of their publication. Other centers in Spanish America for the diffusion of the latest European knowledge were the Economic Societies of the Friends of the Country (Sociedades Económicas de Amigos del País), which had developed in Spain and spread to the New World by the 1780s. The statutes of one of the early societies, that of Santiago de Cuba, indicated that some of the goals were to promote education, employment, commerce, and agriculture, and it was later pointed out that the goals could not be attained without encouraging manufacturing. In general the societies showed a strong tendency to emphasize the natural and physical sciences, agriculture, commerce, and education, as well as to give some attention to political and social questions. Portuguese America had not a single university, but its counterpart of the economic societies was the literary and scientific academies of which there were six, all established between 1724 and 1794 in either Salvador or Rio de Janeiro. Each had a short but apparently active life. The printing presses in Spanish America—Lisbon rigidly prohibited the setting up of a press in its American possessions—contributed significantly to spreading ideas. Among their many publications numbered several outstanding newspapers, all fonts of enlightened ideas and nativism, *Diario Literario de Mexico* (1767–68); *Las Primicias de la Cultura* (Quito), (1792); *Mercurio Peruano* (1791–95); *Gazeta de Guate-*

mala (1797–1810); and *Semanario del Nuevo Reyno de Granada* (1808–11). Their pages were replete with references to, quotations from, and translations of the major authors of the European Enlightenment.

Considerable evidence testifies that the Latin Americans drank deeply from the heady wines of the Enlightenment. The minutes of the meetings of the Economic Societies and the academies, the discussions in clandestine Masonic lodges, and writings, both private and published, indicate that some of the ideas most prevalent among the intellectuals were the equality of all men before the law, the need to open the ports to world trade, the hardships worked by monopolies and restrictions on trade and production, the desirability of expanding educational facilities and opportunities, the benefits of a free press, and the necessity of establishing justice as an independent branch of government. These also were some of the ideas upon which liberals concentrated their attention throughout the nineteenth century. Concerning the role of ideas in the mounting tensions between the Old World and the New, the Argentine statesman and historian Bartolomé Mitre observed, "There can be no revolution until the ideas of men become the conscience of the masses, and until the passions of men become a public force. . . ." A fascination with those ideas, an inclination to experiment, the urge to reason weakened a former blind respect for authority and tradition.

The privileged classes in the New World desired most to reform commerce and trade. The American merchants and planters chaffed under monopolies and restrictions, and the reforms in the eighteenth century were not all welcome. The thrust of those reforms was to accelerate centralism and thus to increase the effective political and economic powers of the crowns. The Americans felt more heavily than before the weight of royal authority, a closer supervision and contact which multiplied tensions between the colonies and the metropolises.

Physiocrat doctrine gained support among Brazilian intellectuals. Timidly at first they began to suggest some changes. Bishop José Joaquim da Cunha de Azeredo Coutinho argued against a higher tax on sugar in 1791 and three years later pointed out the inconveniences of several crown restrictions and monopolies. Other Brazilians spoke out in favor of reducing or abolishing taxes and duties and soon were advocating a greater freedom of trade. From Bahia, João Rodrigues de Brito boldly called for the full liberty for the Brazilian farmers to grow whatever crops they wanted, to construct whatever works or factories were necessary for the good of their crops, to sell in any place, by any means, and through whatever agent they wished to choose without heavy taxes or burdensome bureaucracy, to sell to the highest bidder, and to sell their products at any time when it best suited them. Similar complaints and demands reverberated throughout the Spanish-American empire. Chileans wanted to break down their economic isolation. Reflecting on the potential wealth of Chile and the lingering poverty of its inhabitants, José de Cos Iriberri, a contemporary of the Bahian Rodrigues de Brito, concluded, "Crops cannot yield wealth unless they are produced in quantity and obtain a good price; and for this they need sound methods of cultivation, large consumption, and access to foreign markets." Manuel de Salas agreed and insisted that free trade was the natural means to wealth. And Anselmo de la Cruz asked a question being heard with greater frequency throughout the colonies, "What better method could be adopted to develop the agriculture, industry, and trade of our kingdom than to allow it to export its natural products to all the nations of the world without exception?"

As the American colonies grew in population and activity and as Spain became increasingly involved in European wars in the eighteenth century, breaches appeared in the mercantilistic walls Spain had carefully constructed around its American empire. British merchants audaciously assailed those walls and when and where posssible widened the breaches. For their part, the Spanish Bourbons tried hard to introduce economic reforms which would reenforce Spain's monopolistic economic control. As we saw in the last chapter, they authorized and encouraged a series of monopolistic companies. Doubtless, the Guipúzcoa Company best illustrated the effects of those monopolies and certainly the protests they elicited from a jealous native merchant class.

By the end of the seventeenth century, Venezuela exported a variety of natural products, most important of which were tobacco, cacao, and salt, to Spain, Spanish America, and some foreign islands in the Caribbean. That trade expanded to England, France, and the United States during the early years of the century. Commerce enjoyed in that Spanish colony a reputation as an honest and respectable profession. A small, prosperous—and increasingly influential—merchant class emerged. The Bolívars were one of the most successful of those native merchant families. The creation of the Guipúzcoa Company in 1728 to insure that Venezuela traded within the imperial markets and to eliminate commercial intercourse with foreigners evoked sharp protest from the merchants, who readily foresaw the impending injury to their welfare. They complained that the company infringed upon their interests, threatened their economic well-being, shut off their profitable trade with other Europeans, and failed to supply all their needs. Spain, after all, they quickly pointed out, could not absorb all of Venezuela's agricultural exports, whereas an eager market in the West Indies and northern Europe offered to buy them. Finally, exasperated with the monopoly and discouraged from expecting any results from their complaints, the merchants fostered an armed revolt against the company in 1749, a revolt which took Spain four years to quell. The struggle, both armed and verbal, against the company fostered a hostile feeling toward the crown committed to support the unpopular company. The friction between the local merchants, businessmen, landowners, and population on the one hand and the Guipúzcoa Company and crown on the other continued throughout the rest of the century. The merchants' belief that freer trade would fatten their profits was more than satisfactorily proven when Spain, after 1779, entered the war against England with the consequent interruption caused by the English fleet in the trade between Venezuela and Spain. The merchants took immediate advantage of the situation to trade directly and openly with the English islands in the Caribbean. Their profits soared.

Two new institutions soon organized the protests and activities of the disaffected Venezuelans. The Real Consulado de Caracas, authorized in 1785 and established in 1793, brought together merchants and plantation owners, and it soon became a focal point for local dissatisfaction and agitation. Then in 1797 the merchants formed a militia company to protect the coast from any foreign attack. That responsibility intensified their nativism, or, at that stage, patriotism. Nurtured by such local institutions, the complaints against the monopoly, burdensome taxes, and restrictions mounted in direct proportion to the increasing popularity of the idea of free trade. As one merchant expressed it, "Commerce ought to be as free as air." Popular songs at the end of the eighteenth century also expressed the economic protests:

Todos nuestros derechos	All our rights
los vemos usurpados	We see usurped
con tributos e impuestos	And with taxes and tributes
estamos agobiados	We are bent down
• • •	
Si alguno quiere saber	If anyone wants to know
por que estoy descamisado	Why I go shirtless
porque con los tributos	It's because the taxes
el Rey me ha desnudado	Of the king denude me
• • •	
Los Intendentes ayudan	With much enthusiasm
con mucho afán al Tirano	The Intendents aid the Tyrant
a comerse la sangre	To drink the blood
del pueblo americano	Of the American people

One of the results of these intensifying complaints was the series of armed uprisings in 1795, 1797, and 1799. Great Britain continued to encourage those and other protests against Spain's system of commercial monopoly. Clearly English interests coincided with those of the creole elite who thought in terms of free trade.

Economic dissatisfaction extended beyond the narrow confines of the colonial elite. Many popular elements protested the burdensome taxes and expressed hope for improvements. In fact, a wider segment of the population probably understood and appreciated the economic motivations for independence more than they did the political ones. Popular anti-tax demonstrations rocked many cities in both Spanish and Portuguese America in the eighteenth century. Oppressive economic conditions helped to spark two potentially serious popular uprisings, the Tupac Amaru Revolt in Peru in 1780 and the Comunero Revolt in New Granada (Colombia) in 1781, and to foment the Bahian Conspiracy in Brazil in 1798.

Taking the name Tupac Amaru II and considering himself the rightful heir to the Incan throne, the mestizo José Gabriel Condorcanqui Noguera led a revolt—mainly of Indians, but at least in the beginning with the support of mestizos as well as some creoles—which broke out in November 1780, to protest the most distressing abuses of the Spanish colonial system. Excessive taxation, economic exploitation, and forced labor constituted some of the bitterest complaints of the followers of the Incan pretender. Much blood ran before a well-armed militia checked the Indians, captured their leader, and suppressed the revolt in 1781. Later that same year a leading Lima intellectual, José Baquíjano y Carillo, expounded before the newly arrived viceroy the injustices Spain had perpetuated on the Indians. His emotional discourse rang with ideas from the French philosophers. He subtly questioned not just the abuses of royal power but royal power itself.

Protesting an increase in taxes and burdensome monopolies, creoles and mestizos in New Granada rose up to nullify unpopular Spanish laws. The revolt spread spontaneously through New Granada in 1781. Faced with the growing success of the rebels, the Spanish authorities capitulated to their demands for economic reforms. However, once the *comuneros* dispersed, satisfied with their apparent success, the viceroy abrogated former agreements and arrested the leaders who were executed in 1782 and 1783.

Across the continent in Bahia, another popular conspiracy, this one against the Portuguese metropolis, came to a head in 1798. It exemplified the penetration of the ideas of the Enlightenment into the masses, which, in this case, thought in terms of economic, social, and political reforms, even of independence. The conspirators were simple folk: soldiers, artisans, mechanics, workmen, and so large a number of tailors that the movement somtimes bears the title of the "Conspiracy of the Tailors." All were young (under 30 years old), and all were mulattoes. The conspirators spoke in vague but eloquent terms of free trade, which they felt would bring prosperity to their port, and of equality for all men without distinctions of race or color. They denounced excessive taxation and oppressive restrictions. The plot, after it was uncovered by the colonial officials, caused one Portuguese minister to lament that the Bahians "for some unexplained madness and because they did not understand their own best interests, had become infected with the abominable French ideas and shown great affection for the absurd French Constitution." Dissatisfaction thus pervaded many classes. Its increase during the eighteenth century coincided with many reforms enacted by the Iberian crowns. Perhaps this situation further substantiates Crane Brinton's thesis that revolutions stem from hope not despair, from the promise of progress rather than from continuous oppression. The Latin Americans came to realize that in order to effect the reforms they desired they themselves would have to wield political power.

The enlightenment of the elite (and to a much lesser degree of a small portion of the masses); the growing feeling of nativism which indicated a greater self-confidence on the part of the Latin Americans and certainly a psychological change which diminished former feelings of inferiority; a concern among the Latin Americans with the mighty potential of their region coupled with a frustration because the potential went unrealized; a resentment of the metropolitan exploitation of the colonies; and growing complaints of excessive taxes, restrictions, and monopolies widened the gap between the colonials and the Iberians. The resentment was very noticeable on the highest level between the creoles and mazombos on the one hand and the peninsulares and reinóis on the other. Those born in Latin America seldom received the preferment, positions, or promotions which the crowns lavished on the Iberian born. Only four creoles served as viceroys—and they were the sons of Spanish officials. Of the 602 captains-general, governors, and presidents in Spanish America, only 14 had been creoles; of the 606 bishops and archbishops, 105 were born in the New World. Such a preference aroused bitter resentment among the creoles. In his early seventeenth-century travels, Thomas Gage witnessed and discussed the bitterness arising from creole-peninsular rivalry. One distinguished representative of the creoles, Simón Bolívar stated in 1815, "The hatred that the Peninsular has inspired in us is greater than the ocean which separates us." The Iberian suspicion of the New World elite in effect questioned both their ability and loyalty. One high Portuguese official remarked of Brazil, "That country increases in everyone the spirit of ambition and the relaxation of virtues." A distinguished Chilean, advising the king that all would be better served if the crown would make use of the creoles, concluded, "The status of the creoles has thus become an enigma: they are neither foreigners nor nationals . . . and are honorable but hopeless, loyal but disinherited. . . ." Further, the New World inhabitants resented the flow of wealth into the pockets of the peninsulares and reinóis who came to the Americas to exploit the wealth and return to Iberia to spend their hastily gained riches. A *visitador* to New Spain, José de Gálvez, expressed to the crown an oft-repeated creole grievance: "Spaniards not only don't allow us to share the government of our country, but they carry away all our money."

Obviously the point of view of the Iberian and the American varied. The first came to the New World with a metropolitan outlook. He saw the empire as a unit and catered to the well-being of the metropolis. The latter had a regional bias. His prestige, power, and wealth rested on his lands. Whatever political base he had was the municipal government, whose limited authority and responsibility reinforced his parochial outlook. In short, he thought mainly in terms of his region and ignored the wider imperial views.

During the last half of the eighteenth century, a new position, once again of local significance, was opened to the Latin Americans when the crowns created the colonial militias. The obligation to defend the colonies from foreign attack intensified nativism. Further, the high militia ranks conferred new prestige on creoles and mazombos alike and encouraged their ambitions. They awaited with growing impatience an opportunity to improve their status. The Napoleonic wars provided that opportunity.

Napoleon rocked the foundations of both Iberian monarchies. In 1807, his armies crossed Spain, invaded Portugal, and captured Lisbon. The Portuguese Braganzas, however, did not fall prisoner to the conquering French armies. Prince-Regent John packed the government aboard a fleet and under the protecting guns of English men-of-war sailed from Lisbon for Rio de Janeiro just as the French reached the outskirts of the capital. The transference of a European crown to one of its colonies was unique. The Braganzas were the only European royalty to visit their possessions in the New World during the colonial period. They set up their court among the surprised but delighted Brazilians and ruled the empire from Rio de Janeiro for 13 years.

After seizing control of the Portuguese metropolis, Napoleon immediately turned his attention to Spain. He swept first Charles IV and then Ferdinand VII off the Spanish throne in order to crown his brother Joseph king. The Spaniards detested the Bonapart puppet and renewed allegiance to Ferdinand, a prisoner in France. Rising up against Napoleon, they created a series of juntas to govern the empire in the name of the captive king. Spanish-Americans reacted with equal repugnance to the usurper. Various juntas appeared in the New World to govern in Ferdinand's name. In effect, this step toward self-government constituted an irreparable break with Spain. By abducting the king, Napoleon had broken the major link between Spain and the Americas. The break once made was widened by the many grievances of the Latin Americans against the metropolis.

Most of Latin America achieved its independence during a period of two decades, between the proud declaration of Haiti's independence in 1804 and the Spanish defeat at Ayacucho in 1824. Nearly 20 million inhabitants of Latin America severed their allegiance to France or to the

Iberian monarchs. Every class and condition of men in Latin America participated at one time or another, at one place or another, in the protracted movement. Three distinct aspects of the movement stand out: the slave uprising in Haiti, the popular revolt in Mexico, and the elitist defiance in most of the rest of Latin America.

THE SLAVES DECLARE HAITI'S INDEPENDENCE

Saint Domingue, the western third of the island of Hispaniola, witnessed the only completely successful slave rebellion in the New World. Long, bloody, devastating, it expelled or killed the white masters, terminated French rule, and left the blacks free to govern themselves.

Sugar profits soared in the eighteenth century as the French planters exploited the good soil of the island, adopted the latest techniques for growing and grinding the cane, and imported ever larger numbers of African slaves to work the land and to process the crop. The motherland smiled with satisfaction on its rich Caribbean treasure. A multiracial society had developed, a divided society, which by 1789 counted 40,000 whites and half a million blacks with approximately 25,000 mulattoes. The Code Noir, promulgated in 1685, regulated slavery. Theoretically it provided some protection to the black slave, facilitated manumission, and admitted the freed man to full rights in society. In reality, the European code but slightly ameliorated the slave's dreadful state. In general, slavery on the lucrative plantations was harsh. To meet the demand for sugar, the plantation owner callously overworked his blacks and to reduce overhead he frequently underfed them. An astonishingly high death rate testified to the brutality of the system.

The distant cry of "Liberty, equality, fraternity" echoed in the Caribbean in 1789. Each segment of the tense colony interpreted it differently. The white planters demanded and received from the Paris National Assembly a large measure of local autonomy. Then the Assembly extended the vote to all free persons, a move favoring the mulattoes. The planters' demand for the repeal of that law precipitated a struggle between them and the mulattoes. Then, on August 22, 1791, the slaves demanding their own liberty rebelled in northern Saint Domingue. Over 100,000 arose under the leadership of the educated slave Toussaint L'Ouverture, son of African slave parents. In pursuit of his constant goal of liberating his fellow blacks, he fought for the following decade against —depending on the time and circumstances—the French, British, Spaniards, and various mulatto groups. Victory rewarded his extraordinary leadership and the courage of the blacks. By 1801, L'Ouverture commanded the entire island of Hispaniola. In that year Napoleon resolved to intervene to return the island to its former role as a profitable sugar producer. A huge army invaded Saint Domingue and the French induced L'Ouverture to a meeting only to seize him treacherously. Imprisoned in Europe, he died in 1803. His two lieutenants, Jean-Jacques Dessalines and Henri Christophe took up the leadership. A combination of black strength and yellow fever defeated the massive French effort. On January 1, 1804, Dessalines proclaimed the independence of the western part of Hispaniola, giving it the name of Haiti. Haiti emerged as the second independent nation of the Western Hemisphere, the first in Latin America. For the exploited blacks of the New World, it represented hope; into the hemisphere's plantation owners, it instilled a chilling fear.

AN UNSUCCESSFUL POPULAR REVOLUTION IN MEXICO

Taking advantage of the political vacuum in Spain in 1808, the creoles of New Spain maneuvered to form a local junta to govern the viceroyalty, a move calculated to shift political power from the Spaniards to the Mexican elite. Alarmed by the maneuvering, the peninsulars feared the loss of their traditional, preferred positions. They acted swiftly to form their own junta and thus shoved the creoles aside. The creoles plotted to seize power, but in September 1810, the peninsulars discovered the plan and jailed the leaders. One plotter, Father Miguel Hidalgo, a parish priest in the impoverished town of Dolores, escaped detection. Well educated, indeed, profoundly influenced by the Enlightenment, he professed advanced social ideas. He believed that the Church had a social mission to perform and a duty to improve the lot of the downtrodden Indians. Personally he bore numerous grievances against peninsulars and the Spanish government.

Hidalgo resolved to carry out the exposed plan. Ringing his church bell on September 16, 1810, he summoned his humble parishioners, most of whom were mestizos and Indians, to exhort them to expel the peninsulars from office and to establish a better government. In so doing, Hidalgo unleased new forces. Unlike the creoles who simply wanted to substitute themselves for the peninsulars in power, the mestizo and Indian masses desired far-reaching social and economic changes. The popularity of the revolution, as well as the fury of the masses, amazed the benign churchman. The ranks of his army swelled overnight to awesome numbers. With little difficulty, Hidalgo's forces swept through Guanajuato and Guadalajara and advanced on Mexico City. A swath of massacred peninsulars as well as many creoles lay behind them. With energies released after three centuries of repression, the Indians and mestizos struck out at all they hated. The creoles became as frightened as the peninsulars, and the two rival factions united before the threat from the masses.

Hidalgo did little to discipline the men under him. Indeed, his control of them proved minimal. His ideas were disorganized, vague, at times contradictory. While voicing his loyalty to Ferdinand, he denounced the abuses of the viceregal government—later he declared Mexico free and independent. He threatened the peninsulars with death; he abolished slavery. Poised before Mexico City, he hesitated, then ordered a withdrawal, an action which cost him much of the allegiance of the masses. The Spanish army regained its confidence and struck out in pursuit of the ragtag rebels. It captured Hidalgo and in mid-1811, a firing squad executed him. To Hidalgo goes the credit of initiating Mexico's revolution for independence.

Father José María Morelos, a mestizo parish priest, took command of the revolutionary movement. He defined his program: establish the independence of Mexico; create a republican government in which the Mexican people would participate with the exclusion of the former wealthy, nobility, and entrenched officeholders; abolish slavery, affirm the equality of all men; terminate the special privileges of the Church as well as the compulsory tithe; and partition the large estates so that all farmers could own land. At Chilpancingo, he declared that Mexico's soverignty resided in the people who could alter the government according to their will. He called forth pride in the Mexican—not the Spanish—past. His program contained the seeds of a real social, economic, and political revolution and thereby repulsed peninsular and creole alike. He ably led his small and disciplined army in central Mexico for more than four years. In 1815, the Spaniards captured and executed him. The royalists immediately gained the ascendency in Mexico, and dashed the hopes of the mestizos and Indians for social and economic changes. New Spain returned momentarily to its colonial slumbers.

The conservative elite consummated Mexican independence. The peninsulars enjoyed their comfortable privileges in Mexico so much that they, allied with the creoles, were willing to free themselves from Spain in order to perpetuate them. Spain in 1820 smacked of a liberalism far too extreme for their tastes. A revolt in that year restored constitutional government to Madrid. A current of liberal and anticlerical sentiment characterized the high Spanish officials, much to the annoyance of the peninsulars and creoles in New Spain. They rejected Spanish liberalism just as they earlier had turned away from Mexican liberalism. In their reaction to the events in Spain, they decided to free themselves and thus chart their own destiny. The ecclesiastical hierarchy, fearful of the loss of property and of secular restrictions if the liberals in control of Spain had their way, converted to the independence movement, buttressing it with the Church's prestige and power. The peninsulars and creoles selected a pompous creole army officer, Agustín de Iturbide, who had fought against Hidalgo and Morelos, first as their instrument to effect independence and then as their emperor. The most conservative forces of New Spain ushered in Mexican independence in 1821. They advocated neither social nor economic changes. They sought to preserve—or enhance if possible—their privileges. The only innovation was political: a creole emperor replaced the Spanish king, symbolic of the wider replacement of the peninsulars by the creoles in government. The events harmonized little with the concepts of Hidalgo and Morelos but suited creole desires. The Mexican struggle for independence began as a major social, economic, and political revolution but ended as a conservative coup d'etat. The only immediate victors were the creole elite.

ELITIST REVOLTS

The triumph of the Mexican creole elite paralleled similar victories in other parts of Latin America, where the local aristocrats, occasionally in alliance with some peninsulars, took advantage of the disgust with Iberian rule, the changing events in Europe, the example of the United States of America, and the desires for reform, to declare the independence of their locality and assume power. The actual consummation of independence in Latin America only affected a minority of the area's inhabitants. The masses, composed primarily of Indians, blacks, mestizos, and mulattoes, played an ambiguous role, at times fighting for their Iberian leaders, while at others filling the ranks of the American armies. Their loyalty often depended upon a variety of local factors as well as the abilities, promises, and persuasiveness of rival generals. With the major exception of Haiti and of Mexico during the early years of the wars of independence, the masses gained little. At best there were vague and contradictory promises of change which might improve their lot.

The issues at stake revolved mainly around control of the government and trade policies and as such affected almost exclusively the local aristocracy. The successful urban merchants and rural planters stood to gain the most from independence. The landed gentry enjoyed considerable power and social prestige because of their huge estates and their influence over local government. They identified more closely with local conditions than with either of the distant metropolises. They favored independence in order to expand their own power and to assure a greater freedom of access to international markets. Conservative by nature, they advocated few structural reforms. An influential Brazilian journalist of the period summed up their viewpoint when he pleaded, "Let us have no excesses. We want a constitution, not a revolution." The cities brought together the planters to discuss their common problems and aspirations, while at the same time within the cities a small but vocal class of free persons appeared, neither plantation owners nor slaves nor peasants, an unstable class anxious to improve its status. Most influential of the urban dwellers were the merchants who saw in independence an opportunity to better control their own destiny and hence to increase trade and business. The cities had previously been focal points of discontent and agitation. In them, the waves of nativism crested. Frequently the municipal councils served as the forum of debate and the instrumentality for action by which the cause of independence was furthered.

Representatives of the privileged classes led the hastily recruited American armies whose ranks of patriots as well as adventurers expanded or contracted depending on the forcefulness of the generals and their successes in battle. The wars for independence in South America—in many areas, protracted, bloody, devastating—have been reduced largely to a chronicle of the exploits and brilliance of a handful of able generals: Simón Bolívar, Bernardo O'Higgins, José de San Martín, Antonio José de Sucre, to cite the most oft-mentioned. The narrative and glorification of the biographies of single elitist leaders evolved into a marked characteristic of Latin American historiography. In Brazil, the Visconde de Porto Alegre once announced, "To know the biographies of all the outstanding men of a period is to know the history of those times." The Peruvian historian Francisco García Calderón later echoed that observation, "The history of the South American Republics may be reduced to the biographies of their representative men." Such an outlook obviously eliminated the study of the actions and thoughts of the common man. Increasingly, attention focused on the exploits of two extraordinary representatives of the creole elite, General José de San Martín of Argentina and General Simón Bolívar of Venezuela, who between them led courageous armies through a grand pincers movement which defeated the Spaniards in South America.

In 1810, the movements for independence got underway simultaneously in opposite ends of South America, Venezuela and Argentina. The Argentine movement went practically unchecked, while in the north the Venezuelans battled heroically, although not always with the blessings of Mars. The struggle for Spanish America's independence fell into three rather well-defined periods: the initial thrust and expansion of the movement between 1810 and 1814; the faltering of the patriotic armies and the resurgence of royalist domination, 1814–16; and the consummation of independence between 1817 and 1826. The actual fighting was limited to a few areas, principally Mexico and Venezuela. In large sections of Latin America—Central America, Paraguay, Argentina, and Brazil—no major battles occurred.

In both Venezuela and Argentina some leaders understood that their declarations would be meaningless and their aspirations thwarted so long as a Spanish army remained anywhere on the South American continent. For that reason they expanded their struggle from the regional to the continental stage. From Argentina, the army of San Martín crossed the Andes to contribute in 1817 to Chile's struggle against the Spaniards and then in 1820 invaded Peru, stronghold of Spanish royalism. In the North, Bolívar's army moved back and forth, between Venezuela and Colombia before penetrating southward into Ecuador, Peru, and Bolivia. Although the independence of Spanish South America was virtually guaranteed by Sucre's decisive victory at Ayacucho in late 1824, the wars of liberation really only ended in early 1826 when the Spanish garrison occupying Callao, Peru's principal port, surrendered. Long before then, the new nations of Latin America had declared their independence. In most cases either a specially assembled congress or a local assembly—always dominated by the creoles—issued the declaration. Some, as in the case of Peru, Uruguay, Mexico, Brazil, Colombia, and Venezuela, did so before de facto independence was achieved; and others, Argentina, Bolivia, Central America, Haiti, Paraguay, and Chile, afterward.

The prolonged struggle for independence had some social and economic consequences for the new nations. Class and color lines blurred slightly. None of the newly independent nations continued the legal disabilities once restricting mestizos. In spite of some creole desires it was impossible. In Mexico, for example, the clergy no longer kept the minute records of caste in their parochial books. In fact, some mestizo army officers quickly rose to power in the new nations. Mentally they tended to identify with the creoles. In a few areas, the governments abolished slavery or began the lengthy process of gradual emancipation. Contacts with Europe north of the Pyrenees multiplied with the resultant influx of new ideas. Economically the revolutions brought disaster to many areas. Normal trade and communications routes were interrupted; mines were flooded and equipment destroyed; herds of livestock were slaughtered, confiscated, or dispersed; currency manipulation, depreciation, inflation, the flight of capital, forced loans, confiscation of property, and capricious taxation brought financial ruin; and part of the work force was scattered, maimed, or killed. On the other hand, the ports of Latin America opened to the world and trade policies liberalized, although these changes were not without their disadvantages. Iberian mercantilist policies were abandoned, but in the new order, Great Britain came to exercise the economic hegemony once held by Spain and Portugal. The complex taxation system of the colonial past gave way to a reliance on customs duties as the principal source of national income.

Portuguese America achieved its independence during the same tumultuous years. Like its republican neighbors, Argentina and Paraguay, Brazil entered into nationhood almost bloodlessly, and following the trend evident in Spanish America, the mazombos clamored for the positions of the reinóis, although their ascendancy was more gradual than that of the creoles. The difference lay in the way Brazil achieved its independence.

Under the guidance of John VI, Brazil's position within the Portuguese empire improved rapidly. He opened the ports to world trade, authorized and encouraged industry, and raised Brazil's status to that of a kingdom, the equal of Portugal itself within the empire. Rio de Janeiro changed from a quiet viceregal capital to the thriving center of a far-flung world empire. The psychological impact on the Brazilians was momentous. Foreigners who knew Brazil during the first decade of the monarch's residence there commented on the beneficial effect the presence of the crown exercised on the spirit of the Brazilians. Ignácio José de Macedo typified the elation of his fellow Brazilians when he predicted, "The unexpected transference of the Monarchy brought a brilliant dawn to these dark horizons, as spectacular as that on the day of its discovery. The new day of regeneration, an omen of brighter destinies, will bring long centuries of prosperity and glory." When the royal court returned to Lisbon in 1821, after 13 years of residence in Brazil, John left behind the Braganza heir, Prince Pedro, as regent. The young prince took up his duties with enthusiasm, only to find himself caught between two powerful and opposing forces. On the one side, the newly convened parliament, the Côrtes, in Lisbon, annoyed with and jealous of the importance Brazil had assumed within the empire during the previous decade and a half, sought to reduce it to previous colonial subservience; on the other, Brazilian patriots thought in terms of national independence. As the Côrtes made obvious its intent to strip Brazil of previous privileges as well as to restrict the authority of its prince-regent, Pedro listened more attentively to the mazombo views. He appointed the learned and nationalistic mazombo José Bonifácio de Andrada e Silva to his cabinet, the first Brazilian to hold such a high post. Bonifácio was instrumental in persuading Pedro to defy the humiliating orders of the Côrtes and to heed mazombo opinion which refused to allow Lisbon to dictate policies for Brazil. On September 7, 1822, under the influence of Brazilian nationalism, Pedro declared the independence of Latin America's largest nation, and several months later in a splendid ceremony he was crowned "Constitutional Emperor and Perpetual Defender of Brazil." The evolutionary course upon which Brazil had embarked provided a stability and unity which no other former viceroyalty of the New World could boast.

A Nineteenth-Century Country Home outside Asunción, Paraguay

four

National

Consolidation

Most of Latin America had crossed the threshold to independence by the end of the first quarter of the nineteenth century. The independence was nominal, since the elites of the new nations remained spiritually linked to Iberia, culturally dependent on France, and economically subservient to Great Britain. In general they were ill-prepared to exercise their new political freedom. They lacked the experience and training for the tasks confronting them. They disagreed, sometimes violently, on the course of action to be taken. From their doubts and debates emerged disorder; in some regions anarchy threatened. The sad spectacle of civil discord depressed Bolívar who sighed, "The Americans have risen rapidly without previous knowledge and, what is worse, without previous experience in the conduct of public affairs, to enact upon the world stage the important roles of legislators, magistrates, financial administrators, diplomats, generals, and every position of authority. . . ." Greater perspective on the period has only confirmed the Liberator's judgment. Contemporary Latin American historians agree that independence posed problems too complex for immediate solution. The Mexican historian Daniel Cosío Villegas has lamented, "Mexico could not have been less prepared for its political freedom and to exploit its

A Political Map of Contemporary Latin America

natural riches." The search for answers to some perplexing political and economic questions absorbed the Latin Americans during the first decades following independence and created an atmosphere of tension in the new nations.

THE TRANSFER AND LEGITIMIZATION OF POWER

Who would govern and how they would govern were the most fundamental questions facing the newly independent Latin Americans. They were questions previously unasked. For centuries all authority and power had been concentrated in the Iberian kings who ruled the New World in accordance with an ancient body of laws and customs and by "divine right." For nearly three centuries the inhabitants of the New World had accepted their rule. The monarchies provided their own continuity. The declarations of independence created a gaping political vacuum. The Latin Americans experienced anguish, bloodshed, and chaos in their uncertain and contradictory efforts to fill it.

Brazil alone easily resolved the questions, mainly because of the presence of the royal family in Portuguese America. On hand to lend legitimacy to the rapid, peaceful political transition of Brazil from viceroyalty to kingdom to empire were first King John VI and then his son, Prince Pedro, heir to the throne, who severed the ties between Portugal and Brazil and wore the new imperial crown. The mazombo elite supported the concept of monarchical government and thereby avoided the acrimonious debates between republicans and monarchists which rent much of Spanish America. Obviously facilitating their decision was the convenient presence of a sympathetic prince, a Braganza who had declared Brazil's independence. By his birth and inheritance as well as through the concurrence of the Brazilian elite, Pedro's position and power were at once legitimate. As a Braganza, he inherited his authority. All the symbols of power surrounded him and enhanced his status. Historical precedent strengthened his position. The throne legitimately occupied by a Braganza proved to be the perfect unifier of the new and immense empire.

If there was a genuine consensus as to who would rule, the question remained open as to how he would rule. The emperor and the elite agreed that there should be a constitution, but the contents and limits of that projected document sparked a debate which in turn generated the first major crisis in the Brazilian empire. Elections were held for an assembly which would exercise both constituent and legislative functions. The group which convened on May 3, 1823, composed of lawyers, judges, priests, military officers, doctors, landowners, and public officials, clearly represented the privileged classes of the realm. They came from the ranks of the old landed aristocracy and the new urban elite, neither of which at that time was totally divorced from the other. With few exceptions, they lacked legislative experience. Almost at once, the legislature and the executive clashed, each suspicious that the other infringed on its prerogatives. Furthermore, the legislators manifested rabid anti-Portuguese sentiments and thus by implication a hostility to the person of the young emperor born in Lisbon. Convinced that the assembly not only lacked discipline but scattered the seeds of revolution, Pedro decided to dissolve it. On November 11, 1823, troops closed the assembly hall, and the principal legislative leaders fled into exile.

Despite the dissolution of the assembly, Pedro intended to keep his word and rule under a constitution. He appointed a committee of ten Brazilians to write the document and then submitted it to the municipal councils throughout Brazil for their ratification. After most of them signified their approval, Pedro promulgated the new constitution on March 25, 1824. It provided for a highly centralized government with a vigorous executive. Although power was divided between four branches—executive, legislative, judiciary, and moderative—the lion's share rested in the hands of the emperor. Assisted by a Council of State and a ministry, the emperor exercised the functions of chief executive, a function enhanced by the novel moderative power. That power made him responsible for the maintenance of the independence of the nation as well as the equilibrium and harmony of the other powers and the 20 provinces. The emperor enjoyed a veto over all legislation as well as the right to convoke or dissolve the General Assembly. He chose the presidents of the provinces, the ministers, the ecclesiastical authorities (for he claimed the old royal patronage the Pope had conferred on Portuguese kings), and the senators. He could pardon criminals and review judicial decisions. In short, the emperor was given and expected to use broad powers as an omniscient harmonizer in a far-flung empire whose infinite geographic and human diversity challenged the existence of the state. In the last analysis, the crown was the one, pervasive, national institution which could and did represent all Brazilians. The General Assembly was divided into a senate, whose members were appointed by the emperor for life, and a chamber of deputies periodically and indirectly elected by a highly restricted suffrage. The constitution afforded broad individual freedom and equality before the law. Considering the time, place, and circumstances, it seems safe to conclude that the constitution was a liberal document. Above all it was practical, proven by its subsequent flexibility. It easily allowed amendments and reforms without the necessity of adopting a new constitution. It facilitated an experiment, nearly disastrous for national unity, with federalism between 1834 and 1840 and permitted the evolution of a parliamentary government *sui generis* after 1847. Proof of the viability of the constitution lay in its longevity: it lasted 65 years until the monarchy fell in 1889. It has proven to be Brazil's most durable constitution and one of Latin America's longest lived.

The Brazilians gradually took control of their own government. At first, Pedro disappointed them by surrounding himself with Portuguese advisers, ministers, and prelates. The Brazilians had their independence but were tacitly barred from exercising the highest offices in their own empire. Pedro had been born in Portugal (although he came as a boy to Brazil and always displayed a deep devotion to it), and soon the mazombos accused him of paying more attention to affairs in the former metropolis than to those of the new empire. Indeed, after the death of John VI in 1826, the young emperor became increasingly involved in Portuguese dynastic struggles. Meanwhile, as the Brazilians demanded access to the highest offices of their land, the currents of anti-Portuguese sentiment swelled. Pedro's failure to understand those sentiments and to appoint Brazilians to top positions were among the primary causes of the discontent leading to his abdication in 1831. After his departure for Europe, members of the elite with their roots firmly in the plantation economy replaced the Portuguese-born who monopolized the high posts of the First Empire. In 1840, when Pedro II ascended the throne, a Brazilian—for the adolescent emperor had been born and raised in the New World—even occupied that exalted position. Thus, the mazombo ascendancy was much more gradual than the creole. It began in 1808 when the royal court arrived in Rio de Janeiro and reached its climax in 1840 when a Brazilian-born emperor took the scepter.

Unlike Brazil, Spanish America did not experience the relatively easy transfer and legitimization of power. There the political vacuum stirred winds of disorder and ambition to blow forcefully for many decades. The question of what form the new governments should take absorbed considerable energy and aroused heated debates, particularly over the issues of federalism versus centralism and a republic versus a monarchy. Monarchy harmonized with the past and with the hierarchical, aristocratic structure of Spanish-American society. However, desire to repudiate at least the outward symbols of the Spanish past, an infatuation with the political doctrines of the Enlightenment, and the successful example of the United States strengthened the arguments of the partisans of a republic. Only in Mexico did the monarchists carry the day, but, unable to persuade a European prince to accept the new Aztec scepter, the creoles crowned one of their own, Augustín de Iturbide, whose brief reign lasted from May of 1822 until February of 1823. Still, since Mexico at that time included the territory from Oregon to Panama, it meant that together with Brazil, a majority of Latin America in late 1822 and early 1823 fell under monarchical sway. Iturbide's reign was not a happy one. Like Pedro I, he could not agree with his constituent assembly. Consequently he dictated his own constitution. His power rested firmly on the army and hence on the whims of jealous generals. Unlike Pedro, he enjoyed scant popular and minimal elitist support and none of the tradition which legitimized the Brazilian emperor's position. Falling prices for exports, economic stagnation, and an empty treasury complicated Iturbide's reign. Tired of waiting for delayed salaries, the military officers deserted their creole emperor and adhered to the republican cause, one which seemed to promise a more punctual delivery of paychecks. The army banished Iturbide in early 1823, abolished the empire, and helped to establish a liberal, federal republic. With that, the principle of republicanism triumphed, at least as an ideal, throughout Spanish America. Nonetheless, some would continue to argue the case for monarchy, and, in fact, Mexico experimented with it once again in the 1860s.

The debates over the merits of centralism and federalism reached no immediate conclusion. A reaction against the previous Spanish centralism, a host of local rivalries, and the apparent successful example of North American federalism combined to persuade many of the Latin American leaders to experiment with federalism. Most of the nations, large and small, tried it at one time or another. Indeed, an occasional experiment with it still continues, and several of the republics maintain the fiction of being federal. The experiments at best were unsuccessful, but in the cases of Mexico and the United Provinces of Central America they were a disaster which led to partial or total dismemberment of the nation. Colombia's experiment with a confederation under the Constitution of 1858 nearly dissolved the nation, and only the emergence of a strong caudillo, Tomás Cipriano de Mosquera, restored unity and preserved the nation. The centrifugal propensity in the huge, underpopulated, and poorly integrated nations cautioned against further experiments with federalism and eventually led to the abandonment of the idea in most of the nations.

The question of who should govern posed yet another problem for the new states to solve. The immediate answer was to turn the reigns of authority over to independence heroes, and therefore the first chiefs of state in many lands were the very men who had declared and fought for the independence of those nations. Thus, Bolívar served as president of Gran Colombia (the modern states of Colombia, Venezuela, Panama, and Ecuador); O'Higgins governed Chile; Sucre became the first constitutional president of Bolivia; San Martín ruled as "Protector of Peru," Iturbide wore the crown of Mexico, and so forth. The Latin Americans found it more difficult to select successors to the independence heroes—most of whom were turned out of office as their popularity faded and the nations showed themselves less grateful for past services rendered. Efforts to fill the presidential chair unleashed bitter power struggles among various factions of the elite, struggles conducive to despotism.

The contending factions all too often sought simply to seize, hold, and exercise power for its own sake and its own reward. Only secondarily did the leaders cloak their power with some cloth of legality, a cloth usually of exotic and impractical fabric. During the early decades of independence, elections seldom were held and even more rarely were they honest. Consequently the various factions resorted to violence as the path to power. Once in office, they usually exerted more violence in maintaining themselves in power than they had in achieving it. The strong leaders which emerged in the violence of nineteenth-century politics, known by the Spanish term *caudillo*, were an assorted lot, some were pompous popinjays who sported splendiferous uniforms and adopted sonorous titles, others lived ascetic lives, hidden from public view and attired in somber suits. All radiated a mystique and exercised compelling leadership.

Attracted and dominated by his personality, at least a sizeable portion of the population gave its allegiance to the caudillo. In truth, caudillismo offered a return to the more familiar—perhaps more comfortable—patriarchal patterns of the past. Since all power, all authority emanated from the caudillo, he played, in short, the role of the "king," but in practice he exercised more control over his "subjects" than the Spanish monarchs ever dared to. The caudillos shared power with no one. As one remarked, "I neither want nor like ministers who think. I want only ministers who can write, because the only one who can think am I, and the only one who does think am I." Neither convictions nor principles necessarily guided the caudillo. He favored expediency an ideological irresponsibility in which his will and whim were supreme. To rule, the caudillo employed force with impunity. Nor did his measures stop with imprisonment, confiscation, or exile. He could and did impose the death penalty as he saw fit. The general lack of restraints on his power permitted him to tax and spend as he pleased, a situation conducive to financial abuse, if not outright dishonesty.

To balance the picture, it should be noted that many of the caudillos bestowed some benefits on the nations they governed. Those disturbed by the chaos, or anarchy, of the early decades of independence, welcomed the order and stability characteristic of caudillismo. The early caudillos unified some of the nations, and there can be no doubt that their great strength in several notable cases prevented national disintegration so easily facilitated by the difficult geography and isolation of many communities. Later caudillos liked to cast themselves as modernizers and in that role bequeathed material improvements on the nations they governed. They built roads and imposing government buildings, lay railroad tracks, strung telegraph wires, and renovated ports. They even built schools with the intention of propagating their own virtues in them.

An archetype of the Spanish-American caudillo who defended independence and imposed national unity was Dr. José Gaspar Rodríguez de Francia who ruled Paraguay during its first 29 years. In 1811, he served as part of the ruling junta of the newly independent mediterranean nation. By 1814, he was ruling alone, and it was not long before a popular assembly made him dictator for life, a position he held until his death in 1840. While chaos engulfed the rest of the Platine region, Francia imposed order and hard work on Paraguay, and the new nation enjoyed a certain degree of prosperity and well-being. Fearful of the imperialistic pretensións of both Brazil and Argentina, particularly the latter, he isolated his inland country from the world and thereby, in all likelihood, guaranteed its independence.

Argentina, too, partially owes its unity to an early caudillo. The old Viceroyalty of La Plata disintegrated in the early nineteenth century: Paraguay declared its independence, Brazil momentarily absorbed Uruguay, Bolivia went its own way, and Argentina itself split into a variety of squabbling regions each under the iron command of a local caudillo. The idea of Argentine unity was kept alive, and even the concept of a vast modern state replacing the old viceroyalty did not entirely disappear, but local rivalries defeated any effort at unification. Sharpest was the rivalry between the port and province of Buenos Aires, growing prosperous through their trade and close ties with Europe, and the interior provinces, backward, impoverished, and wracked with civil wars. Buenos Aires advocated a centralized government in which it fully expected to dominate, while the interior provinces favored federalism in order to prevent the hegemony of the port. The bitter struggle between Buenos Aires and the interior delayed Argentine unification until Juan Manuel de Rosas strode onto the political stage. He had lived and worked in gaucho country before being elected governor of Buenos Aires in 1829 and he judiciously paid lip service to federalism, although he acted as a centralist. An American diplomatic representative in Buenos Aires, John M. Forbes, noted the appeal of Rosas to the rough men of the provinces in 1829:

> Rosas, however, differs from anything we have in our country, inasmuch as he owes his great popularity among the gauchos, or common peasantry, to his having assimilated himself to the greatest extremity to their most singular mode of life, their dress, their labors, and even their sports; and it is said that he excels in every gymnastic exercise, even the most active and adroit, of that half savage race of men.

Rosas steadily increased his control over most of the area composing contemporary Argentina, eliminating one regional caudillo after another until by the mid-1830s he held supreme power. He succeeded in imposing his will and keeping the nation unified for nearly two decades. A later U.S. diplomat, John S. Pendleton, termed his regime "the most simple and rigorous despotism in the civilized world." In the first Argentine novel, *Amalia*, José Marmol denounced the brutality of the Rosas regime and provided a wealth of detail on life in Argentina during those years. Rosas successfully met both internal and external threats until his defeat in 1852 in the Battle of Monte Caseros by a regional caudillo commanding his own troops as well as soldiers from Uruguay and Brazil. Rosas then fled into a European exile. The basis for Argentine unity was the legacy he bequeathed his nation.

Not all the early caudillos left a positive mark on their national histories. Antonio López de Santa Anna, who dominated Mexico from 1829 to 1855, combined all the negative qualities of the caudillo without the mitigating influence of those positive achievements characteristic of the regimes of some of his Spanish-American contemporaries. During those decades he contributed to the chaos which swept Mexico, kept the treasury in a state of perpetual bankruptcy, prevented the noble attempts at liberal reform urged by Valentín Gómez Farías, José María Luis Mora, and other able statesmen and intellectuals, and was partially responsible for the loss of half of Mexico's territory to the United States. Mexican historians have found very little good to say about Santa Anna. One popular Mexican school text refers to the "unbearable tyranny" of his rule.

None of the new republics escaped caudillo rule. For Chile, the experience was mild, brief, and transitory. The other republics spent most of the nineteenth century in the shadow of one or another caudillo. A few knew of no other form of government. Bolívar's unhappy prediction, "Many tyrants will arise upon my tomb," proved to be all too accurate. Perhaps little else could be expected considering the low level of development, the extremes of poverty and wealth, the concentration of land and resources in the hands of a few, the staggering degree of illiteracy, the minimal level of nutrition, the rigidity of class lines, and the lack of preparation for self-government.

Although the caudillos did not have to concern themselves with public opinion—for all intents and purposes it did not exist—they did seek the support of at least three groups, individually or in combination, to buttress their personal power: the rural aristocracy, the Roman Catholic Church, and the army. The early caudillos were more often than not members of or related to the rural landowning class, men notable for their desire to preserve the prestige, wealth, and power of their class and opposed to land reform, extension of the suffrage, and popular government. The caudillos usually represented their interests. Of course, they ruled from the capital cities (although they might spend long periods of time on their estates), but they tended to suppress the influence of the more liberal urban elements. The Church as an institution was a conservative force suspicious of reforms and usually in open conflict with the liberals who proposed them. Indeed, a high percentage of the men in the higher echelons of the Church hierarchy had not even supported the movement for independence. Church leaders —with a few notable exceptions—rallied to endorse any caudillo who respected and protected Church interests and property.

The army, the only really national institution, immediately emerged as a political force. Its strength revealed the weakness of the political institutions. In many countries it was the dominant political force and has so remained. Since few of the republics developed satisfactory means to select or alter governments, revolutions or palace coups—in which the military always had a role—became the customary means to effect political shifts. The military then exercised the dual role of guaranteeing order on one hand and changing governments on the other. No caudillo or president would willfully alienate the military. Consequently the officers enjoyed generous salaries and rapid promotions. The Latin American armies became and have remained top-heavy with brass. Thus, the army not only retarded the growth of democracy through its political meddling but also slowed down economic growth by absorbing a lion's share of the national budgets. It spent the capital needed for investment. Prior to 1850, the military received over 50 percent of the national budgets. Mexico provides one of the most shocking examples: between 1821 and 1845 the military budget exceeded the total income of the government on 14 occasions. Chile was the first—and for a long time the only—of the Spanish-speaking nations to regulate the army to its proper position as the defender of the fatherland from foreign attacks. After 1831 and until the civil war of 1891, the army kept out of Chilean politics. Few other nations could boast of a similarly well-behaved military.

As the question of who was going to rule was never properly answered in most of the republics during the first decades after independence—at best satisfactory *ad hoc* solutions were provided—so too did the problem of how the nations should be governed remain largely unsolved. Almost without exception the elite, as well as most of the caudillos, imbued with a long legalistic tradition, desired a written constitution, even though, in most cases, the document proved to be more theoretical than practical. The elite and their political representatives espoused an idealism, thanks to their flirtation with the Enlightenment, far removed from the archaic institutions, paternalism, and backward environment in which they lived. In their compulsive writing and re-writing of their constitutions, they eschewed local experience to import the latest ideas from abroad. Apparently the more novel the idea the better, so long as it originated in one of the nations they regarded as progressive. The most popular models for the many nineteenth-century Latin American constitutions were the North American and French constitutions as well as the Spanish Constitution of 1812, considered in the early nineteenth century as a splendid example of liberal thought. In defense of the framers of the Latin American constitutions it should be emphasized that they had minimal experience or tradition on which to draw. Lacking experience they were seduced by theories. On the other hand, the desire to alter fundamentally the system was probably superficial, an intellectual enthusiasm or exercise out of touch with reality. The creoles found the system they inherited from the Spanish colonial past far too comfortable for them to want to stray too far from it in practice.

The Latin Americans promulgated and abandoned constitutions with numbing regularity. It has been estimated that in the century and a half after independence, they wrote between 180 and 190 of them, a large percentage of which were adopted during the chaotic period before 1850. Venezuela holds the record with 22 constitutions since 1811. The four major Latin American nations have a somewhat stabler constitutional record. Brazil's constitution promulgated in 1824 lasted until 1889. After several trials and errors, Chile adopted a constitution in 1833 which remained in force until 1925. Argentina's Constitution of 1853 survived until 1949 but was put into force again in 1956. Mexico promulgated a constitution in 1857, which remained the basic document until 1917.

Generally the constitutions invested the chief executive with paramount powers so that both in theory and practice he exercised far greater authority than the other branches of government, almost invariably subservient to his will. In that respect, the Latin Americans reverted to their experience of the past. The presidents played the omnipotent role of past kings. Chile and Brazil experimented with parliamentary government. By the mid-nineteenth century, all the Latin American governments shared at least three general characteristics: strong executives, a high degree of centralization, and restricted suffrage (the vote invariably was limited to literate and/or propertied males). In effect, then, the new governments were by, of, and for the elite. The masses stood silent witnesses to political events.

THE TENSE SOCIETIES

Tension characterized the early governments. A feeling of insecurity complicated the search for political formulae. The new governments felt threatened by internal challenges, aggression from their neighbors, and the possibility of European reconquest. There was the psychological insecurity of those uncertain of their new positions of power, of those pressing for class fluidity—the restive commercial class and educated mestizos—and of those apprehensive over political change and its implications for the future.

From the start, the fear existed that Spain or Portugal, alone or in union with other European governments, might try to recapture the former colonies in the New World. The conservative monarchies of Russia, Austria, and Prussia formed the Holy Alliance, which numbered among its goals the eradication of representative government in Europe and the prevention of its spread to areas where it was previously unknown. The Alliance boldly intervened in a number of European states to dampen the fires of liberalism. At one time, it seemed possible that the Holy Alliance might help Spain in an effort to reassert its authority over its former American colonies, a possibility as displeasing to the United States as it was to Latin Americans. National self-interest, menacing European rhetoric, and Russian settlement advancing down the western coast of North America prompted President James Monroe to issue his Monroe Doctrine in 1823 declaring that the Americas were no longer open to European colonization and that the United States would regard any intervention of a European power in the Americas as an unfriendly act against the United States. Desirous of keeping open the lucrative markets of the newly independent nations, English statesmen agreed with the substance of the defiant declaration. The doctrine received a mixed reception from the Latin Americans, some of whom had as much reason to suspect the North American motives as they did those of the Europeans. The Spanish-American nations never officially recognized the doctrine nor gave it hemispheric legitimacy. At best they only tacitly accepted it. Brazil, to the contrary, always accorded the doctrine a cordial welcome. Less than two months after its issuance, the Brazilian government recognized the new doctrine and spoke of an offensive and defensive alliance with the United States. Brazil, more than any other of the Latin American states, saw in the doctrine a defense of its newly proclaimed independence and protection from European aggression.

Latin American fears of European intervention were not unfounded. Several European governments did physically intervene in the new republics. Spain made several feeble attempts to invade Mexico and Central America in 1829 and 1832. Later, in the decade of the 1860s, Spanish imperialism threatened the former colonies again. Spain made war on Peru, seizing one of its guano-producing islands, and bombarded the Chilean port of Valparaíso. During that same decade, the Dominican Republic, a sad spectacle of chaos, invited Isabel II to accept the return of a contrite nation to the Spanish fold. Spain reasserted its authority in 1861, but the insular nation proved so unruly and expensive that Spain withdrew in 1865 leaving the Dominican Republic independent once again and as the unique example of a former colony which voluntarily, if temporarily, returned to its colonial status. France and Great Britain also intervened in the New World. The French occupied Vera Cruz, Mexico, in 1838, in order to force Mexico to pay alleged debts and blockaded Buenos Aires in 1838–40, and again in 1845–48, this time in conjunction with the British, to discipline Rosas. The Argentine adventures proved to be far less successful than the Mexican one. The most brazen European intervention occurred in Mexico during the 1860s. Responding to some grandiose schemes of Napoleon III, a French army in 1862 marched into central Mexico to set the hapless Maximilian of Austria on an unsteady Aztec throne. The French remained until 1866, when, defeated by geography and the determination of the troops under the command of Benito Juárez, they withdrew. These examples show that Latin American anxieties over European intervention were well-founded. For half a century, those apprehensions—or, on occasion, the interventions themselves—increased local tensions as well as diverted resources and energy which more profitably could have been invested in national development.

To diminish the threat of invasion from the former mother countries as well as from other European states, the new nations sought international recognition of their independent status. The European governments hesitated to extend a hand of friendship before the former mother countries did so. Portugal, due to a family pact among the Braganzas who occupied the thrones both in Lisbon and Rio de Janeiro, extended the promptest recognition, accorded to Brazil in 1825. France delayed its recognition of Haitian independence, declared in 1804, until 1825. Spanish recognition was tardiest and most complicated. The death of Fernando VII in 1833 ended unrealistic Spanish intransigence and opened the way for negotiations with the former colonies. In 1836, Spain and Mexico agreed "to forget forever the past differences and dissensions which unfortunately have interrupted for so long a period the friendship and harmony between two peoples." Spain then recognized Mexico, and gradually over the decades extended similar recognition to the other republics, the last being Honduras in 1894.

Unlike the European nations, the United States felt no need to consider the feelings of the Iberian monarchs before acting, although other considerations—the desire to obtain Florida from Spain, for example—did delay recognition. In 1822, the process began when the Department of State recognized Argentina, Gran Colombia, and Mexico, followed in 1823 by the recognition of Chile, and in 1824 of Brazil and Central America. The United States maintained a high degree of interest in Latin America. Of the ten legations provided for by the Department of State's budget in 1824, five were in Latin America. By 1821, commerce with the southern neighbors already accounted for over 13 percent of United States trade. Although formal recognition might have made the new states feel somewhat more secure and reduced by a small degree the tensions disturbing the new societies, it did not in and of itself eliminate foreign threats or even deter interventions.

The threats were by no means all external. The national unity of the new states proved to be extremely fragile, and the forces which shattered it more often than not were internal. Geography provided one major obstacle to unity. Vast tracks of nearly empty expanse, impenetrable jungles, mountain barriers, and lonely deserts separated and isolated population pockets among which communication was tardy and difficult and transportation often nonexistent and where existent hazardous and slow. The rainy season halted all communication and transportation in many regions. Such poor communications and transportation made it impossible to exchange goods, services, and ideas on a national basis. It was easier and cheaper to ship a ton of goods from Guayaquil, Ecuador, to New York City via the Straits of Magellan than to send it 200 miles overland to the capital, Quito. Rio de Janeiro could import flour and wheat more economically from England than from Argentina. Likewise the inhabitants of northern Brazil found it easier to import from Europe than to buy the same product from southern Brazil despite the fact that sailing vessels connected Brazil's littoral population nuclei. Most of the population lived within easy reach of the coast. To penetrate the interior, the Brazilians relied on inland waterways—in some areas generously supplied by the Amazon and Plata networks—or cattle trails. A journey from Rio de Janeiro to Cuiabá, capital of the interior province of Mato Grosso, took eight months in the 1820s. The situation was comparable in Spanish America. The trip from Vera Cruz, Mexico's principal port, to Mexico City, a distance of slightly less than 300 miles, over the nation's best and most used highway took about four days of arduous travel when Madame Frances Calderón de la Barca made the journey under the most favorable conditions in 1839. She described the road as "infamous, a succession of holes and rocks." The English merchant-traveler Robert G. Dunlop praised the government of Costa Rica in 1845 for maintaining the best roads in Spanish America, but then revealed: "The road from San José to Punta Arenas, though far from rivaling such works in Europe, is quite passable for the carts of the country, each of which conveys half a ton of coffee from the capital to the port, a distance of 25 leagues [between 80 and 90 miles] over a country naturally of the impassable nature, in four or five days." In the 1820s a journey from

Buenos Aires to Mendoza, approximately 950 miles inland at the foot-hills of the Andes, took a month by ox cart or two weeks by carriage, although a government courier in an emergency could make the trip in five days on horseback. With the outstanding exception of the good road connecting Valparaíso and Santiago, built in 1795, roads in Chile were scarcely more than "bridle paths." Chile's sea-links with its neighbors offered tedium mixed with adventure: around Cape Horn from Valparaíso to Buenos Aires took 45 days if the traveler were lucky and up the coast to Callao the voyage averaged 30 days.

Distance, difficult geography, slow communication and transportation, and local rivalries, in part spurred by isolation, encouraged the growth of a regionalism hostile to national unity. Experiments with federalism intensified that regionalism. With the exception of Brazil, the former viceroyalties engendered almost no feelings of cohesion among their widely dispersed residents who tended to give their loyalty to their political subdivisions—the captaincies, kingdoms, and presidencies—which seemed closer in harmony with regional realities and needs. As a result, soon after independence the former territories of the Spanish viceroyalties disintegrated. None splintered more than the Viceroyalty of New Spain. In 1823, Central America, the former Kingdom of Guatemala, seceded. In turn, in 1838–39, the United Provinces of Central America broke into five republics. Texas left the Mexican union in 1836, and during the war of 1846–48 the United States detached California, Arizona, and New Mexico. Gran Colombia failed to maintain the former unity of the Viceroyalty of New Granada: Venezuela left the union in 1829 and Ecuador followed the next year. Chile and Bolivia felt no loyalty to Lima, and consequently the Viceroyalty of Peru disbanded even before the independence period was over. In a similar fashion, Paraguay, Uruguay, and part of Bolivia denied the authority of Buenos Aires, thus spelling the end of the Viceroyalty of La Plata. By 1840, the four monolithic Spanish viceroyalties had split giving rise to all of the Spanish-speaking republics of the New World except Cuba and Panama which appeared in the wake of a new, aggressive American imperialism at the end of the nineteenth and beginning of the twentieth centuries.

The maintenance of Brazilian unity while the Spanish American viceroyalties disintegrated begs an explanation. Perhaps the constant fear of the small mazombo landholding class of a slave rebellion caused the widely dispersed elite to hold similar opinions and to advocate similar actions, a harmony which might not have characterized them had there been no common fear. Certainly the reasons for unity will not be found in the common language, religion, cultural heritage, and contiguous territory. On that basis, Spanish America would have remained unified too. Permissive Portuguese colonial institutions, amazingly ill-defined in contrast to those of Spain, allowed a more leisurely formation of the colony and permitted a flexibility uncommon in the more rigid Spanish bureaucracy. Apparently, unlike Spain's, they could be bent without breaking which permitted them to change to meet new situations. Further, the presence of the Braganzas starting in 1808, with all the centralization of control and power that involved for the colony, unified the colony during its final years of dependency, at the very time when Napoleon's campaigns were breaking the bonds between Spain and its colonies, a break which came suddenly and without any preparation on the part of the creoles. Certainly, 81 years of highly centralized monarchy with, until the end, few questioning or challenging the emperor's authority, goes a long way in helping to explain Brazilian unity. Other scholars have pointed to the vast Brazilian frontier as an instrument of unity. Cattle paths and water networks crisscrossed to link the interior together, a matrix holding also the coastal population nuclei together. Of course, within that unity existed—still exists—an immense variety which the regions exemplify. There has been conflict between the forces of unity and diversity, that is, between centralism and regionalism. The scales at one time or another have tipped both ways. In the long run, however, the two forces have maintained a certain balance. The essential fact is that despite stress and threat the Brazilian union remained intact. National unity and homogeneity are achievements of which Brazilians can be justifiably proud. They stand in contrast to the fate which befell the four Spanish American viceroyalties.

None of the 18 new nations had clearly defined frontiers with its neighbors, a problem destined to cause war, bloodshed, and ill-will ever after. In some cases, commercial rivalries added to the difficulties. Further, the rapid multiplication of new states raised hemispheric trade barriers which in turn complicated and intensified those rivalries. In short, former colonial regional rivalries took on a nationalistic tone after independence. The resultant suspicion and distrust among the 18 states accelerated the tensions felt within the new societies. On all too many occasions, those tensions gave rise to war as neighbor fought neighbor in the hope of gaining a trade advantage, greater security, or additional territory.

Argentina and Brazil struggled in the Cisplatine War (1825–28) over possession of Uruguay and in an exhausted stalemate agreed to make the disputed territory independent; Chile attacked Peru and Bolivia in 1836 to prevent the federation of the two neighbors and during the War of the Pacific (1879–83) the three fought for possession of the nitrate deposits of the Atacama Desert; the Dominican Republic battled Haiti in 1844 to regain its independence; westward expansion brought the United States into conflict with Mexico, 1846–48; and throughout the nineteenth century the five Central American republics challenged each other repeatedly on the battlefield. This catalog of conflicts is only representative, not inclusive. The major conflict of the century pitted tiny, landlocked Paraguay against the Triple Alliance, Argentina, Brazil, and Uruguay, in a clash of imperialistic pretensions in the strategic La Plata basin, one phase in a constant and continuing struggle to maintain the balance of power there. It took the allies five years, 1865–70, to subdue plucky Paraguay. That war solved two difficult problems which had troubled the region since independence. First, it definitively opened the Plata River network to international commerce and travel, a major concern of Brazil which wanted to use the rivers to communicate with several of its interior provinces. Second, it freed the small states of Uruguay and Paraguay from further direct intervention from Argentina and Brazil which came to understand the importance of the independence of the two small Platine states as buffer zones. The two large nations might try to sway one or both of the small nations to its side, but neither Brazil nor Argentina physically intervened again.

Relations between the new states and the Roman Catholic Church created tensions of another sort to disturb domestic tranquility in all the states. On occasion conflict between church and state degenerated into civil war, as the history of Mexico amply illustrates. The Roman Catholic Church had penetrated every region of Latin America. Almost all Latin Americans in the early nineteenth century professed to be at least nominal Catholics.

Due to efficient organization, able administration, and the generosity of the pious, the Church continued to amass riches in the New World. At the end of the eighteenth century, the traveler Humboldt estimated that in some provinces of New Spain the Church controlled as much as 80 percent of the land. That, however, constituted only part of the Church's wealth. Lucas Alamán, a devout Catholic, leader of the clerical party in Mexico during the first half of the nineteenth century, and one of the most reputable Mexican historians of that century, revealed,

> The wealth of the clergy did not consist so much of the estates that it possessed, although these were numerous, especially the urban properties of the principal cities like Mexico City, Puebla, and others, as of capital invested in quitrent mortgages. Collecting interest made every chaplaincy and religious brotherhood a sort of bank. The total property of the secular and regular clergy in estates and loans of this type was certainly not less than half of the total value of the real estate of the country.

Wealth begot considerable power for the Church, but the Church's strength rested on other foundations as well. The clergy, one of the best educated segments of society, enjoyed a tremendous prestige, particularly among the masses, a prestige which often made a mere suggestion carry the weight of a command. The clerics often entered politics, held high offices in the new governments, or endorsed political candidates. The clergy exerted its influence within the educational system; in almost all of the new countries they monopolized education from the primary school through the university. It was obvious then that in the early national period the Church wielded great influence not only in the spiritual lives of the new nations but also in economics, politics, society, and the intellectual pursuits. Alamán concluded, "The influence of the clergy was great for three reasons: respect for religion, remembrance of its great benefactions, and its abundant riches." Favorable as he was toward the Church, Alamán discerned potential danger in the authority of the clerics:

> This respect, which reached fanatical devotion, had nothing dangerous in it so long as it was given to men worthy of veneration because of their virtues; and the government, to which they were faithful and obedient, found in these exemplary ecclesiastics its strongest support; but it might come to be most dangerous if, the customs of the clergy being corrupted, this body should for personal advantage wish to abuse its influence. . . .

Under the influence of the ideas of the Enlightenment, a vociferous body of critics began to accuse the clergy of just such abuse.

Any criticism of the Church was aimed not at religion itself, or at dogma, but rather at the secular power and influence of the institution and its servants. Religious discontent had not been a cause for the wars of independence. Rebellion against the Church was unthinkable at the time. Indeed, the revolutionaires and their early successors offered to Catholicism recognition of its traditional position and privileges. The new constitutions revealed the respected status of the Church. But many of the leaders of the new states quickly became apprehensive of the overwhelming power wielded by the privileged Church, far better organized and efficient than the state and more often than not better financed. They felt it necessary to subordinate the Church to the state by control of the patronage in a manner characteristic of the former Iberian arrangement with the Vatican. They sincerely believed that the independence of the new states could not be guaranteed if they did not exercise some temporal control over the Church. For that reason, the Latin American chiefs of state claimed the right to exercise national patronage as heirs of the former royal patronage. The Pope in turn announced that the patronage had reverted back to the papacy, its original source, with the declarations of independence. In their open sympathy with the Spanish monarchy the popes antagonized the Latin American governments. In 1824, Pope Leo XII issued an encyclical to archbishops and bishops in America to support Ferdinand VII, confirmation in the eyes of the Latin American leaders that the Vatican was in league with the Holy Alliance. The new governments found it necessary to expel a number of ranking clerics because they refused to swear allegiance to the new state. Such a fate befell Archbishop Ramón Casaus y Torres of Guatemala in 1830, for example.

Out of consideration for the feelings of Madrid, the Vatican for a long time refused to recognize the new American states much to the chagrin of their governments, which were fearful that the discontent of the American Catholics with their isolation might endanger independence. Rome began to change its attitude toward the Latin American states in 1826, when the Pope announced his willingness to receive American representatives strictly as ecclesiastical delegates which in no way implied political recognition. The next year the Roman pontiff began to preconize candidates presented by the American governments. With the death of Ferdinand VII in 1833, he no longer felt any Spanish constraints on his policy in the New World. In 1835, the Vatican recognized New Granada and the following year accredited to Bogotá the first papal nuncio. The recognition of New Granada signified the end both of the problem over political recognition and of Spanish influence over the Vatican's diplomacy in and relations with Spanish America. However, other questions remained unsolved and for the remainder of the century the difficulties between Church and state centered on such questions as lay teaching, secularization of the cemeteries, civil marriage, the establishment of a civil register for births, marriages, and deaths, ownership of religious property, and patronage.

The religious questions were the surest, the universal division between the two strongest political currents of the nineteenth-century Latin America, liberal and conservative. On other issues the stands of the liberals and conservatives might have varied from country to country or even region to region but not so on the Church. The conservatives invariably favored the status quo of the Church, supporting its spiritual and temporal powers, privileges, and prestige. On the other hand, just as invariably, the liberals challenged the temporal powers of the Church. They uncompromisingly demanded that the state exercise patronage and thus temporal control of the Church.

The disputants often failed to settle their differences by compromise or conciliation. On more than one occasion, armies took to the field to settle them. Mexico, in particular, suffered from the conflict over the question of the proper place of the Church within the new states. The early constitutions established Roman Catholicism as the state Church but endorsed the principle of national patronage. The liberals campaigned to reduce the privileges of the Church, and, in 1833, during the brief tenure of Valentín Gómez Farías as chief of state, reforms were enacted to secularize the California missions and to confiscate their funds, to secularize public education, to abolish compulsory tithes, to give members of the religious orders the option of retracting their vows, and to strengthen the principle of national patronage. Santa Anna removed Gómez Farías from power in 1834 and annulled those reforms. Under the succeeding conservative governments, the Church regained its privileged status. During those years, Mexico expended much of its energy and resources against the rebels in Texas, to thwart French intervention, and to attempt to halt or deflect the expansion of the United States into the northern provinces. The attendant bankruptcy and disappointments paved the way to power for a new generation of liberals, an outstanding group of intelligent and honest men, the most prominent of whom was Benito Juárez, a full-blooded Indian. Never deviating from his liberal principles, he held the liberals together during a decade and a half of stress. In their Plan of Ayutla issued in 1854, the liberals called for the overthrow of Santa Anna and a new constitution. They came to power the following year but were repeatedly challenged. Of all the issues at stake, the religious question predominated. Neither side showed any willingness to compromise on that question.

The liberals initiated their religious reforms in 1855 with the Ley Juárez, which restricted the privileges of military and ecclesiastical courts by ending their jurisdiction in purely civil cases. In 1856, the Ley Lerdo required all corporations to sell their lands, the intention of which was to divest the Church of all its property not strictly devoted to religious purposes. The well-intentioned law had several unfortunate consequences for Mexico. In the first place, the Church lands were more often than not the most efficiently run and productive and hence a major contributor to the national economy. Further, income from those lands supported a wide variety of essential charities. The requirement that all corporations sell their lands included the Indian *ejidos*, and in that manner the liberals contributed to divesting the Indian communities of their lands. The *hacendados*, owners of the large estates, found as a result of the enforcement of the Ley Lerdo considerable new land on the markets which they snatched up to add to their already considerable holdings. The new constitution promulgated in 1857 incorporated both the Ley Juárez and the Ley Lerdo and went on to nullify compulsory observance of religious vows and to secularize education. The conservatives and the Church denounced the new laws and constitution. Pope Pius declared, "We raise our Pontifical voice in apostolic liberty . . . to condemn, to reprove, and to declare null and void the said decrees and everything else that the civil authority has done in scorn of ecclesiastical authority and of this Holy See." The clergy and military united to defend their privileges and attacked the liberals, initiating the bloody War of Reform, 1858–61. The bold challenge to the liberal government unleashed an avalanche of anticlerical laws upon the Church: the nationalization of cemeteries, civil marriage, abolition of tithes, nationalization of all real property of the Church, separation of Church and state, suppression of all monasteries, and the prohibition of novitiates in nunneries.

Defeated on the battlefields, the conservatives resolved to seek foreign intervention rather than accept the triumph of Juárez. They persuaded the ambitious Napoleon III to intervene in their favor in 1862 by supporting the restitution of the monarchy in the person of the Austrian Archduke Maximilian, who arrived in 1864. Much to the annoyance of the conservatives, Maximilian accepted the religious reforms. To oppose the French intervention and monarchical restoration, the liberals took up arms again. Napoleon found it necessary to commit 34,000 regular troops to support the unsteady throne of Maximilian. Even so, the monarchy never extended its authority over more than a fraction of Mexican territory and never enjoyed the support of more than a minority of the Mexican population. The French withdrawal in 1866 condemned the monarchy to an early extinction. The following year the liberal army captured and shot Maximilian. Juárez returned to Mexico City and the herculean task of rebuilding a ravaged Mexico. The Church had lost considerable wealth, prestige, and power during its prolonged struggle with the state, but the battles were by no means over. They flared up later and extended well into the twentieth century.

Mexico represents an extreme in the Church-state struggles which added much to the tensions of nineteenth-century Latin America. Although such bitter warfare might not have characterized the rest of the hemisphere, no new nation escaped entirely the conflict. The struggle over patronage and to reduce the Church's powers continued throughout the nineteenth century. It complicated and strained relations between the Vatican and Latin America and gave rise to considerable national tension.

ECONOMIC STAGNATION

A major paradox has always characterized Latin America: the potential richness of the land and the abject poverty of the majority of the people who work it. The contrast between what could be and what is confounds all careful observers and begs explanation. Luís dos Santos Vilhena, a Portuguese professor of Greek who resided 12 years in Salvador da Bahia at the end of the eighteenth century, posed the sad question about Brazil, "Why is a country so fecund in natural products, so rich in potential, so vast in extent, still inhabited by such a small number of settlers, most of them poor, and many of them half-starved?" He answered his own question frankly, putting the blame for underdevelopment on slave labor, the latifundia, and inefficient or obsolete agricultural methods. Across the continent at exactly the same time, the Chilean intellectual José de Cos Iriberri asked an identical question: "Who would imagine that in the midst of the lavishness and splendor of nature the population would be so scanty and that most of it would be groaning under the oppressive yoke of poverty, misery and the vices which are their inevitable consequences?" He blamed the sad economic condition of Chile on the unequal distribution of the land which favored a few large landowners but condemned most of the population to the role of peasants. What they said about Brazil and Chile could be applied to all of Latin America.

Independence provided no panacea for Latin America's economic ills. The trend established during the colonial period to subordinate the economy to Europe's needs continued unaltered. In fact, during the nineteenth century, if anything, Latin America's economy became increasingly and more inextricably integrated into the widening network of international capitalism. During the first half of the century, Europe and the United States entered an active period of population growth and accelerated industrialization and urbanization. They demanded raw products: food for the urban centers and materials for the factories. In turn, they sought markets in which to sell growing industrial surpluses. The newly independent nations of Latin America with their abundant natural wealth and limited industries were pressed into a working relationship with the burgeoning capitalist centers: they exported the raw materials required in Europe and the United States and imported the manufactured goods pouring from the factories. Latin America's exports depended upon and responded to the requirements of Europe and the United States. In catering to the caprices of an unpredictable market, the Latin Americans encouraged the growth of a reflex economy, little different, except perhaps more hazardous, than the previous colonial economy. External factors, over which the Latin Americans had little or no influence, determined whether the economies prospered or vegetated. The economic cycles of boom and collapse repeatedly reoccurred in all regions of Latin America. Responding to the needs and requirements of Europe and the United States condemned most of the area to remain on the periphery of international capitalism.

Between 1800 and 1850, world trade tripled, and Latin America participated in that growth. After recovering from the wars of independence, it shipped ever greater amounts of agricultural produce abroad. While two or three ships a year had handled trade between Chile and England in the 1815–20 period, more than 300 carried Chilean exports to England in 1847. The value of exports leaving Buenos Aires nearly tripled in a quarter of a century, 1825–50. During the fiscal year 1830–31, Venezuela exported 60,181 bags of coffee, 38,008 bags of cacao, 1,525 head of cattle, and 45,000 hides, which increased in the fiscal year 1847–48 to 200,998 bags of coffee, 66,660 bags of cacao, 15,832 head of cattle, and 365,554 hides.

Improving international transportation put Europe and the United States into closer contact with Latin America. Faster sailing vessels and then the introduction of the steamship, which was being used successfully in North Atlantic crossing in the 1830s, were responsible. The steamships appeared in the waters of Brazil in 1819 and of Chile in 1822. By 1839, a steamship line connected Rio de Janeiro with the northern provinces of the empire. A dramatic event in 1843 impressed the Brazilians with the importance of the steamship for their future development. In that year the puffing and chugging *Guapiassú* churned the waters of the Amazon for the first time. The steamship journeyed from Belém to Manaus, 900 miles upstream, in nine days and returned in half the time, a remarkable record considering that hitherto the sailing vessels required two to three months to ascend and a month to descend. Much of Latin America was witnessing at that time a similar rapidity which the steamship afforded international commerce.

In 1840, the British chartered the Royal Mail Steam Packet Company to provide regular twice monthly steamship service to the entire Caribbean area, touching most of the islands and all the mainland ports from Paramaribo to Tampico. Meanwhile, they were founding a steamship company for the Pacific coast of South America. A prospectus of 1838 indicated the potential value of such a line:

> No part of the world is better calculated for steam navigation than the shores of the Pacific. . . . Land communication is everywhere difficult and in many places impracticable, and navigation by sailing vessels is tedious and uncertain at every season. Voyages now occupying 20 to 25 days may be accomplished by steam in 40 or 50 hours. . . . H. M. Government, having determined to establish steam packets between England and the West Indies, these two proposed plans will together ensure a greatly accelerated communication between Europe and the western coast of South America. The voyage to Lima will then, by the Isthmus of Panama, be reduced to one of about 30 days; by Cape Horn it occupies four months.
> . . .

In 1840, the Pacific Steam Navigation Company began to provide steamboat service to the western coast of South America. Frail engines of 150 horsepower turned the wooden paddle wheels to propel the ships measuring approximately 200 feet in length and 50 feet in breadth. In 1868, the Valparaiso-Liverpool line began operations. Meanwhile, in 1851, the Royal Mail Steam Packet opened service from England to

Brazil, and at Rio de Janeiro the company transferred passengers and cargo to a smaller steam vessel for La Plata. The English inaugurated direct steam service to the Río de la Plata in 1853. At the same time, the United States expanded its international steamship service which reached Latin America in 1847 with the foundation of the Pacific Mail Company. Those improved communication and transportation systems further meshed the economies of Latin America with those of the United States and Europe and most particularly with that of Great Britain.

Great Britain quickly replaced the two Iberian kingdoms as the dominant economic force in Latin America and held that primacy throughout the nineteenth century. The English provided a model for change which the Iberian nations never could have furnished. As soon as Portugal and Spain fell to Napoleon, eager British merchants began to move in large numbers into Latin America to capture the markets they had so long craved. By 1810, approximately 120 merchants resided in Buenos Aires alone; by 1824, the English community in that strategic port numbered 3,000. It has been estimated that by that time about 100 English commercial houses operated in Spanish-American cities. The British sold more to Latin America than anyone else and in some cases almost monopolized the imports into certain countries. British firms handled the lion's share of Latin America's foreign trade, and British bottoms carried much of it to distant ports. The English government maintained men-of-war in Latin American waters to protect British commerce, to safeguard the rights of Englishmen, and on occasion to transport specie. London supplied most of the loans and investments to the new nations. Already by 1822, four Latin American loans had been floated, in 1824 five more were and the following year an additional five. In the years immediately after independence, British investors readily subscribed to joint-stock companies being formed in Latin America, particularly the mining companies—almost all of which failed. The British government successfully wrested from the Latin Americans agreements and treaties favorable to its merchants, traders, and bankers. Brazil's experience was classic. The new empire provided the English merchants and manufacturers with their most lucrative Latin American market. Exports to Brazil in 1825 equaled those sold to the rest of South America and Mexico combined and totaled half those sent to the United States. Naturally the British wanted to keep their Brazilian market. In exchange for arranging Portugal's recognition of Brazilian independence in 1825, London exacted a highly advantageous commercial treaty from Pedro I. It limited the duty placed on English imports to 15 percent and bound Brazil not to concede a lower tariff to any other nation. The treaty thereby assured British manufacturers domination over the Brazilian market and postponed any Brazilian efforts to industrialize.

Captivated by foreign political ideologies which bore little relevance to local conditions, the Latin American elite also showed a penchant for economic doctrines more suitable to an industrializing Europe than to an underdeveloped New World. Adam Smith mesmerized many Latin American intellectuals who embraced free trade as a solution to their nation's economic problems. In the words of Mexico's *El Observador* in 1830, the country needed "absolute and general freedom of commerce" to promote prosperity. In reaction to the former mercantilism they had deplored, the Latin Americans adopted policies of economic liberalism which they associated with the triumph of the Enlightenment but which bore no relation to the requirements of Latin America. Consistently modest tariffs deprived the new governments of sorely needed incomes and facilitated the flood of European manufactured articles inundating the New World to the detriment of local industrialization. Mexico, for example, opened its ports in 1821 to all foreign goods at a uniform tariff of 25 percent ad valorem. Artisan manufacturing immediately declined. A petition to the national government in 1822 from Guadalajara for protection blamed the liberal tariff for putting 2,000 artisans out of work in that city alone.

Latin America's early economic woes cannot be blamed exclusively on the flirtations of the intellectuals with European ideologies. The destruction wrought by the wars for independence in many parts of the hemisphere and unsettled conditions during the early decades of the national period inhibited economic growth. The chronic political instability so characteristic of most of the new countries did not provide the proper climate for development. Politics rather than economics absorbed most of the attention and energy of the new nations. At the same time the quality of public administration deteriorated. Many trained public administrators departed with the defeated Spanish armies or returned to Lisbon with John's court. Recruitment seldom was based on talent; rather, positions in the civil service came as a political reward, and the frequent changes of government hindered the training of a new professional civil service. The national treasuries lay bare. Public financing was precarious and the fiscal irresponsibility of the governments notorious. Scant capital for investment existed. The elite possessed little and had only limited access to any. Early unhappy experiences frightened away foreign capital. By 1850, foreigners had invested only a limited amount of capital, most of which was British. The most successful investments were in trading firms.

Legal changes in the labor system further threatened the precarious Latin American economies. The governments abolished Indian tribute (in theory, if not always in practice) and slowly freed the blacks. Central America and Chile ended slavery in 1823; Bolivia, in 1826; Mexico, 1829; Uruguay, 1830; Colombia, 1851; Ecuador and Argentina,

1853; and Peru and Venezuela, 1854. Brazil forbade further importation of African slaves after 1850. As usual, however, the resourceful landowners found a variety of ways of observing the letter of the law while changing but slightly the patterns of labor employment. They perfected systems of apprenticeship and debt peonage to that end.

Mining and manufacturing suffered the most during the decades after independence. With some mines flooded and machinery destroyed during the fighting, the labor system in flux, and investments lacking, the production of the once fabled mines plummeted. The decline continued steadily in Mexico and Peru until mid-century. The Bolivian mines did not revive until around 1875. Industry fared no better. The availability of cheap European manufactured goods reversed the industrial advances made during the final decades of Iberian rule, decimated the handicraft industries, and put local artisans out of work.

After the initial shock and decline, agriculture recovered and improved. The markets of Europe and the United States readily absorbed many of the agrarian products and some of the natural wealth of Latin America, and their sale provided the basis for any prosperity in the decades before 1850. The large estates survived intact the turmoil of the independence period. In the national period, as in the colonial past, land retained its primary importance as the principal source of wealth, prestige, and power. The landed gentry immediately took control of the new governments. The chiefs of state owned large agricultural estates and/or were intimately connected with the landowning class. Representatives of that privileged class filled the legislatures. Indeed, the voting requirements of property ownership and/or literacy almost restricted the franchise to that class. The courts represented them—from the ranks of the elite came the lawyers and judges—and invariably decided cases in their favor. In fact, the times were propitious for the landlords to extend their holdings. The governments put the lands of the Church, Indian communities, and public domain on the market. The hacendados and fazendeiros bought them, accelerating the concentration of land in the hands of the few. The governments acquiesced in the extension and perfection of debt peonage to insure an adequate and docile labor supply for those expanding estates. The restraints a distant king once had imposed on the landed aristocracy existed no longer. That aristocracy, after independence, ruled for its own benefit, identifying national well-being with its own.

The landlord was a patriarch chief who ruled family, servants, slaves, tenant farmers, sharecroppers, peasants, and even neighbors—unless they were large estate owners like himself—with absolute authority. The vastness of the estate, its isolation from the seat of government, the relative weakness of local bureaucrats, and the propensity of the government to side with the landed class all strengthened his power.

Furthermore, the estate chaplain and local parish priest orbited around him like satellites, lending the prestige of the Catholic Church to augment his authority. From the comfort and security of his house, because naturally the "big house" was the focal point of the estate's activity, the patriarch administered his holdings, listened to petitions from his subordinates, dispensed justice, and in general held court. Those large, strong, and sometimes well-furnished houses sat in the midst of barns, stables, carriage houses, warehouses, workshops, granaries, sheds, and a chapel. In the lowland plantations the slave quarters stood nearby; in the highlands the Indian peons lived in small villages on the estate. The estate contained fields for growing the commercial crop as well as food for the residents, orchards, pastures for pack animals, cattle, and sheep, and forests for firewood. Still, only a fraction of the extensive estates was put to use. As far as possible, the estates were self-contained. Carpenters, smithies, bakers, seamstresses, candlemakers, and a host of skilled and semi-skilled workers satisfied nearly all the simple, local demands. There was scant need for contact with the world beyond the estate's boundaries. Those estates were a way of life, a society unto themselves. The slaves or peons were born, lived out the dull routine of their lives, and died right on the estate. Only a very few of them on the most infrequent occasions ever left that self-contained rural world. A rough road, probably not serviceable during the rainy season, led to the next estate and nearest village. Occasionally a traveling merchant appeared to peddle his wares. More importantly the road served to carry away the estate's principal crop to the nearest port. The patriarch and part of his family visited the nearest town and the nation's capital from time to time to purchase from the outside world a few luxury items for themselves and to savor the conviviality and pleasures of urban life. The wealthiest landlords maintained city homes. Often they or a member of their families served in the local municipal government.

Foreign visitors to Latin America in the nineteenth century have left us vivid accounts of the large estates. After having been a guest in numerous Mexican country homes in the early 1840s, Frances Calderón de la Barca generalized:

> As for the interior of these haciendas, they are all pretty much alike, so far as we have seen; a great stone building, which is neither farm nor country-house (according to our notions), but has a character peculiar to itself—solid enough to stand a siege, with floors of painted brick, large deal tables, wooden benches, painted chairs, and whitewashed walls; one or two painted or iron bedsteads, only put up when wanted; numberless empty rooms; kitchen and outhouses; the courtyard a great square, round which stand the house for boiling the sugar, whose furnaces blaze day and night; the house, with machinery for extracting the juice from the cane, the refining rooms, the places where it is dried, etc., all on a large scale.

If the hacienda is, as here, a coffee plantation also, then there is a great mill for separating the beans from the chaff, and sometimes also there are buildings where they make brandy. Here there are 400 men employed, exclusive of boys, 100 horses, and a number of mules. The property is generally very extensive, containing the fields of sugar cane, plains for the cattle, and the pretty plantations of coffee, so green and spring-like, this one containing upwards of 50,000 young plants, all fresh and vigorous, besides a great deal of uncultivated ground, abandoned to the deer and hares and quails, of which there are great abundance.

Included in her visits was one hacienda the awed woman described as "princely." "This beautiful hacienda . . . is 30 leagues in length and 17 in width [roughly 1800 square miles]—containing in this great space the productions of every climate, from the fir-clad mountains on a level with the volcano of Toluca, to the fertile plains which produce corn and maize; and lower down to fields of sugar cane and other productions of the tropics."

Huge plantations dominated the Brazilian countryside as well. To all appearances, those fazendas remained the same in structure and operation as they had for hundreds of years. One observant traveler, Daniel F. Kidder, visited a fazenda at Jaraguá in the interior of São Paulo at mid-century. The estate belonged to an enterprising woman who resided most of the year in the city of São Paulo. The variety of the products grown on the fazenda impressed Kidder: sugar cane, manioc, cotton, rice, and coffee. He left this description of part of it:

Around the farm-house as a centre, were situated numerous out-houses, such as quarters for negroes, store-houses for staple vegetables, and fixtures for reducing them to marketable form.

The engenho de cachassa was an establishment where the juices of the sugar-cane were expressed for distillation. On most of the sugar estates there exist distilleries, which convert the treacle drained from the sugar into a species of alcohol called cachassa. . . . The apparatus for grinding the cane was rude and clumsy in its construction, and not dissimilar to the corresponding portion of a cider-mill in the United States. It was turned by four oxen.

He then went on to describe the customs of the plantation house and of his hosts:

Our social entertainments at Jaraguá were of no ordinary grade. Any person looking in upon the throng of human beings that filled the house when we were all gathered together, would have been at a loss to appreciate the force of a common remark of Brazilians respecting their country, viz that its greatest misfortune is a want of population. Leaving travelers and naturalists out of the question, and also the swarm of servants, waiters, and children—each of whom, whether white, black, or mulatto, seemed emulous of making a due share of noise—there were present half a dozen ladies, relatives of the Donna, who had come up from the city to enjoy the occasion. Among the gentlemen were three sons of the Donna, her son-in-law, a doctor of laws, and her chaplain, who was also a professor in the law university, and a doctor in theology. With such an interesting company, the time allotted to our stay could hardly fail to be agreeably spent. . . . It is a pleasure to say, that I observed none of that seclusion and excessive restraint which some writers have set down as characteristic of Brazilian females. True, the younger members of the company seldom ventured beyond the utterance of Sim Senhor, Não Senhor, and the like; but ample amends for their bashfulness were made by the extreme sociability of Donna Gertrudes. She voluntarily detailed to me an account of her vast business concerns, showed me in person her agricultural and mineral treasures, and seemed to take the greatest satisfaction in imparting the results of her experience on all subjects.

Kidder spoke favorably of the food. The national diet revolved around the basic staples of rice, beans, manioc, flour, sugar, coffee, corn, and dried meat. Apparently the fazenda offered its guests considerably more. Our traveler noted:

There was a princely profusion in the provisions for the table, but an amount of disorder in the service performed by near a dozen waiters, which might have been amply remedied by two that understood well their business. The plate was of the most massive and costly kind. The chairs and tables were equally miserable. The sheets, pillow-cases and towels, of the sleeping apartments, were of cotton, but at the same time ornamented with wide fringes of wrought cambric. Thus the law of contrast seemed to prevail throughout.

Life in the large plantation seemed genteel enough—for the owners, that is. It represented a traditional comfort to which they had accustomed themselves.

The continuity between the 30 years after independence and the colonial period is remarkable. Economic changes were few. Agriculture and the large estate retained their prominence, and the new nations became as subservient to British economic policies as they once had been to those of Spain and Portugal. The wars of independence had shaken and weakened some of the foundation stones of society but the edifice stood pretty much intact. A small, privileged elite ruled over the muted masses. Less than one in ten could read and less than one in 20 earned enough to live in even modest comfort. Land remained the principal source of wealth, prestige, and power, and only a few owned the land.

The continuity, however, was not perfect. Two major political changes marked the early national period. The first and most obvious was the transmission of power from the Iberians to the creole and mazombo elites. Political power no longer emanated from Europe; it had a local source. The second was the emergence of the military in Spanish America as an important political institution destined to play a decisive role in Latin American history.

five

The Emergence
of the
Modern State

Rio de Janeiro in the Early Twentieth Century

The many problems faced by the new nations after independence found no easy solution—indeed, no nation yet, after a century and a half of effort, has succeeded in solving all of them. Still, by the mid-nineteenth century it was possible to see that some of the nations, of which Brazil and Chile served as outstanding examples, were progressing toward political stability and economic prosperity. Foreign threats had diminished; the republican principle had triumphed everywhere but in Brazil; centralized government had been generally accepted. Nationalism became a better defined force as more and more citizens in the various states expressed greater pride in their homeland, appreciated its uniqueness, and sought its progress.

If political change and instability had marked the first half of the nineteenth century, economic and social innovations as well as political stability characterized the last half. An accelerating prosperity —at least for the favored classes—encouraged material growth and attracted a wave of immigrants, particularly to Argentina, Brazil, and Chile. The combination of stability and prosperity helped to accelerate three trends, industrialization, urbanization, and modernization, which in turn threatened to alter some of the established patterns inherited from the colonial past.

POLITICAL STABILITY

With civil disorder on the wane, the chiefs of state consolidated and extended their authority. They governed supremely with few if any checks from the congresses and the courts which they customarily dominated. In some cases, they selected their own successors who were assured of impressive electoral victories. Nonetheless, a greater respect for legal forms prevailed, and some caudillos even appeared to be more legally conscious and circumspect than their predecessors. At any rate, they paid more lip service to constitutional formalities and some even showed an occasional indication of heeding the constitution.

In somber frock coats representatives of the elite discussed and debated the political issues of the day. The earlier division of political proclivities into conservative and liberal prevailed. Those of liberal suasion often flirted with federalist schemes, maintained a theoretical interest in the rights of man, demanded an end to the Church's temporal powers, embraced laissez-faire economic doctrine, and professed a willingness to experiment with new ideas and methods. The conservatives, on the other hand, lauded centralism, defended a hierarchical society, approved the privileges and prerogatives of the Church, and felt more comfortable with a controlled or regulated economic system. Neither political division expressed any desire to tamper with the major land, labor, and social systems. The latifundia and debt peonage continued. Indeed, in most cases they grew. Nor did either party become seriously concerned with extending the suffrage. Consequently on many fundamental issues the two major political divisions harmonized rather than diverged. In Brazil, the Visconde de Albuquerque wryly remarked, "There is nothing quite so much like a Conservative as a Liberal in office." More distinctive than party labels were the personalities. The individual, rather than a vague catalog of political ideas, attracted or repelled support. The politician as a man, as a leader, exercised far more strength than the more abstract institution, the party.

In some countries, the formalization of political beliefs into two major divisions did contribute to political stabilization. The parties helped to train young men for politics and they provided the means for nominating and electing men to office. The contributions of parties to political regularization were very noticeable in Chile and Brazil, two major countries where the landed aristocracy drew together after independence and enforced stability. On the other hand, examples exist in which the division of political beliefs into conservative and liberal created not two debating societies but two war camps. Nicaragua provided the perfect example. The Liberals centered in León, while the Conservatives concentrated in Granada. They fought back and forth throughout the nineteenth century. The victory trophy was the presidency. Colombia furnished a similar example. The tumult exacerbated by party strife in Colombia and Nicaragua contrasted vividly with the more tranquil experiences of party politics in Chile and Brazil.

Brazil had enjoyed stability during the First Empire (1822–31); but during the regency established after the abdication of Pedro I, centrifugal forces began tugging at the huge empire. One province after another, from the far north to the far south, rebelled against the government in Rio de Janeiro. To save national unity, the Brazilians proclaimed the young Pedró II emperor in 1840, four years before he was legally of age to ascend the throne. As expected, the monarchy, the only truly effective national institution in Brazil, provided the ideal instrument to impose unity on the disintegrating nation. Brazil's nearly disastrous experiment with federalism ended when Pedro II reimposed a high degree of centralism on the nation. The Brazilian-born emperor succeeded in restoring order and stability to his badly shaken realm. The last rebellion broke out in 1848. After mid-century, the opposition no longer resorted to violence but relied on constituted and orderly channels to voice disagreement. Before the end of the 1840s Pedro was more than a figurehead; he was tightly controlling the reigns of government. As the constitution prescribed, he functioned on a plane above politics, the grand manipulator of all the instruments of government. He ruled benevolently but firmly. As the years of his long reign waxed, he preferred to exercise power more indirectly, but nonetheless his presence was always felt. During most of his reign, Pedro enjoyed the devotion and respect of his subjects. In manner he was calm, deliberate, and serious, eschewing military uniforms for somber black suits and preferring books and study to the active life of the outdoors. He practiced a morality in both private and public life which few could equal and thereby imposed a Victorian morality on the court and government in an otherwise relaxed nation. By all accounts, and his portraits and photographs verify it, he was an imposing and handsome man. Foreigners who met him universally praised him. The Protestant clergymen D. P. Kidder and J. C. Fletcher, whose accounts of nineteenth-century Brazil are among the best written and most informative, were no exception. In the early 1850s, they witnessed the emperor's behavior at the gala opening of the legislature and reported:

> The Emperor is indeed a Saul—head and shoulders above his people; and in his court-dress, with his crown upon his fine, fair brow, and his sceptre in his hand, whether receiving the salutes of his subjects or opening the

Imperial Chambers, he is a splendid specimen of manhood. His height when uncovered is six feet four inches, and his head and body are beautifully proportioned: at a glance one can see, in that full brain and in that fine blue eye, that he is not a mere puppet upon the throne, but a man who thinks.

In 1847, the emperor created the post of President of the Council of Ministers, and a parliamentary system *sui generis* developed. The emperor saw to it that the two political parties, the Liberals and the Conservatives, alternated in power. Between them they formed 36 different ministries during the 49 years of the Second Empire. Guided by the emperor, the parties accepted the give-and-take of politics in a manner rare on the continent.

The fall of the Liberal ministry of Zacharias de Góis e Vasconcelos in 1868 divided the political history of the Second Empire. The Liberals blamed the heavy hand of the emperor for their loss of power, in their opinion nothing short of a coup d'etat. As a result, the following year the Liberals issued a reform manifesto calling for the abolition of the moderating power, the Council of State (they regarded it as the stronghold of conservatism), the National Guard (they denounced the privileges of the officers), and slavery and favoring the establishment of direct elections, expanded suffrage, periodical elections for senators for a limited term of office, popular election of provincial presidents, an independent judiciary, more educational institutions, and other reforms. If enacted, their program would weaken the government in Rio de Janeiro because in effect what the Liberals envisaged was federalization with its consequent decentralization. At the same time, the Federal Republican Party emerged, and in a manifesto issued in December of 1870 it denounced the monarchy and called for a federal republic. By 1870, some major structural reforms—of which the abolition of slavery, the substitution of a republic for a monarchy and federalism for centralism, and the expansion of the political base were the most significant—had been suggested, injecting into politics more substantial issues than was usually the case. Some of these reforms were enacted during the following decades.

The foundations of the monarchy slowly weakened. In the early 1870s, a display of regalistic ire annoyed many churchmen. It began when the Bishop of Olinda carried out a papal order, unapproved by the emperor, to expel Masons from the lay brotherhoods of the Roman Catholic Church. Pedro II ordered the bishop to remove the penalty. His refusal to comply challenged the emperor. The government arrested and jailed the churchman along with another bishop, both of whom the royal courts found guilty of disobedience of civil law. That controversy with the Church and the resultant imprisonment of the bishops created religious enemies for the crown. In a mood of sullen resentment the once devoted Church cooled toward the monarchy. The manumission of the slaves in 1888 without any compensation to the owners distressed part of the landowning class, which also turned its back on the emperor. Emancipation had been brought about largely by urban groups. They did not identify closely with the monarchy which they felt did not represent their interests. They viewed the aging emperor as a symbol of the past, anathema to the modernization they preached. It was among those urban groups that republican doctrine spread. That doctrine, as well as the urban mentality, pervaded the army officer corps. Pedro had ignored the military officers, an increasingly restless group in the 1880s. In them, the disgruntled clergy, landowners, and urban dwellers found their instrument for political change. The republican cause won many military converts, particularly among the junior officers who equated a republic with progress and modernization. The fate of the monarchy was sealed when the principal military leader, Marshal Deodoro da Fonseca, switched his allegiance and proclaimed himself in favor of a republic. Under his leadership on November 15, 1889, the army surrounded the royal palace, occupied the important governmental buildings, and silenced Rio de Janeiro. The military overthrew the monarchy and declared Brazil to be a republic. Brazil's foremost novelist of the period, Machado de Assis, ably caught the mood of the times, a general ambivalence, in his brilliant novel, *Jacob and Esau*. The old emperor abdicated and, like his father before him, sailed into European exile. There was no turmoil. The transition was bloodless. A new constitution, presidential, federal, democratic, and republican was promulgated on February 24, 1891.

Chile, too, found its stability early. In fact, by 1830, Chile's search for national order was over. The small and powerful landowning class consolidated quickly and from the ranks of the conservatives emerged one of Chile's ablest leaders of the nineteenth century, Diego Portales. Through his force, efficiency, and skill, he imposed conservative rule in 1830, and it lasted until 1861. He never served as president, although he held various ministerial portfolios, Interior, Foreign Relations, War, and Navy until his assassination in 1837. Matters of power, discipline, stability, and order concerned him, not social or economic reforms. In sharp contrast to what was happening in the rest of Spanish America, he succeeded in subordinating the army to a civilian government and thereby removing the military from nineteenth-century politics. He also framed the Constitution of 1833, which lasted until 1925. It guaranteed aristocratic influence for nearly a century.

Presidential mandates lasted five years and could be renewed for an additional five. Three conservative leaders each held the office for ten years, enforcing the remarkable stability imposed by Portales. Manuel Montt, who served from 1851 to 1861, accepted a moderate, José Joaquín Pérez, to succeed him. The 30 years, 1861–1891, were a period of liberal rule tempered by conservative opposition, in direct contrast to the preceding three decades. The major reforms enacted by the liberals indicated the direction and degree of change they advocated: private liberty of worship in houses and schools, the establishment of cemeteries for non-Catholics, the abolition of the privileged Church courts, civil marriage, freedom of the press, no reelection of the president, a modification of the electoral reform law to substitute a literacy test for property qualifications, greater autonomy for municipal governments, and the power of congress to override a presidential veto. As is obvious, none of these altered the power structure in Chile, none attempted to shift the social and economic imbalance of the country. Chile's record of stability and order encouraged economic prosperity and a high degree of material progress.

Argentina and Mexico, on the other hand, experienced greater difficulty in their search for political stability. After Rosas fell in 1852, the city and province of Buenos Aires refused to adhere to the new Argentine union, fearful that they would have to surrender too much power. The old struggle between the port and the provinces continued until 1862, when the prestigious and powerful Governor of Buenos Aires, Bartolomé Mitre, was able to impose his will on the entire nation. His force and ability reunited the nation. A succession of able presidents, each of whom served for six years, followed him. Those presidents wielded almost total power. The Argentine historian Ricardo Levene concluded, "The presidency absorbed and centralized all the power of the democracy, in such a manner that the fortunes of the candidates did not depend upon the electoral struggle of political parties but upon the wish of the president." In 1880 the thorny question of the city and province of Buenos Aires was finally solved. New legislation separated the city from the province, federalized the city and declared it the national capital, a role it had previously played. The rich province then went its own way with a new capital, La Plata. Meanwhile, the nation was investing the energy once given to political struggles into economic development.

Mexico's search for stability was one of the most difficult in Latin America, complicated by questions of federalism and the position of the Church in the new nation. The bloodshed and drama which began in 1810 lasted well over half a century and exhausted the nation. Finally a mestizo strongman, Porfirio Díaz, who had risen through the military ranks to become general and in the process had fought against Santa Anna, the French, and Maximilian, brought peace to Mexico in 1876, an iron peace as it turned out. For the next 34 years, he imposed a conservative, centralized government on Mexico while ruling under the liberal, federal Constitution of 1857. His government brought order and stability to a degree unknown since the colonial period. The strength and political longevity of Diaz rested on a powerful supporting alliance he created. The Church, the army, foreign capitalists, and the great landowners found it beneficial to back his regime, and they reaped substantial material rewards for their allegiance. On the other hand, the wily Díaz manipulated them at will for his own ends. Under his guidance, Mexico made outstanding material progress and witnessed a prosperity surpassing the best years of colonial mining.

The supporting alliance Díaz formed proved to be the most effective combination of forces to buttress political stability. To varying degrees the chiefs of state of other nations made use of similar combinations to buttress their power. The two key groups obviously were the army and the landowners. Where the elites were generally in concurrence and worked in harmony—as, for example, in Chile and Brazil—order came early in the national life; where those elites found it more difficult to concur—Argentina and Mexico are examples—order was delayed. Of course, there were nations in nineteenth-century Latin America—Bolivia, Uruguay, and Nicaragua, for example—in which no concurrence at all was reached with the consequence that order and stability eluded them throughout the century. Once political order was imposed, the Latin American nations sought to institute at home some of the technical and material progress they admired abroad. In doing so, they initiated the process of modernization.

MODERNIZATION

The Latin American elite was acutely aware of the progress being made in Great Britain, France, Germany, and the United States. Many of them had mastered French, the second language of the elite, and a few had a knowledge of English or German, so that they had direct access to the information and literature from the nations whose progress impressed them. The newspapers carried full accounts of what was happening in the leading nations of the Western world, and the programs of the learned societies featured discussions of the technical advances of the industrializing nations. Many members of the elite traveled abroad and were exposed to the innovations firsthand. They returned to their quieter capitals in the New World with a nostalgia for Paris and the irrespressible desire to ape everything they had seen there. Of course, the imports bore testimony to larger segments of the population of the manufacturing skill and ingenuity of those technically advanced societies. Clearly the new inventions, techniques, methods, and ideas fascinated the Latin Americans. The process of modernization in Latin America was largely one of following the models set by the United States and by those nations of Western Europe which the elite and middle sectors most admired. A direct correlation between class status and attitudes toward modernization existed. Broadly speaking, in the upper levels of society people more readily accepted modern values. They were the ones most in contact with the world and knew what was going on. They more readily imitated the advances and changes which most struck their fancy.

The individual who subscribed to the process of modernization was willing to experiment, to change, to alter his environment to suit his needs. On the other hand, those immersed in tradition adjusted to life, accepting it as it was. Apathetic, fatalistic, less sure of themselves in a modernizing society, they clung tenaciously to patterns and methods sanctioned by time. Agriculture testified to that, for as basic as agriculture was to the prosperity of the new nations, by mid-century few changes had been made in timeless production methods. The son used what his father had used, and the father copied his father. The traveler Albert M. Gilliam observed in the mid-1840s: "The plough universally in use in Mexico is the instrument handed by the Romans to their posterity." That indictment could be repeated about most practices, particularly in the countryside. An agricultural report on northern Brazil in the early 1860s termed the local agrarian practices as "primitive" if compared to those observed on the farms of Western Europe and the United States. The hoe was the single farm implement, and the workers faithfully followed past procedures without any thought of improving them or effort to change. In comparison to the modernizing nations of Europe and to the United States, Latin America appeared backward, behind the times, too traditional. Many members of the elite, in particular those who lived in the cities or were closely connected with urban life, sought to bring their nations materially up-to-date.

Stability released energy and resources, which were invested in the process of modernization. It is not surprising therefore, that Brazil and Chile were among the first Latin American nations to experiment with the inventions and innovations offered by Europe. The steam engine made an early appearance in those two nations. In 1815, Bahia boasted its first steam-driven sugar mill. Two years later Pernambuco also possessed one. By 1834, there were 64 of them in operation, a number which rose to 144 by 1852 and then increased rapidly thereafter. At the same time, the coffee processors were beginning to acquire steam-driven machinery. In Chile, the first steam-powered flour mill went into operation in 1839. By 1863, Chile counted 132 steam engines used in sawmills, distilleries, blower furnaces, flour mills, and coal mines.

None of the innovations had more impact than the railroad. Its steel rails helped bind together nations, an effective agent to counteract the centrifugal propensities always at work in the larger Latin American nations. The Argentine intellectual Juan Bautista Alberdi concluded, "Without the railroad, political unity cannot be possible in a nation where distance weakens centralized political power." The railroad served a vital economic as well as political function. Penetrating distant regions the railroads tapped new sources of economic prosperity. Bulky and perishable products could be rushed over long distances to eager markets. True, the railroads also had their negative aspect. The governments contracted heavy debts to pay for them. These debts often led to foreign complications and always to some sacrifice of economic independence. One brazen example of foreign intervention precipitated by railroad funding occurred in Venezuela. In 1903, German gunboats appeared off the coast to force the government to pay 1.4 million pounds sterling for loans associated with railroad building.

Cuba can boast of the first railroad in Latin America. The line from Habana to Güines, approximately 30 miles, began operation in 1838. Chile initiated its first railroad in 1852 and a decade later had laid 543 miles of tracks. A new Brazilian law in 1852 provided favorable conditions for any entrepreneur who would undertake to construct a railroad. The capitalist Viscount Mauá accepted the challenge and in 1854 inaugurated a line of ten miles. By 1874, there were approximately 800 miles of tracks. After 1875, construction increased rapidly: in 1875–84, 2,200 miles were laid; in 1885–89, 2,500. By 1889, then, trackage totaled approximately 6,000 miles. Argentina's railroad era began in 1857 with the inauguration of a seven-mile line. The government offered a variety of inducements to encourage its expansion: the duty-free entry of materials and equipment, interest guarantees, and land grants. British capital readily responded and dominated rail construction. Britain supplied technicians and engineers as well and then sold English coal to the railroad companies to run the steam engines. By 1885, Argentina had 2,290 miles of rails; then the building boom began and the mileage jumped to 10,200 in 1889; 15,000 in 1908; and 21,700 in 1914. Argentina boasted the most extensive railroad network in Latin America and the eighth largest in the world. In total, South America's railroad mileage grew from 2,000 in 1870 to 59,000 in 1900.

Mexico began its railroad construction very slowly. When Diaz took power in 1876, only 400 miles had been laid. He pushed rail construction with the result that approximately 15,000 miles of rails were put down during his long regime. Argentina, Brazil, Chile, Mexico, Cuba, and Uruguay developed a reasonably extensive network of railroads covering much of the effective national territory, but in the rest of Latin America the railways were short, feeder lines for seaports, unconnected and unrelated with each other.

Along the newly laid rail lines, at rail junctions, and at railheads sprang up villages and towns. Older settlements took on a new life. Hastings Charles Dent, an English engineer in Brazil in 1883–84 to survey the route for the Minas Gerais Railroad, observed one such impact of the railroad on urbanization. He commented on the phenomenal growth of the town of Queluz, Minas Gerais, during the brief span of 11 months: "There are great changes in this place since I was here on July 1, last year. The town of Queluz is up on a hill; the station Lafayette . . . which last July was in course of construction, and an isolated building, is now the centre of a large colony of houses, inns, 'armazens,' etc." At about the same time another Englishman, Sir Horace Rumbold, was making a similar observation on the impact of the railroad on Argentina where he resided for two years: "Villages and towns spring up in its [the railroad's] wake with mushroom growth, and stud, in an incredibly short space of time, those vast empty tracts which on the map were marked before only with the sites of former Indian encampments or a few simple names indicative of barbarian chase or travel." The railroad brought the countryside and the city into closer contact and as a result the neofeudalistic and paternalistic aspects of plantation and hacienda life were challenged as never before. The railroads opend new markets for the incipient industries of the large cities and brought into the hinterlands a greater variety of goods than those populations had hitherto seen. Railroads thus helped to promote the fledgling industries. The railroad also provided some amusement during its early years. When the railroad finally reached Guatemala City in the 1880s, it became a custom for the capital's inhabitants of all social levels to congregate at the railroad station for the semiweekly arrivals and departures of the train. On those occasions, the National Band played in the plaza in front of the station for the further entertainment of the crowd.

The telegraph furthered the communications revolution in Latin America. Both Chile and Brazil began service over short lines in 1852. In Chile, the telegraph linked Santiago and Valparaiso. In Brazil, the first line connected the imperial palace at São Cristóvão, on the outskirts of the capital, to the military headquarters in the capital. The outbreak of the Paraguayan war caused a flurry of activity to string lines southward toward the battlefields. In a record time of six months a telegraph line joined Rio de Janeiro to the southernmost province of the empire. In the opposite direction, the lines reached Belém, at the mouth of the Amazon, in 1886, and thereafter penetrated the interior. In 1861 there were ten stations with 40 miles of wire transmitting

233 messages. By 1885 there were 171 stations with 6,560 miles of lines handling over 600,000 messages. Argentina began to string telegraph wires in the 1860s, and by 1875, 60 stations were transmitting messages. In 1869, Costa Rica became the first Central American republic to inaugurate telegraphic service, connecting Puntarenas on the Pacific with the capital in the highlands. Twenty years later, there were 389 miles of wire and 30 stations.

While on the one hand the telegraph contributed to national unity, on the other it helped to bring nations closer together. In 1866, a cable connected Buenos Aires and Montevideo; and the following year the United States opened cable communication with Cuba. The transandine telegraph united Buenos Aires and Santiago in 1872. Brazil inaugurated telegraphic contact with Montevideo in 1879 and with Buenos Aires in 1883. From the United States, the Central and South American Cable Company, formed in 1879, began stretching its cables southward into Middle America and then beyond. By 1882, its line reached as far south as Lima and in 1890 it extended to Santiago where it connected with the Transandine Telegraph Company. Transatlantic cables put Latin America in instantaneous communication with Europe. Pedro II dictated the first message to be cabled from Brazil to Europe in 1874. Significantly, then, Rio de Janeiro was linked to Europe by cable long before it could communicate by telegraph with other parts of its own empire.

The number of international steamship lines serving Latin America increased rapidly during the last half of the century. The principal ports of the Austro-Hungarian Empire, Italy, Spain, France, Great Britain, Germany, and the United States were in direct and regular contact with those of Latin America. Sailings became increasingly frequent; ships carried more cargo; service improved. The major ports underwent renovation with the addition of new and larger warehouses, faster loading and unloading machinery, larger and sturdier wharfs, and the dredging of deeper channels.

The concern with improved transportation and communication exemplified a growing dedication to progress. To a large extent, material advances measured that progress. How many miles of railroads, how much horsepower generated by steam engines, how many tons handled per hour in the ports, how many miles of telegraph lines? The higher the number given in the response to those questions, the greater was the progress which the nation could credit itself. Little wonder then that some members of the elite warmly embraced the new philosophy of Positivism, formulated in Europe during the second quarter of the nineteenth century by Auguste Comte. Positivism emphasized material growth and well-being. It favored a capitalist ideology, and it regarded private wealth as sacred. Indeed, private accumulation of wealth was a sign of progress as well as an instrument for progress. Because of the weakness of domestic, private institutions, the state had to assume the role of directing progress. Of course, to promote capitalism and to direct progress, the state, according to Positivist doctrine, had to maintain order and impose stability. With its special emphasis on order and progress, Positivism reached its height of influence between 1880 and 1900. It became almost an official doctrine of the Díaz regime in Mexico; some of his principal ministers, who, very significantly, were known as the *científicos*, had imbibed deeply of Comte's doctrines and tried to offer a scientific solution to the problems of organizing national life. In Brazil, too, Positivism attracted many adherents, particularly among young army officers who believed that the monarchy retarded national progress. Most of the other Latin American nations had their disciples of Comte who preached the new method of achieving national progress and prosperity.

Clearly not all of Latin America shared fully in the progress. One astonished visitor to the highlands of Ecuador and to Quito in 1885 gasped, "The country does not know the meaning of the words progress and prosperity." At that time, the only communication between Quito, the capital high in the Andes, and Guayaquil, the Pacific port, was still by mule path, a route impassable during six months of the year because of the rainy season. Under optimum conditions, it was possible to make the journey in eight or nine days over the same route in use for centuries. As a port, Guayaquil was in contact with the world and showed signs of modernization long before the isolated capital did. The public streetcar, gas lighting, and other amenities reached Guayaquil years before they could be seen in the capital. Not until the end of the first decade of the twentieth century did a railroad link Guayaquil with Quito. The 227-mile railroad climb from the port to the capital took two days. The slower development of Ecuador was not unique; it characterized many of the nations which lagged behind the leadership of Argentina, Brazil, Chile, and Mexico.

The elite proudly regarded the new railroads, steamships, telegraph lines, and renovated ports as ample physical evidence of the progressive course on which their nations had embarked. In their satisfaction, they seemed oblivious to another aspect of modernization: that those very steamships, railroads, and ports tied them and their nations ever more tightly to a handful of industrialized nations in Western Europe and North America which bought their raw products and provided manufactured goods in return. They failed to take note of the significance that many of the railroads did not link the principal cities of their nations but rather ran from the plantations or mines directly to the ports, subordinating the goal of national unification to the demands of the industrial nations for agricultural products and minerals. As foreign investment rose, the voices of foreign investors and bankers spoke with greater authority in making economic decisions for the host countries. Local economic options diminished. In short, modernization magnified Latin America's dependency.

Economic prosperity contributed heavily to the growing political stability and modernization. Much of that prosperity was based on the increasing influx of foreign investments and the growing volume of exports.

The demands of the industrialized nations for raw products continued to rise throughout the last half of the nineteenth century. Not only was there a rapidly increasing number of consumers in Western Europe and the United States but their per capita purchasing power was ever greater too. It was during that half-century that the United States emerged as the principal industrialized nation of the world and as the foremost consumer of Latin America's exports. As the industrial centers bought more agricultural and mineral products from Latin America, the region's trade underwent a dramatic expansion. Plantation owners and miners produced larger amounts of grain, coffee, sugar, cotton, cacao, bananas, livestock, copper, silver, tin, lead, zinc, and nitrates for export. The natural products—such as palm oils, nuts, woods, rubber, and medicinal plants—also found a ready market abroad, and their exportation rose sharply.

Foreign observers marveled at the rapid rate of increase of Latin American trade. An official United States report in 1890 stated:

> People who have not studied the subject have very little conception of the magnitude and value of the foreign commerce of Central and South America . . . which amounts to $1,000,000,000 annually, nearly evenly divided between exports and imports. . . . The total value of the foreign commerce of these countries increased from $709,000,000 in 1870 to $1,014,000,000 in 1884, a gain of $304,732,000, or 43 percent.

By comparison, during the same period British trade increased by 27.2 percent. The five principal areas engaged in foreign commerce were Brazil, Argentina, Cuba, Chile, and Mexico, which together accounted for more than three-quarters of Latin America's trade. With the exception of Argentina, they exported more than they imported. Trade statistics for the individual nations were impressive. Argentine exports jumped sevenfold between 1853 and 1873 and doubled again by 1893.

Mexican exports quadrupled between 1877 and 1900. The smaller nations benefited too. Exports of coffee from Costa Rica increased fourfold between 1855 and 1915, and tin shipments from Bolivia quadrupled during a four-year period, 1897–1900, and tripled again by 1913.

In Brazil, the value of foreign trade increased by six to seven times between 1833 and 1889, a record made possible by coffee, a relatively new export. At the time of independence, coffee accounted for only about a fifth of Brazil's exports, a figure which rose to two-thirds by the time of the fall of the monarchy, 1889. Those figures indicated an increase from 190,060 to 5,586,000 in the number of sacks of coffee beans shipped to world coffee markets in a 67-year period. The value of the coffee sold during those years equaled that of all the exports during the entire colonial period. The coffee industry flourished first in the Paraíba Valley in the province of Rio de Janeiro from where it spread into the neighboring provinces of Minas Gerais and São Paulo.

During the harvesting season, the plantation required long and hard hours from the workers. An observant American traveler to Brazil, Herbert H. Smith, visited a modern and efficient plantation in full operation in the Paraíba Valley in the 1870s and reported the following schedule for the slaves:

> The negroes are kept under a rigid surveillance, and the work is regulated as by machinery. At four o'clock in the morning all hands are called out to sing prayers, after which they file off to their work. At six coffee is given to them; at nine they breakfast on jerked beef, mandioca meal, beans and corn-cake; at noon they receive a small dram of rum; at four o'clock they get their dinner, precisely like the breakfast, and, like that served in the field, with the slightest possible intermission from work. At seven the files move wearily back to the house, where they are drawn up to the sound of a bugle. From the tripod at one side a bright fire half illumines, half conceals, the dark figures, sending flashes over the walls beyond, and casting long shadows on the ground. The tools are deposited in a storehouse, and locked up; two or three of the crowd, perhaps, advance timidly to make requests of the master; after that all are dispersed to household and mill-work until nine o'clock; then the men and women are locked up in separate quarters, and left to sleep seven hours, to prepare for the seventeen hours of almost uninterrupted labor on the succeeding day. On Sunday there is a nominal holiday, which, practically, amounts to but three or four hours; none of the Catholic holidays are celebrated here, and even Christmas is passed unnoticed.

Obviously it was at the cost of enormous labor that the coffee beans were prepared for market.

A number of inventions, among them the railroad, barbed wire, and refrigerator ship, facilitated the exploitation of Argentina's hitherto untamed pampas, potentially one of the world's most fertile regions. The sailing of the first, primitive refrigerator ship, *Le Frigorifique,* from Buenos Aires to Europe in 1876 changed the course of Argentine economic history. The successful voyage proved that chilled and frozen beef could be sold in lucrative European markets. Measures were taken at once to improve the quality of the beef. By 1900, 278 refrigerator ships plied between Great Britain and Argentina. During the decade of the 1870s, Argentina also made its first wheat shipments to Europe, a modest 21 tons in 1876. In 1900, wheat exports reached 2,250,000 tons. During the same period, the cultivated acreage on the pampas jumped 15 times. Exports rose fivefold from 30 million gold pesos in 1870 to 150 million by 1900. That extraordinary economic boom made Argentina the most prosperous nation in Latin America.

Most governmental leaders paid far more attention to the international economy than to the national, domestic economy. The export sector of the Latin American economy grew more rapidly than the domestic sector, and income from foreign trade contributed an unusually high percentage of the gross national product. Foreign trade emphatically did not mean commerce among the Latin American states. They were total strangers in each other's marketplaces. Their economies developed to complement the demands of the distant major capitalistic economies in Western Europe and the United States.

Mounting foreign investments were the second outstanding characteristic of the Latin American economy in the last half of the nineteenth century. Europe generously sent capital, technology, and technicians to Latin America to assure the increased agricultural and mineral production its factories and urban populations required. The more pronounced stability of Latin America engendered greater confidence and generosity among foreign investors. The politicians of Latin America, and none more so than the caudillos, discovered the advantages of foreign investment. It created new wealth, which caudillos, politicians, and elite alike enjoyed. In a pattern being well established throughout the hemisphere, Porfirio Díaz meticulously paid off Mexico's foreign debts and decreed laws favorable to foreign investors. Foreign investment poured into Mexico.

To handle the new flow of money, banks, both national and foreign, sprang up with amazing rapidity in the major Latin American cities. Only one bank existed in Brazil in 1845, but in the following 12 years 12 new banks were founded as the Brazilians began to rapidly expand their banking system. Foreign banks made their appearance in Brazil for the first time with inauguration of the London and Brazil Bank in Rio de Janeiro in 1862. In that same year, the Bank of London and the River Plate was established in Buenos Aires. The London Bank of Mexico and South America opened in Mexico City in 1864. Spanish,

Portuguese, Italian, French, German, and North American banks followed. In Central America, Costa Rica witnessed the founding of the first bank in 1857 by an enterprising local capitalist. Its existence was brief. In 1863 the Anglo-Costa Rican Bank was established and four years later the Bank of Costa Rica. The banks facilitated international trade and investment. They also brought to an end most of the personal financial transactions characteristic of the decades after independence. Impersonal institutions of growing resources, they multiplied the power and importance of the city and conversely diminished the prestige of the landowners whose debts to the urban banks increased.

By the eve of World War I, foreign investments totaled $8.5 billion. The English invested the heaviest, $5 billion, or 20 percent of British overseas investment. The French were second with $1.7 billion, followed very closely by the United States with $1.6 billion. Germany was fourth with somewhat less than $1 billion. The largest share of the money went to Argentina, Brazil, and Mexico, and the most popular investments were railroads, public utilities, and mining. British investments predominated in South America; those of the United States capitalists in Mexico and the Caribbean area.

During the last half of the century, the larger and stabler nations began to industrialize in order to meet growing internal demands for manufactured goods, to develop more balanced economies, and to protect the national economies from extremes of fluctuation in international trade. Some farsighted statesmen believed that without that industrialization the Latin Americans would be doomed to economic dependency and backwardness. The Chilean Manuel Camilo Vial, Minister of Finance during the administration of Manuel Bulnes (1841–51) preached, "Any nation in which agriculture dominates everything, in which slavery or feudalism shows its odious face, follows the march of humanity among the stragglers. . . . That future threatens us also, if we do not promote industry with a firm hand and a constant will." The governments raised the tariffs, particularly during the final decades of the century, to encourage and protect the new industries and from time to time promulgated other legislation such as tax incentives and permission to import machinery duty-free to give further impetus to the process. Despite such disadvantages as limited capital, unskilled labor, low labor productivity, lack of coal, limited markets, and a mentality emphasizing the continued reliance on the exploitation of mineral and agricultural possibilities, industrialization grew gradually in the last decades of the nineteenth century. As an official report of the Costa Rican government expressed it in 1890:

> The scarcity of working people and the absence of capital were formerly the greatest barriers to the progress of industry, while at the same time the

abundance and relative cheapness of imported articles rendered useless all attempts at home production. There is now a new aspect of affairs; for judicious economic principles have changed the conditions that so long existed.

In the beginning, industrialization was primarily concerned with the processing of natural products for local consumption or export. Flour mills, sugar refineries, meat-packing plants, tanning factories, lumber mills, wineries, and breweries developed wherever the requisite resources were at hand. Then service industries appeared: gas and electric utilities, repair shops and foundries, and construction enterprises. Finally, protected industries began to manufacture other goods for home consumption, principally textiles or processed food.

In Brazil, the textile industry was by far the most important. The nine cotton mills in 1865 multiplied into 100 before the fall of the empire. The new republican government which came to power in 1889 visualized an industrial expansion for the nation. Symbolic of their ambitions, the Republicans changed the name of the Ministry of Agriculture to the Ministry of Industry. As further encouragement, they promulgated a protective tariff in 1890 which raised to 60 percent the duty on 300 items, principally textiles and food products, which competed with nationally produced goods. Conversely they lowered the duty on primary goods used in national manufacturing. The tariff rose again in 1896 and still higher in 1900. Fundamental to any industrialization, the government established four new engineering schools in the 1890s.

The Argentine government began to turn its attention seriously to the encouragement of industrialization during the 1870s. In 1876, it enacted a high protective tariff. Industrialization concentrated in and around Buenos Aires, which by 1889, counted some 400 industrial establishments employing approximately 11,000 workers. Of that number 41 had existed before 1869; 73 were established between 1870–79; 101 between 1880–84; and 112 between 1885–89. (The dates of the rest are unknown.) During the last decade of the century, larger factories appeared and industry began to penetrate other regions, although Buenos Aires would always remain the focal point. The census of 1895 listed the number of factories and workshops as 23,000 with 170,000 employees (small workshops employing less than ten workers were by far the most common); the next census, 1914, raised the number of factories and workshops to 49,000 and the number of employees to 410,000. By that time, Argentina manufactured 37 percent of the processed food its inhabitants consumed, 17 percent of the clothing they wore, and 12 percent of the metals and machinery they used.

Other nations, certainly Chile and Mexico were foremost among them, followed the industrial leadership of Argentina and Brazil. The process of industrialization not only challenged and changed timeworn economic structures, but also brought in its wake some political and social innovations.

THE SOCIAL MILIEU

Modernization and industrialization accompanied the growth of cities in size and number. In fact, the three trends of modernization, industrialization, and urbanization, were inextricably intertwined, each acting as a catalyst for the others. Together they challenged the traditional values and patterns of the past and modified, if they did not always change, them. For purposes of definition, most of the Latin American nations classify as urban those localities which have some type of local government and a population of at least 1,000 or 2,000 inhabitants.

The cities played ever more important roles in the development of each nation. The governmental and administrative apparatus, commerce, and industry were located in the cities. Increasingly they served as hubs of complex transportation and communications networks. Further, they provided important recreational, cultural, and educational services. Rapid urban growth resulted from the arrival of greater numbers of foreign immigrants, a constantly increasing population (Latin America counted 60 million inhabitants in 1900), and a "push-pull" effect of the city on the countryside. Promises of better jobs and a better life lured thousands each year from the countryside to the city, a road which became increasingly more heavily trodden. On the other hand, even where that promise was lacking, the grinding poverty of the countryside pushed many desperate peasants into urban areas.

Urban culture imposed a particular mentality on city dwellers which in turn shaped an outlook quite diverse from that of the rural inhabitant. In an urban environment, traditional relationships tended to bend or to disintegrate as necessity or example indicated newer ones. In very general terms, the more intimate living conditions of the city and the great familiarity of the city dweller with foreign cultures exposed the urban inhabitant to different ideas and other values. In every way, he behaved like an activist. He read newspapers and participated in public events. He was aware of the changes the world was undergoing; he knew of the opportunities open to the trained and talented and was willing to strive for those opportunities. Consequently he laid plans for his future, and exerting every effort to realize those plans, he worked to shape his own destiny. The educational opportunities, varied careers, and job possibilities afforded by the city encouraged him to aspire toward upward mobility.

The statistics on Latin America's urban boom are impressive. Argentina's urban population doubled between 1869 and 1914, so that in the latter year the urban sector represented 53 percent of the population. In 1869, Buenos Aires had a population of a quarter of a million, a figure which increased eightfold by 1914 to encompass a quarter of the national population. Brazil witnessed a similar urban growth. Between 1890 and 1914, the government created approximately 500 new municipalities. During the three decades after 1890, the population of the major cities jumped: Recife and Rio de Janeiro doubled in size, Niterói and Porto Alegre tripled, and São Paulo increased eightfold. São Paulo grew faster than any other major Brazilian city, in fact it was one of the fastest growing cities of the world. In 1890, it had 64,000 inhabitants; a decade later it counted 240,000. It increased at a rate above 25 percent every five years after 1895. In 1910, the distinguished British diplomat and author James Bryce described São Paulo, a city then approaching half a million, as "the briskest and most progressive place in all Brazil. . . . The alert faces, and the air of stir and movement, as well as handsome public buildings rising on all hands, with a large, well-planted public garden in the middle of the city, give the impression of energy and progress."

Chile well represented the urban surge in Latin America. In 1875, approximately 27 percent of the population could be classified as urban dwellers, but a quarter of a century later the figure reached 43 percent. Santiago's population shot up from 160,000 in 1880 to 400,000 in 1910, while the population of the second city and principal seaport, Valparaiso, more than doubled to 200,000 during the same period. Foreign visitors always had praise for the modernity of Chile's two major cities. Frank Vincent, who called at Valparaiso in 1885, rhapsodized:

> I was struck by the very civilized look of the famous Chilean seaport. . . . In the dining-room of the hotel the electric light was used, as well as in very many of the stores. In the streets is a "Belgian" pavement, and the sidewalks are smoothly and neatly flagged. The architecture of some of the buildings is very fine, and there are several rich and elegant churches. The principal streets are threaded by tramways. The trams, or cars, are of two stories as in Paris and other European cities. But a Valparaiso conductor is not paralleled in any other city anywhere—for it is a woman.

Visitors to Chile usually commented on those female streetcar conductors. However, the Chilean women of the lower classes held a variety of jobs in the cities by the end of the nineteenth century. In addition to running the streetcars, they did most of the street-cleaning and sold meats, vegetables, and fruits in the markets and on street corners. Visitors invariably commented on the beauty of Chilean women. A well-known figure in Chilean society at the time was Isadora Cousiño, one of the wealthiest persons in Latin America, if not in the world. She administered her vast estates, said to number in the millions of acres, mines, and factories, with a business acumen few could equal and lived amid a splendor that would have been the envy of European monarchs.

Foreign visitors to the capital admired the cleanliness, bustle, and progress. W. D. Boyce, who was there during the first decade of the twentieth century, marveled:

> No city in the world has a finer location. There are many beautiful drives. . . . The Alameda Avenida Delicias, the great boulevard of Santiago, is six hundred feet wide and runs the full length of the city. The finest private houses front on the Alameda. The largest of these are of Spanish style, being built around a courtyard, or patio. . . . Sixty-seven miles of electric tramways are operated by a private company, which also supplies electric light. . . . There are many churches in Santiago, and the great cathedral facing the large Plaza de Armas, in the center of the city, is one of the handsomest structures in the world. It occupies the entire side of the street on the west of the plaza. The public buildings are very fine structures and are substantially built.

By the beginning of the twentieth century, nearly all the capitals and many of the largest cities boasted of electricity, telephones, streetcar service, covered sewers, paved streets, ornamental parks, and new buildings reflecting French architectural influence.

Nurtured in an increasingly prosperous urban environment, intellectual activity flourished. Some of Latin America's most prestigious newspapers were founded: *El Mercurio* in Chile and the *Jornal do Commércio* in Brazil, both in 1827; *El Comercio* in Peru in 1839; and *La Prensa* in 1869 and *La Nación* in 1870 in Buenos Aires. Starting with the University of Chile in 1843, the major universities of Latin America began to publish reviews, journals, annuals, and books, an activity which further stimulated intellectual development. Romanticism, with its individuality, emotional intensity, and glorification of nature held sway in literary circles for much of the nineteenth century. José Marmol of Argentina, Jorge Isaacs of Colombia, and José de Alencar of Brazil were masters of the romantic novel. Excesses in romanticism prompted literary experiments by 1880 in modernism and realism, already in vogue in Europe. The brilliant Nicaraguan poet Rubén Darío helped to introduce modernism into Latin America, and by the end of the century he dominated the field of poetry. Critics considered him one of the most original and influential poetic voices of his time. With two notable exceptions, Latin American culture aped European trends, particularly those set in Paris. They were Ricardo Palma, whose original *"tradiciones peruanas,"* delightful historical anecdotes of Peru, recreated with wit and imagination his country's past; and the Gaucho poets, foremost of whom was the Argentine José Hernández, creator of *Martín Fierro*, a true American epic, picturing life among Argentina's rugged cowboys.

Education continued to be a privilege of the elite. Overwhelming numbers of the masses remained illiterate. What few schools there were could be found concentrated in the larger cities. In Brazil, the illiteracy rate never dropped below 85 percent in the nineteenth century. In the 1880s, with a population exceeding 13 million, the number enrolled in primary schools totaled less than a quarter of a million. Three Argentine presidents, Bartolomé Mitre, Domingo Faustino Sarmiento, and Nicolás Avellaneda dedicated much of their energy and the nation's budget to improving education. As a result, literacy in Argentina rose from 22 percent in 1869 to 65 percent in 1914, an enviable record throughout most of Latin America. In Uruguay, during the 1870s, José Pedro Varela preached that education should be free, obligatory, co-educational, and secularly controlled. Under his direction, the Uruguayan educational system expanded rapidly and the illiteracy rate dropped proportionately. Chile, too, extended its schools to ever larger numbers of children. During his long administration (1873–85), President Justo Rufino Barrios of Guatemala devoted as much as 10 percent of the national budget to education. Still, at the end of his regime, Guatemala had only 934 schools enrolling 42,549 pupils, out of a population of approximately 1.25 million. In truth, despite the efforts of a number of farsighted statesmen, the illiteracy rate remained high throughout Latin America during the last half of the nineteenth century, varying from 40 to 90 percent. It was always much higher in the countryside than in the city. A marked contrast existed between the well-educated few and the ignorant many. The unschooled masses silently witnessed the events which surrounded and affected them but in which they could play only the most limited role. A small minority, the emerging urban middle sectors and the traditional aristocracy, enjoyed the benefits of an educational system closely modeled after European examples and consequently quite unrealistic for Latin America.

The rising national income, gross national product, and level of technology changed the standard of living of the masses little if at all. Their condition remained constant throughout the nineteenth century. On the other hand, the landowners grew richer, while the middle sectors shared in the prosperity as well. Amorphous and small throughout much of the nineteenth century, the middle sectors began to take a more definite shape and increase in numbers during the last half and certainly the last quarter of the nineteenth century. Members of the liberal professions, schoolteachers and professors, bureaucrats, military officers, businessmen, merchants, and those involved in the nascent industrialization composed the ranks of that group. The common denominator of the middle sectors rested on the fact that they were neither admitted to the ranks of the traditional elite nor associated with the lower and poorer ranks of society. The observant James Bryce noted during his tour of South America at the end of the first decade of the twentieth century, "In the cities there exists, between the wealthy and the workingmen, a considerable body of professional men, shopkeepers, and clerks, who are rather less of a defined middle class than they might be in European countries." They possessed a strong urge to improve their lot and tended to imitate, as far as it was possible, the elite. Still, they were not cohesive enough or sufficiently defined to compose a "class," and for that reason the purposely chosen, more nebulous term "middle sectors" is applied to them. Although the heirs of the creoles and mazombos tended to predominate in the middle sectors, increasing numbers of mulattoes and mestizos entered. Education and military service provided two of the surest paths of upward mobility, but the climb was too steep for any but the exceptional or the favored. Although few in number, the dominant presence of the middle sectors in the capital city of each nation allowed them to wield influence far out of proportion to their size. A high percentage of the intellectuals, authors, teachers, and journalists came from their ranks, and they had a powerful voice in expressing what passed for public opinion in the late nineteenth century.

Only an educated guess permits some approximation of the size of the middle sectors. At the end of the nineteenth century it is estimated that Mexico had an urban middle group numbering roughly three-quarters of a million, while another one-fourth of a million constituted a rural middle group. In contrast, there was an urban proletariat of over one-third of a million and a huge peon class of eight million working on the haciendas. In Mexico, Chile, Brazil, Argentina, and Uruguay, the middle sectors may have included as many as 10 percent of the population by the turn of the century. In many of the other countries, it fell far short of that.

The swelling tide of foreign immigration contributed to the growth of the middle sectors. Many of the new arrivals were from the lower classes, but still a high percentage represented Europe's middle class, and besides there was a high incidence of upward mobility among the immigrants in the lands of their adoption. Argentina was one of the largest recipients of immigrants in modern times. Between independence and 1914, approximately three million arrived, a majority of them Italians and Spaniards. In 1914, 30 percent of the Argentines were foreign-born. Those immigrants provided 60 percent of the urban proletariat and held 46 percent of the jobs associated with the middle sectors. Half of the population of Buenos Aires in 1914 was foreign-born. About 100,000 Europeans migrated to Chile before World War I. They constituted at that time only 4 percent of the population. Yet, the foreign-born owned 32 percent of Chile's commercial establishments, and 49 percent of the industries. Brazil welcomed large numbers of Europeans, particularly Italians, Portuguese, and Spaniards. Between 1891 and 1900, approximately 112,500 immigrants arrived annually. The trend continued and reached record yearly averages just before World War I. From 1911 through 1913, half a million immigrants entered. However, the proportion of immigrants to the total population in Brazil never was more than 6.4 percent, a figure reached in 1900. Nonetheless, because of their concentration in the south and southeast, and particularly because of their importance in the cities of those two regions, they exerted an influence far greater than their numbers might indicate. The traditional elite soon grew wary of the immigrants and blamed them for many of the ills the burgeoning urban centers were beginning to experience. The new ideas, methods, and skills introduced by the immigrants helped to accelerate modernization.

CONTINUITY AND CHANGE

During the last half of the nineteenth century, new forces appeared which challenged the hoary social, economic, and political instiutions deeply rooted in the colonial past. Urbanization, industrialization, and modernization formed a trinity menacing to tradition. Once introduced, those mutually supporting forces could not be arrested. The center of political, economic, and social life once located on the plantations and haciendas shifted gradually but irreversibly to the cities.

In the cities the middle sectors grew in size and influence. The white descendants of the creoles and mazombos no longer dominated that group unchallenged. In many of the Latin American nations, the mestizos and/or mulattoes formed the larged part of the population. Mexico, Guatemala, Ecuador, Peru, Bolivia, and Paraguay, for example, had large mestizo populations, while the Dominican Republic, Venezuela, and Brazil had large mulatto populations. Representatives of the mestizos and mulattoes entered the middle sectors in larger numbers during the last decades of the nineteenth century and claimed their right to play a political and economic role in their nation's destiny. In some cases, the traditional social elites accommodated their ambitions; in others their frustrations mounted as they were excluded from positions of control, prestige, or wealth.

By the beginning of the twentieth century, some of the Latin

American states—certainly Argentina, Brazil, Chile, and Mexico—conveyed at least the outward appearance of having adopted the patterns and modes of the most progressive European states and of the United States. Their constitutions embodied the noblest principles of Western political thought. The governmental apparatus followed the most progressive models of the day. Political stability replaced chaos. Expanding transportation and communications infrastructures permitted the governments to control a larger area of their nations than they ever had before. New industries existed. An ever larger banking network facilitated and encouraged commerce. Society was more diversified than at any previous time. In the capitals and the largest cities, the architecture of the new buildings duplicated the latest styles of Paris—in how many Latin American cities do the local citizens proudly point to the opera house and claim it to be a replica of the Paris Opera? To the extent that some of the Latin American states formally resembled the leading nations of the Western world which they consciously accepted as their models of modernity, it is possible to conclude that those nations qualified as modern. However, many would argue that such modernity was only a veneer.

All was by no means new in Latin America. Much of the past still predominated. The rural aristocracy still enjoyed power; their estates remained huge and generally inefficient; their control over their workers was complete. The latifundia actually grew rather than diminished in size during the nineteenth century at the expense of the Indian communities and their traditional landholdings, the properties confiscated from the Church, and the public domain. One visitor to Chile in the early twentieth century noted:

> The owner of the land, however, has much more authority over his tenant than obtains in the United States. He is usually the local magistrate, and does not hesitate to adjudicate cases in which he is personally interested. He also runs a store to supply his tenants with necessary articles, and as credit is easily obtained, the tenant is seldom free from debt.

With 25 years of residence and travel in South America, Albert Hale observed of Brazil in 1906, "There exist traces of a feudal system, in that sharp line which divided the upper class, the aristocracy, from the lower class, the laborers. . . . The monarchy was so recently destroyed that in their [the laborers'] minds an aristocracy of blood still prevails, but this aristocracy is really one of land, of money." In 1910, James Bryce vividly described the large planter in Brazil as living "in a sort of semi-feudal patriarchal way" in his "little principality." He compared the situation to that in England a century earlier, when country squires controlled local affairs and selected the members of Parliament.

The wealthiest and most powerful class in Latin America in general was white or near white in complexion. Heirs of the creoles and mazombos, they enjoyed age-old economic advantages to which after independence they added political power. The group which surrounded Porfirio Díaz spoke of themselves, symbolically enough, as the "New Creoles."

The residues of social inequality, of neofeudalism, and of paternalistic rule clearly were incompatible with the new trends started during the last half of the century. The Chilean intellectual Miguel Cruchago Montt pointed out in his *Estudio sobre la organización económica y la hacienda pública de Chile* (Study of Chile's Economic Organization and Public Finances), published in 1878, that the colonial past hindered development. In his opinion outdated institutions prevented progress. Tradition and modernization could not exist peacefully side by side indefinitely. The course was charted for conflict.

THE PRESENCE OF THE UNITED STATES

Foreign influence—and none more so than Great Britain's—shaped much of Latin America's development in the nineteenth century. The primary challenge to British interests came from the United States, determined to spread across the North American continent and to dominate the Caribbean. By the early twentieth century, the United States had succeeded in doing both and was well on its way to replacing Britain's century-long domination of Latin America.

After the bold proclamation of President Monroe in 1823, officials in Washington chose to ignore his Doctrine for several decades. The British reoccupied the Falkland Islands despite vigorous Argentine protests, the French intervened in Mexico and the Plata area, and the French and British blockaded Buenos Aires, all without the United States reminding those European interlopers of the content or intention of Monroe's statement. Only when the British and French maneuvered to thwart the union of Texas with the United States did President John Tyler invoke the principles of the Doctrine in 1842 to warn the Europeans to keep out of hemispheric affairs. Indeed, as later used, the Doctrine provided a handy shield for North American expansion, well underway by the mid-1840s. As President James Polk gazed westward toward California, he notified the Europeans that his country opposed any transfer of territory in the New World from one European state to another or from a nation of the Western Hemisphere to a European nation. However, by his interpretation the Monroe Doctrine did not prohibit territorial changes among the nations of this hemisphere. Such an interpretation complemented the annexation by the United

States of Texas in 1845 and of Arizona, New Mexico, and California later in the decade. Expansionist sentiment rose to a fever pitch as the Stars and Stripes fluttered across the continent toward the Pacific Ocean. An editorial in the influential *De Bow's Commercial Review* in 1848 expressed the ebullient mood of a confident nation:

> The North Americans will spread out far beyond their present bounds. They will encroach again and again upon their neighbors. New territories will be planted, declare their independence, and be annexed. We have New Mexico and California! We will have Old Mexico and Cuba!

Such rhetoric aroused cheers in the United States. Reacting quite differently, the Latin Americans watched with apprehension the division of Mexico and debated how best to stem the expansion of the menacing "Colossus of the North." Their old fears of European intervention faded as the shadow of the United States lengthened.

Great Britain served as the major check on United States expansion southward into Middle America and the Caribbean during the mid-nineteenth century. British interests in the area were considerable; United States interests were growing; and the diplomatic maneuverings between the two to protect and extend those interests intensified. The best the United States could arrange at the time was an agreement in 1850, the Clayton-Bulwer Treaty, in which both nations promised not to occupy, fortify, colonize, or otherwise exercise domination over Central America. The treaty temporarily checked the territorial expansion of both nations into troubled and tempting republics which otherwise stood helpless before the two aggressive Anglo-Saxon powers. At about the same time the attention of the United States focused inward once again as a divided nation girded itself for internal strife.

While civil war rent the United States, several European nations pursued their own adventures in the New World. Spain reannexed the Dominican Republic and fought Peru and Chile. France intervened in Mexico. Only after it became apparent that the North was winning the Civil War and determined to oppose European adventures in this hemisphere did Spain depart from the Dominican Republic and return the Chincha Islands to Peru. When Napoleon III hesitated to withdraw French forces from Mexico, the government in Washington dispatched a large army to the Mexican border to help the French emperor make up his mind. Once those European threats to Latin America had ended, the United States seemed content to ignore the region—at least for the moment—while the nation concentrated its energies on reconstruction, railroad building, and industrialization.

Rapid industrial growth eventually prompted United States businessmen and leaders to search for new markets and none seemed more promising than Latin America, long the domain of European salesmen. One of the most remarkable Secretaries of State, James G. Blaine, understanding the need for friendship and cooperation among the nations of the hemisphere, sought to stimulate more intimate commercial relations as a logical means to solidify the inter-American community. The United States had long appreciated the strategic importance of Latin America but had been slow to develop its trade relations with the huge area. During the last half of the nineteenth century North American commerce with and investments in Latin America rose gradually. In the vigorous industrial age which had begun in the United States, Secretary of State Blaine envisioned a fraternal hemispheric trade in which the United States supplied the manufactured goods and Latin America the raw products. With such an idea in mind, he presided over the first Inter-American Conference, held in Washington in 1889–90. Although cordiality characterized the sessions, it became increasingly obvious that the Latin Americans were less interested in placing orders for the new industrial products than they were in containing the expansion of an ambitious neighbor by obtaining a promise of respect for the sovereignty of their nations. The times augured ill for such a promise. In fact, at that very moment, a rising tide of sentiment favoring expansion once again swept the United States.

Others in the United States realized as Blaine did that Latin America contained great wealth and potential, but unlike the Secretary of State they showed less subtlety in coveting it. In the eyes of many, the Latin Americans appeared too slow in fulfilling the destiny nature had charted for the area. Doubtless some "Protestant virtues and Yankee know-how" were needed to turn potential into reality—or at least so thought a growing number of citizens of the prospering United States, well satisfied that they had discovered the secrets of success. The Reverend Josiah Strong summed up much of the opinion of his fellow countrymen in his influential book *Our Country*, published in 1885, when he asked, "Having developed peculiarly aggressive traits calculated to impress its institutions upon mankind, [the United States] will spread itself over the earth. If I read not amiss, this powerful race will move down Central and South America, out upon the islands of the sea, over upon Africa and beyond. And can anyone doubt that the result of this competition of races will be the 'survival of the fittest?'" Imbued with the Spencerian and Darwinian philosophy popular at the time, the good Reverend spoke with the enthusiasm, confidence, and arrogance of his generation. Other powerful voices soon echoed those views. Henry Cabot Lodge spoke of "our rightful supremacy in the Western Hemisphere." Alfred T. Mahan lobbied for a bigger and better navy. Albert J. Beveridge put his faith in still a more potent force:

"God has marked the American people as His chosen Nation to finally lead to the regeneration of the world . . . . We are trustees of the world's progress, guardians of its righteous peace." Secretary of State Richard Olney announced to the world in 1895 that the United States was supreme in the Western Hemisphere where its will would be done.

Thus, by the end of the nineteenth century, government and business leaders alike spoke approvingly of expanding world markets and of a global foreign policy. Their talk soon led to action: American overseas expansion into the Pacific and the Caribbean. Significantly that expansion began after the conquest of the western frontier, several decades of impressive industrial growth, and during the economic difficulties of the 1890s. The United States challenged Spain in 1898 and easily wrested from its remaining empire the Philippine Islands, Cuba, and Puerto Rico. The easy victory marked the debut of the United States as a world power embarked upon a new international course of extracontinental expansion, which one influential journalist of the day characterized admiringly as "the imperialism of liberty." Washington annexed Puerto Rico and made Cuba a protectorate, a state of dependency which officially lasted 35 years. The United States intervened in the island republic frequently and for long periods of time. The first three decades of the twentieth century were busy years for the U.S. Marines who scurried around the Caribbean intervening in a number of unhappy and unstable republics: Haiti, the Dominican Republic, and Nicaragua. In the cases of the Dominican Republic and Haiti, the marines landed to forestall threatened European intervention to collect debts; in Nicaragua the chaotic finances partially explained the United States presence but probably more significant was the rumor that the Nicaraguan government might sell exclusive canal rights through its territory to either Japan or Great Britain. United States intervention was not limited to the small republics in the Caribbean area. Both Colombia and Mexico felt the weight of its neighbor's might.

Opinion in the United States favoring the construction of an interoceanic canal grew, spurred by military and commercial considerations. The first step toward the realization of a canal was to abrogate the old Clayton-Bulwer Treaty. Under international pressure, London agreed in the Hay-Pauncefote Treaty in 1901 to permit the United States to build, operate, and fortify a canal across the Isthmus. Washington then proceeded to negotiate with Colombia for rights across Panama, but the Senate in Bogotá balked at the terms suggested. At that point, the Panamanians seceded from Colombia, declared their independence, and offered Washington a favorable canal treaty. Not unprepared for that turn of events, the United States protected the new nation to which it extended immediate recognition. The two nations promptly signed a treaty giving the United States in perpetuity a ten-mile wide canal zone. Work on the canal began in 1904 and terminated a decade later. Controversy over the canal and the treaty which made it possible has raged between the United States and Panama ever since. The intervention of the United States in Mexico during the second decade of the twentieth century will be discussed in the next chapter.

The trespassing of the North American giant on Latin American sovereignty evoked protest and aroused distrust. Many Latin American intellectuals of the period, such as José Enrique Rodó of Uruguay, Manuel Ugarte of Argentina, Eduardo Prado of Brazil, and Rufino Blanco-Fombona of Venezuela, spoke out to denounce "the Yankee imperialism." Physically unable to prevent those interventions, Latin American governments sought recourse in international law. They labored long and determinedly to persuade Washington to renounce by treaty recourse to intervention. Meanwhile, the United States was eclipsing Great Britain as the dominant foreign influence in Latin America. In 1904, the Brazilian Foreign Office classified Washington as the "number one" diplomatic post and the following year opened its first embassy in the North American capital. Investments from the United States rose rapidly after 1900. (They quintupled between 1897 and 1914.) New steamship lines and telegraphic cables tightened the links between the United States and Latin America.

six

The

Past

Repudiated

José Clemente Orozco, "The Revolutionary Struggle"

By the beginning of the twentieth century, a desire for reform characterized much of Latin America. Traditional institutions and attitudes came under ever sharper attack. Differing from their nineteenth-century predecessors, the new reformers demanded a redistribution of the land, more effective curbs on the wealth and power of the Church, a limitation on the control that foreigners exerted over the national economies, and a wide range of social benefits and political innovations. New elements in the Latin American societies—larger urban middle sectors, immigrants, new businessmen and industrialists—brought stronger pressure to bear on the established elite and the governments they dominated to break with the past, to eradicate the many vestiges of the colonial era still prevalent. In short, the ambitious new elements in an increasingly complex Latin American society opposed those rigid institutions which impeded their rise. They opted for a more fluid society. They sought to change their society, and if the old institutions and elite proved unwilling to accommodate their ambitions they then were determined to use force to transform the traditional society.

THE MIDDLE SECTORS IN POLITICS

By the end of the nineteenth century, those middle sectors whose previous emergence was noted in the last chapter reached sufficient numbers and had enough direction to exert an influence then and increasingly thereafter on the course of events in some nations, most particularly in Argentina, Brazil, Chile, Mexico, Uruguay, and Costa Rica. Only later were they developed and articulate enough to wield a similar influence in other countries. Commerce, business, and industry contributed heavily to the widening ranks of the middle sectors, and foreign immigrants continued to compose a disproportionately large percentage of their numbers. Certain characteristics of the middle sectors increasingly became evident. The majority of those so classified lived in the cities and boasted of an above-average education. Their income status placed them between the wealthy few and the impoverished many. Although the heterogeneous middle sectors never unified, on occasion a majority of them might agree on certain goals, such as improved or expanded education, further industrialization, or more rapid modernization, and on certain methods, such as the formation of political parties or the exaltation of nationalism. They consented to the use of the government to foment change, and with minimal dissension welcomed the government's participation in—even direction of—the economy. Still, political preferences within their ranks varied from far right to far left.

Always small in numbers they increased their strength by allying with other sectors. At the turn of the century, they showed a willingness on specific occasions and for specific purposes to unite with the urban working class since both sought the structural changes and social fluidity denied by the traditional ruling elites. Except for those occasions when their self-interests wedded them to the oligarchy, the middle sectors at the end of the nineteenth century and beginning of the twentieth supported reforms sufficiently innovative to make them important agents for change. Generally the programs they advanced were moderate. They definitely favored reform over revolution. Their rise to power initially challenged the oligarchy, and their use of the new power modified old institutions and patterns in Latin America.

In Brazil, the middle sectors were strong enough to help overthrow the monarchy in 1889 and for a time, in conjunction with the military, to rule the nation. The composition of Brazilian society had altered considerably in the nineteenth century. At the time of independence the new empire counted barely 4 million inhabitants of whom probably half were slaves of African birth or descent. Sixty-five years later there were 14 million Brazilians, roughly 600,000 of whom were slaves.

At the other end of the social scale stood 300,000 plantation owners and their families. Most of the population fell somewhere between the two extremes. True, most of them were impoverished, illiterate peasants who unknowingly contributed to the status quo. But there was an important, growing body of urban dwellers, many of whom qualified for the ranks of the middle sectors. The gulf between the countryside with its many vestiges of the colonial past and the city with its increasingly progressive outlook widened during the last decades of the nineteenth century. The urban dwellers were less favorably disposed to two basic institutions inherited from the past, slavery and monarchy, than was the rural population. They saw those institutions as buttresses of the position of the elite and uncomplementary to their own best interests. Indeed, they viewed those two institutions as the means by which the traditional rural elite retained most of what was colonial in Brazilian society and in the economy while still rejecting, in the stricter legal sense, colonial status. The military, hostile to slavery, ignored by the emperor, and restless, shared the view of the urban middle sectors to whom the officers were closely related both by family ties and philosophy. Together, they brought an end to both slavery and monarchy.

Not surprisingly the new republican government established by the military in 1889 reflected the goals and aspirations of Brazil's middle sector. The new chief of state, Deodoro da Fonseca, was son of an army officer of modest means, and his cabinet consisted of two other military officers, an engineer, and four lawyers. They were the sons of the city with their university degrees, a contrast to the aristocratic scions who had formed previous governments. During its early years, the republic was identified with both the military and the urban middle groups much more than the monarchy had ever been. As one of their goals, they hoped to transform the nation through industrialization. The government raised the tariff on items which competed with national goods and lowered the duty on primary goods used in national manufacturing. To augment the number of technicians, four new engineering schools were opened in the 1890s. A high income from coffee exports, generous credit from the banks, and the government's emission of larger amounts of currency animated economic activity to a fever pitch. Speculation became the order of the day. Bogus companies abounded, but unfortunately for Brazil the speculation resulted in little real industrial progress. Further, the rate of foreign exchange plummeted, inflation robbed the money of its former value, and fiscal instability deprived the nation of its former confidence. In 1893 a political crisis complicated the economic distress. The navy revolted and the southern state of Rio Grande do Sul rose in rebellion; together they threatened the existence of the republic.

The powerful coffee planters with their wealth and control of the state governments of São Paulo, Minas Gerais, and Rio de Janeiro held the balance of power between the government and the rebels. They promised aid to the government in return for a guarantee of an open presidential election in 1894. Both kept their sides of the bargain, and in the elections the coffee interests pushed their candidate into the presidential palace. The political victory of the coffee interests reflected the predominate role coffee had come to play in the Brazilian economy. Cheap suitable land, high profits, large numbers of immigrant workers, and a rising world demand made coffee a popular and lucrative crop. By the end of the nineteenth century, it composed half of the nation's exports, and the export tax on the coffee bean accounted for a large share of federal income.

The alliance of the coffee planters and the federal government in 1894 superseded all previous political arrangements. Thereafter, the political dominance of the coffee interests characterized the First Republic 1889–1930). The new oligarchy, principally from São Paulo but secondarily from Minas Gerais and Rio de Janeiro, ruled Brazil for its own benefit for 36 years. The coffee interests arranged the elections of presidents friendly to their needs and dictated at will the policies of the governments. Sound finances, political stability, and decentralization were the goals pursued by the coffee presidents.

The urban middle groups, whose unreliable ally, the military, was torn by disunion and bickering, lost the power they had exercised for so brief and unsettled a period. Those middle groups increasingly resented the economic and political monopoly the large planters wielded in the republic. They decried the many favors the government lavished on those planters. Occasionally they supported a presidential candidate, such as Ruy Barbosa in 1910, who understood their aims and objectives. For the elections of 1922, the urban groups and the military united in an unsuccessful effort to wrest the presidency from the coffee elite. They failed. Thereafter, violent protest erupted in Brazil.

In July of 1922, shortly after the coffee interests had once again imposed their presidential preference on the nation, a handful of junior officers revolted in Rio de Janeiro in a quixotic effort to overthrow the moribund republic. It signaled the beginning of an eight-year period of unrest which climaxed in 1930 with the fall of the republic. Military uprisings—once again dominated by junior officers—of a more threatening nature broke out in 1924. Survivors of that rebellion marched 14,000 miles through the Brazilian interior in the mid-1920s hoping to stir up peasant revolt. However, the peasants were still too much under the powerful sway of the local landowners to be enlisted into the ranks of rebellion. The countryside never had been the place to foment change in Brazil. The failure of the efforts in the mid-1920s proved it still was not. The discontented elements centered in the cities. The leaders of the march never made contact with the urban protesters and consequently never tapped that potential reservoir of support. Within the cities the criticism of the "coffee governments" mounted, denouncing the selfish regional monopolization of power, manipulated elections, the continuation of patriarchalism and colonialism, and consistently sterile policies.

By 1926, the movement of the junior military officers, known in Portuguese as *tenentes* (meaning lieutenants) had acquired a somewhat more identifiable philosophy, even though it never became precise. The tenentes maintained a mystical faith that somehow the military could alter the habits of the country and provide the impetus to propel it into the modern age. Their primary concern was not democracy but reform. For the remainder of the discussion reform denotes a gradual change or modification of established economic, political, or social structures. The tenentes wanted to retire the entrenched politicians and modernize the nation. Then, and only then, they would consent to return the nation to constitutional rule. They hoped to expand the base of the government and to eradicate regionalism. They favored a very strong, centralized government. Revealing "social democratic" tendencies, the tenentes proposed government recognition of trade unions and cooperatives, a minimum wage, maximum working hours, child labor legislation, agrarian reform, nationalization of natural resources, and expanded educational facilities. Obviously much of the program advocated by the tenentes favored the urban middle groups. However, those groups failed to understand that the various military rebellions and movements in the 1920s could have been turned to their advantage. Indicative of the weakness of the middle groups was their inability to coordinate their desires for modernization with the similar desires of the young officers. Still, by the end of the decade of the 1920s, the middle groups had made some accomplishments: they had helped to abolish slavery, to bring down the empire, to encourage education, to promote industrialization, and to stoke the fires of nationalism, but they did not achieve the influence their counterparts did in some of the Spanish-speaking nations.

In Argentina, elements representative of the urban middle groups founded the Unión Cívica Radical in 1892. That party campaigned for free elections; obviously under the rigged elections perpetuated by the oligarchy it had scant hope of reaching office. An enlightened president, Roque Saenz Peña, promulgated laws in 1912 to guarantee the secret ballot for all males, a reform which paved the way of the middle sectors to power. In the next presidential election, 1916, the candidate for the Radicals, Hipólito Irigoyen, won.

The Radicals had worked hard for their victory, but once in office they revealed a lack of commitment and a confusion of objectives. Irigoyen showed an interest in and sympathy with the poor, unusual for an Argentine president. To reward his working-class supporters, he saw that some mild social welfare legislation was enacted. He encouraged unionization, but, on the other hand, he was not reluctant to suppress brutally strikes in Buenos Aires in 1919 when he felt the workers had become too violent. Characteristic of the middle sectors everywhere in Latin America, the Radicals gave encouragement to education and made a great fetish of democracy. Irigoyen recognized the inequity of land distribution and hoped to rectify it by making land available on the frontier; he thereby sidestepped the issue of the predominance of the latifundia in the most fertile and populous area of the nation. He also established a national petroleum agency to develop that vital natural resource. By preventing foreign exploitation of oil and thereby opting for greater national economic independence, his action became a model for nationalists both in Argentina and in other Latin American nations.

In retrospect, the achievements of the Radicals over a period of a decade and a half were disappointingly few. As it turned out, once in office, the middle sectors manifested a conservatism not too far removed from that of the displaced oligarchy. Enjoying their taste of power, they muted their cries for reform. During the years the Radicals enjoyed power, they made no structural or institutional changes in Argentine society or economy. In the crisis of 1930 precipitated by the international economic depression, the Radicals proved incapable of reacting. The army swept them from power and returned the government to the traditional oligarchy, although thereafter the military remained as the arbiter of the nation's political destiny.

In Chile, the middle sectors allied with the working classes in 1918 to form the Liberal Alliance, an electoral force dominant enough to win control of the Chamber of Deputies that year. The Alliance under the banner of the popular Arturo Alessandri went on to win the presidency in a closely contested election in 1920. Alessandri had promised many socioeconomic reforms, but once in office he found his efforts to fulfill those promises frustrated by the conservatives in congress hostile to his program. The conservatives from their stronghold in the Senate clearly represented the traditional values of the oligarchy as they fought off the efforts of the urban middle and working groups to implement change. A congressional election in 1924 favored Alessandri by giving him a working majority. The new congress promptly enacted his broad social welfare program. It recognized labor unions and assured their independence. Alas, Congress voted itself a handsome pay raise at an economically inopportune moment when paychecks to the military had been delayed. Contrary to its previous constitutional behavior, the army rebelled and sent Alessandri packing in September of 1924. A liberal counter-coup in 1925 brought him back from exile. He served six more months in office during which time he was able to push a new constitution through congress, a document which replaced the 92-year-old constitution written by Portales. It ended Chile's experiment with parliamentarianism and returned to the president the full measure of power he had lost in 1891. It also contained advanced labor and social welfare provisions and authorized the state to intervene in social and economic matters. The middle sectors have remained a dominant force in Chilean politics ever since the Alessandri presidency.

In Urugauy, the Latin American middle sectors won their greatest victory in the early twentieth century. Uruguay changed dramatically under the government of the middle sectors, providing one of the best such examples of peaceful change in Latin America. Independent Uruguay emerged in 1828 as a result of the stalemate between Argentina and Brazil which had continued the centuries-old Luso-Spanish rivalry over the left bank of the Río de la Plata. Uruguayans divided into two political camps, the Conservatives (Blancos) and the Liberals (Colorados). From independence until 1872 they fought each other almost incessantly for power. When the Liberals got power in 1872, they managed to hang onto it, despite challenges from the Conservatives and the military, until 1959. During the last decades of the nineteenth century, relative peace settled over the small republic, by then in the process of an economic metamorphosis. Prosperity helped to pacify the nation. Exports of wool, mutton, hides, and beef rose. New methods of stock breeding, fencing, the refrigerated ship, and railroad construction (the mileage jumped five times from 200 to 1,000 miles between 1875 and 1895) modernized the economy.

During the same period, Uruguay constructed the foundation of its enviable educational system. New teacher-training institutes and public schools multiplied. Uruguay was on its way to becoming Latin America's most literate nation. Expanded and improved education was among the foremost concerns of the middle sectors, and the attention given to education in Uruguay reflected their increasing influence.

The outstanding political representative of the middle sectors at that time, not only in Uruguay but in all of Latin America, was José Batlle. He first exerted influence as the articulate editor of a prominent newspaper in Montevideo which spoke for the interests of the middle sectors and by providing them with a voice helped to organize that always amorphous group. By the end of the nineteenth century, he led the Colorado Party. He served twice as president (1903–7; 1911–15), but his influence over the government lasted until his death in 1929.

During those decades, he sought to expand education, restrict foreign control, enact a broad welfare program, and unify the republic. He succeeded brilliantly in each instance and through his force and foresight he transformed Uruguay into a model bourgeois nation.

At the turn of the century, the Conservatives controlled some of the departments (local territorial units) to the extent that they were virtually free of the control of the central government. Batlle extended the power of his government over them by assuring the Conservatives proportional representation in the central government. He managed to balance the budgets, repay foreign creditors, and strengthen the national currency. National banks grew in confidence and were able to lend to Uruguayans so that they no longer had to look abroad for much of their capital. To protect national industry, congress raised the tariffs. The government began to enter business, taking over light, power, insurance, and many other formerly private enterprises, and continued to do so on an ever-increasing scale. The government entered the meat-packing business to offer competition to the foreign companies which had long been engaged in that industry so vital to a nation dependent on stock raising. The enactment of advanced social welfare legislation guaranteed the worker his right to unionize, minimum wages, an eight-hour day, pensions, accident insurance, and paid holidays. Batlle felt the government should play a positive role in improving the living conditions of the less favored citizens. On one occasion he announced, "There is great injustice in the enormous gap between the rich and the poor. The gap must be narrowed—and it is the duty of the state to attempt that task." Those reforms like others taking place in Latin America at the time (with the exception of Mexico) affected only the urban areas and never extended into the countryside. Strong as Batlle was, he never directly challenged the landowners or the rural socioeconomic structures. In fact, he saw no reason to, as he stated in 1910: "There is no pressing agrarian problem requiring the attention of the government. The division of the landed estates will take place in response to natural forces operating in our rural industries." It was a point of view shared by the middle sector leaders of the period. Thus they permitted the continuation of the oldest, the most fundamental land and labor institutions. Obviously such a neglect restricted national reforms and circumscribed the limits of change. The neglect of those rural reforms reflected either the middle sectors' fear of the power of the landowners, their preoccupation with the city, their own intermarriage and connections with the landowning families and a desire to acquire estates of their own, or, what is more likely, a combination of all those reasons.

The climax of the Batlle reforms came in the new constitution, written in 1917 but promulgated in 1919. It provided a model of the type of government the middle sectors of the period wanted, one, of course, which guaranteed them power. It authorized direct elections, reduced the powers of the president and created a National Council of Administration to share the presidential powers (with the hope to eliminate any future threat of dictatorship), established a bicameral legislature elected by means of a proportional representative system, reduced the military to a minor institution, separated the Church and State, and provided a comprehensive program of social welfare. In creating the first welfare state in the Western Hemisphere, the middle sectors acknowledged their debt to the working classes and rewarded them for their support.

Uruguay prospered in the years after World War I thanks to a lively demand abroad for products from the nation's fertile pampas. The good times were auspicious for the new reforms. Batlle died in 1929, just before the Great Depression challenged his democratic, welfare state. In the first three decades of the twentieth century, Batlle demonstrated to the Latin Americans how a nation once immersed in chaos, tyranny, illiteracy, social inequality, and foreign exploitation could change peacefully. Compact in size, with a small and homogeneous population, with rich land and no adverse geography, Uruguay enjoyed advantages of which few other nations could boast. Those advantages doubtless smoothed the path to reform. Still, Uruguay provided an example of a nation which could peacefully alter its course. In the three decades during which Batlle exerted his greatest influence, he accomplished much of what many progressive Latin Americans of the period desired. He separated the Church and State, limited foreign control, increased social fluidity, democratized political institutions, and reduced military interference in politics. His constitution provided the blueprint for Uruguay's development in the twentieth century. The middle sectors throughout Latin America venerated it.

MEXICO'S VIOLENT RESPONSE TO THE PAST

In Mexico, class alliances and change took different forms. The urban working class and the rural peasants united to alter violently many of the nation's oldest institutions. In doing so they precipitated Latin America's most profound revolution of the first half of the twentieth century, one of the world's major social upheavals. In certain aspects the Mexican Revolution (as a landmark in Latin American history, this Revolution merits capitalization) continued the movement initiated and directed by Hidalgo and Morelos from 1810 to 1815. Many consider it the prototype for nationalistic revolutionary change in twentieth-century Latin America. For the remainder of the discussion of the twentieth century, revolution means sudden, forceful, and violent overturn of a previously relatively stable society and the substitution of other institutions for those discredited. Change by revolution thus denotes the destruction of old social, political, and economic patterns in favor of newer ones. Use of this definition divides genuine "revolutions" from the more numerous palace coups, military takeovers, civil wars, and the wars of independence, which were nothing more than shifts in the holding of power within the same or similar groups unaccompanied by fundamental economic, social, or political changes.

Mexico in 1910 clung tenaciously to its neocolonial structures and institutions. Porfirio Díaz and the "New Creoles" had ruled for 34 years without popular mandate for the benefit of a privileged native elite and foreign investors. The economy still depended upon foreign whims and direction. The masses were brutally suppressed. The real wages of the working class declined throughout that long period. Land, a principal source of wealth, remained in the hands of a few. Ninety-five percent of the rural population owned none. Not even 10 percent of the Indian communities held land. Fewer than 1,000 families owned most of Mexico. In fact, fewer than 200 families owned one-quarter of the land, while foreigners had another quarter. Private estates reached princely proportions. The De la Garza hacienda in the state of Coahuila totaled 11,115,000 acres; the Huller estate in Baja California sprawled over 13,325,650 acres. Productivity was low; absentee landlords were common. The fact that a majority of the Mexicans lived in the country and worked in agriculture made the inequity of the land distribution all the more unjust. The desire among the repressed peasantry to cultivate its own land was welling into an irrepressible force.

An economy reminiscent of colonial mercantilism and with vestiges of feudalism prevented the growth of democracy. It condemned liberal reform to failure. It goaded the growing mestizo urban classes also to express dissatisfaction with the inequitable institutions inherited from the past. The mestizos had grown rapidly in number over the centuries. By the end of the nineteenth century they surpassed the Indians in number and totally overshadowed the tiny "creole" class. It was obvious from their size, skill, and ambitions that the mestizos held the key to Mexico's future. The mestizo working and middle sectors of the cities voiced discontent with their inferior and static position in Porfirian Mexico. The inflexibility of Mexico's neocolonial institutions retarded their mobility and inhibited their progress. In common with the peasantry, they advocated change in order to improve their conditions.

A political event, rather than vague aspirations for change, set in motion those forces culminating in the Revolution. The Mexicans tired of the long Díaz dictatorship and the electoral farces which perpetuated the aging *jefe* in office. In the elections scheduled for 1910, Francisco I. Madero, a liberal landowner from the North announced his intention to run against Díaz. To the surprise of no one, Díaz declared his victory at the polls and took office for the eighth time. Madero, by that time, had seen the popular response his political opposition to the old dictator had aroused. In November of 1910, he crossed the frontier from the United States into Mexico with the intention of overthrowing the government. His Plan of San Luis Potosí announced the simple political motivation of his movement: the forced resignation of Díaz and electoral reforms. Repeatedly his followers voiced the slogan "Effective suffrage and no reelection," a clue to the exclusively political, urban, and middle sector origin of the Revolution. Díaz resigned in May, 1911, and fled to a European exile. (He died in Paris in 1915.)

Madero took office quite unprepared for the task he faced. His political platform contained some vague planks on political reform and almost nothing solid on social or economic change. He represented the traditional liberalism of the nineteenth century, which at last many realized had not benefited Mexico. Anyway it did not harmonize with the newer demands being made. Madero's importance derived first from his significance as a symbol of the revolt against the Porfirian past and second from the political freedom he permitted for open discussion in which the needs and aspirations of the nation were thoroughly ventilated.

While Madero demonstrated his incompetence, the demand for agrarian reform mounted, encouraged by Emiliano Zapata in his Plan of Ayala in 1911. Crying "Land and Liberty," he and his determined peasant followers demanded land, and in many cases they seized haciendas for themselves. A new force had been unleashed and it represented what distinguished the Mexican Revolution from previous movements in Latin America: the stirring of the masses. It became clear that a social revolution had begun.

To enact change or to redirect the course of the Revolution required power and many were the leaders vying for it. In February 1913, General Victoriano Huerta, a representative of the *porfiristas*, overthrew the ineffectual Madero and then permitted his assassination. Uniting to oppose the reactionary general, Venustiano Carranza, Álvaro Obregón, Plutarco Elías Calles, Francisco Villa, and Emiliano Zapata, all of whom played fundamental roles in the Revolution, marched against Huerta's armies. After Huerta fell in March of 1914, the victors began to struggle among themselves for supremacy. To broaden his support, Carranza appealed to those who regarded the Revolution as a social movement. By mid-1915, he and his allies emerged to direct the Revolution, but Zapata in the South and Villa in the North continued to challenge him until 1919 and 1920 respectively. In May of 1920, Carranza, attempting to rig the presidential elections, was deposed, then assassinated. The moderates made one final effort to gain control of the Revolution in 1924 but failed.

In all the political changes and chaos of the preceding years, one major political fact stood out: the era in which the "creole" had commanded was over. The mestizo dominated Mexican politics after 1914, and he was determined to recreate Mexico in his own image. The emerging leadership of the Revolution was overwhelmingly mestizo: Zapata, Villa, Obregón, Calles, Cárdenas, et al. Impoverished, sons of peasants, virtually illiterate in their childhood, looking more to their Indian than to their Spanish past, unknown, unheralded, they rose to positions of prominence during the Revolution. The Revolution made them and propelled them to the forefront.

During the early years of the Revolution, as the winds of change blew with gale force across Mexico, the absence of a plan, a philosophy, intellectual leadership, or a directing party became painfully obvious. No clear statement of the aims of the Revolution emerged. The Revolution assumed its general characteristics slowly. In time, it became apparent that many of the institutions closely identified with the Spanish past, foremost of which, and most fundamental, was the land tenure system, would be destroyed or altered beyond recognition. To solve national problems, the Mexicans looked deeply inward into themselves for an answer. As a result, the Revolution became increasingly native and conversely more antiforeign.

The Revolution swept all before it. The destruction was as total as the chaos. It cost more than a million lives. It ruined much of the agrarian, ranching, and mining economy. No major bank or newspaper which predated the Revolution survived. Exceptions to the economic dislocation were the henequin and oil industries whose output rose. By 1921, Mexico ranked third among the world's oil producers, furnishing one-quarter of the world's total. From the disorder and destruction which lasted throughout most of the period 1910–20, a new Mexico arose.

The constitution promulgated in 1917 contained the blueprint for the future, the first general statement of the aims of the Revolution. Carranza called a constituent assembly, expecting it to approve a document similar to the liberal Constitution of 1857, but it quickly became apparent that he exercised little control over the proceedings. Ideological differences split the delegates. The radicals, supported by Obregón, gained control and imposed their views. The constitution which emerged after two months of bitter debate at Querétaro contained many of the traditional enlightened ideas characteristic of the former constitution. In the customary Latin American fashion, the constitution conferred strong authority on the president. However, it went on to alter significantly some fundamental and traditional concepts, to eliminate some hoary institutions, and to point the way to new solutions for old problems.

The new constitution exalted the state and society above the individual and conferred on the government the authority to reshape society. The key articles dealt with land, labor, and religion. Article 27 laid the basis for land reform and for restrictions on foreign economic control. It declared government ownership of mineral and water resources, subordinated private property to public welfare, gave the government the right to expropriate land, annulled all alienations of ejidos since 1857, and recognized communal ownership of land. Article 123 protected the Mexican workers from exploitation by authorizing the passage of a labor code to set minimum salaries and maximum hours, provide accident insurance, pensions, and social benefits, and guarantee the right to unionize and to strike. Since foreign investment in Mexican industrialization was heavy, this article potentially could be used as one means of bridling the operations of the foreign capitalist. Finally, Article 130 placed restrictions on the Church and clergy: churches were denied juridical personalities, they could not own property, states could limit the number of ministers by law, no foreigner could be a minister, ministers could not vote, hold office, or criticize the government, and the Church could not participate in primary education.

Carranza dutifully promulgated the constitution, but he evinced scant intention of carrying out most of its provisions, many of which were not put into effect for years. For example, 14 years passed before a labor code was enacted to give body and meaning to Article 123. Nonetheless, the Constitution stands as the single most important event in the history of the Revolution, marking off Mexico's neocolonial past from the modernized nation which was arising from the holocaust of destruction. It provided the point of departure for the creation of a new national state based on local experience. The history of Mexico since its promulgation has been the story of the struggle to carry out the provisions of the document and thereby to put into effect the social, economic, and political changes it envisaged.

With the inauguration of Obregón in 1920, the first efforts were made to implement the socioeconomic changes authorized by the Constitution. After years of slogans, the land reform program got underway. Obregón distributed three million acres to the peasants. To combat illiteracy, the president appointed the energetic José Vasconcelos as

Minister of Education. Accelerated school construction and teacher-training programs received an impetus from him. With the encouragement of the Revolution, educational opportunities continued to expand, and illiteracy, from a high of 80 percent in the early 1920s, slowly declined. Vasconcelos was a fiery cultural nationalist, in the vanguard of a movement enveloping Latin America. He made available space and funds to encourage Diego Rivera, José Orozco, and other artists to paint their monumental murals glorifying Mexico's Indian past. With his encouragement, Carlos Chávez composed music in a Mexican idiom. Desirous of an authentically Mexican culture, Vasconcelos declared the nation's spiritual and cultural independence of Europe: "Tired, disgusted of all this copied civilization . . . we interpret the vision of Cuauhtémoc as an anticipation of the . . . birth of the Latin American soul. . . . We wish to cease being [Europe's] spiritual colonies." Mexico's intellectuals rallied to the cry. A new sense of nationality and pride engulfed Mexico, brilliantly evident in art, architecture, music, dance, and literature.

Calles, who became president in 1924, carried forward the trends begun during his predecessor's administration, but he soon found himself embroiled with the Roman Catholic Church. The Constitution horrified the Catholic hierarchy who saw in several of its articles the power to debilitate the Church. The Church-State issue was enjoined in 1926 when Archbishop José Mora y del Rio publicly announced, "The Episcopate, the Clergy, and all Catholics disavow and combat Articles 3, 5, 27, and 130 of the present Constitution." The government reacted by enforcing those articles much more rigidly than ever before. In response, the Church went on strike. The priests refused to perform their functions, although the government kept the churches open for the faithful. Conservative Catholics revolted against the government, and blood flowed anew in Mexico. Not until the late 1930s did the Church and State show more tolerance toward each other and since then relations have gradually improved.

The bullet of a religious fanatic felled Obregón before he could return to the presidency to which he was reelected in 1928. Calles continued to dominate politics, and in 1929 he founded the National Revolutionary Party (PNR) to help fill the political vacuum. The PNR assumed responsibility for selecting and electing presidents as well as insuring that the transfer of power took place—and took place peacefully. It thus helped to solve a problem which had nagged Mexico, indeed most of Latin America since the declarations of independence. In 1938, the party reorganized as the "official party" under the name of Mexican Revolutionary Party (PRM) and broadened its base of support.

In 1946, the party once again changed its name, this time to Party of Revolutionary Institutions (PRI). With each change the party strengthened itself so that it, an institution not individuals, came to dominate Mexican politics. It gave Mexico a remarkable poltical stablity, a sharp contrast to the nation's own past and unusual in Latin America.

As stability increased, the role of the military diminished. The Constitution assigned the military the conventional tasks of maintaining order and defending the nation from outside attack, and the officers accepted their more restricted position. After 1929, the budget provided increasingly less funds for them. In that year, one-third of federal expenditures went to the military; by 1950, the figure had dropped to one-fourteenth; by 1964, to one-thirtieth.

Basic to the Revolution was land reform. If carried out successfully, it threatened to destroy the hacienda, perhaps the most debilitating and influential institution from the past, and substitute for it communal and small private holdings. Obregón modestly initiated the redistribution of the land, and his successors continued the policy. The titles the presidents handed out conferred on the small farmers a new dignity, a vital step in changing them from abused peasants into responsible citizens. The reform put into use formerly idle or inefficiently cultivated lands. It also strengthened the powers and prestige of the government, which could grant land to or withhold it from the peasants for political considerations. Lázaro Cárdenas, president from 1934 to 1940 (the presidential term had previously been extended from four to six years), accelerated the redistribution of land by handing out titles to 45 million acres, a staggering amount when one considers that between 1910 and 1945 the grand total of land redistributed was 76 million acres. Between 1945 and 1965, another 44 million acres were distributed to the peasants. Only about 0.5 percent of the total value of the land was paid. After 1940, following a period of decline, agricultural productivity began to rise. It increased 46 percent during the following two decades, far above the world's average increase of 12 percent and contrary to the general decline in Latin America's agricultural output. One prominent Mexican economist, Edmundo Flores, affirms that the rapid industrialization of his nation has been achieved only because of the reformed agrarian structures which made possible political stability, high rates of capital formation, and increased agricultural production and productivity.

In many respects, the six-year term of Cárdenas marked the apogee of the Revolution. Cárdenas based his energetic use of the presidency on the support of the peasants and the urban laborers, who in turn benefited the most from his reaffirmation of revolutionary principles.

He was the first Latin American president to shift the power base to the popular masses. He also well understood the potential force of economic nationalism. Cárdenas boldly declared Mexico's economic independence by nationalizing the railroads in 1937 and the oil companies in 1938. The foreign oil companies, accustomed to a privileged status in Mexico, had refused to accept a decision of the Mexican Supreme Court ruling as legal the pay raise requested by the workers. In answer to the defiance of those companies of the court, Cárdenas expropriated the oil firms and thus became a national hero. All Mexicans, of every level and background, vociferously supported the government. Even the Church nodded its approval, the first gesture of cooperation between the two in several decades. What was more, Mexico proved to itself, to the former oil monopolies, and to the world that it could produce its own oil, and contrary to predictions it proceeded to do so more efficiently than the foreigners had done. Oil production climbed. By 1950, it doubled the output reached during the low point of 1932; by 1963 it doubled again. Furthermore, the bulk of Mexican oil no longer flowed to Western Europe and the United States to buttress their industrialization. The Mexicans refined and used it at home as an intricate part of national industrialization, which was then moving forward at an accelerating pace. Using their own oil for national development, the Mexicans challenged and changed old economic patterns, all too reminiscent of the mercantilism of the past. In addition, the state began to remove from foreign control the production of electrical power and to direct that vital industry itself. Mexico was in the process of redeeming itself, of limiting foreign control over its land and its industry.

The major governments of Western Europe and the United States endorsed none of those changes. The endangered investments of their citizens prompted them to complain bitterly to the Mexican government about the new laws, to apply pressure to thwart them, to threaten reprisals, and to speak of intervention. Also, the Roman Catholic Church maintained strong pressures on other governments to force the Mexican officials to accommodate themselves to the interests of the Church. No nation intervened in Mexican affairs more vigorously than the United States whose officials, with the exceptions of Ambassador Dwight W. Morrow and President Franklin D. Roosevelt, lacked even the haziest notion of the significance of the Mexican Revolution. Ambassador Henry Lane Wilson unabashedly supported General Huerta, although the brutal assassination of Madero shocked President Woodrow Wilson into refusing to recognize the Porfirian general. The United States Navy blockaded the Gulf coast in 1914, then shelled and occupied the port of Vera Cruz. After Villa raided Columbus, New Mexico, and killed

17 Americans, President Wilson ordered General John Pershing and an army into northern Mexico in a quixotic search of nearly a year for the evasive Villa. The Constitution of 1917 caused further concern in Washington over United States investments in Mexico as talk of confiscation circulated. The United States did not want Article 27 to be applied retroactively. Because of the violent death of Carranza, the Department of State refused to recognize Obregón when he became president in 1920. It used the issue of recognition as a lever to pry from the Mexicans an agreement to pay compensation for any land expropriated. Relations between the two neighbors improved in 1927, when Dwight W. Morrow arrived as ambassador to Mexico. Astute and able, he understood the significance of the Mexican Revolution and attempted to deal fairly with the Mexicans in their drive for rapid change. Later, President Roosevelt possessed a similar perceptiveness and withstood heavy pressures from the Roman Catholic Church and the oil companies for intervention. Mexico's agreement to compensate the oil companies and the improvement of Church-State relations within Mexico in the late 1930s lifted at least part of the pressures on him and improved relations between Mexico and the United States were the results.

Cárdenas was the last strong man to dominate Mexico. After 1940, Mexican presidents derived their power from the office they held, not from their own personal strength, prestige, or following. In short, the institution possessed greater strength than the individual, a new development in Mexico and Latin America. At the same time, public opinion grew in influence to the point where it exerted considerable pressure on the government. The Revolution created a novel social flexibility, and as one consequence the middle sectors grew both in size and importance. It became increasingly apparent after 1940 that the Revolution clearly had entered its Thermidor phase. It too, precisely as the party name, Party of Revolutionary Institutions, indicated became institutionalized. The Revolution still stands as a major landmark in Latin American history, dividing the past from the present and the future. Culturally, socially, economically, and politically it transformed Mexico. It violently uprooted institutions from the distant past and firmly implanted new ones more complementary to the Mexican experience.

Impressive as the material results of the Revolution were, the psychological changes in the Mexicans surpassed them. The hacienda system was not uprooted nor the oil expropriated just for economic benefits. Those measures were taken to give the Mexican people greater control over their own destiny and to enhance the dignity of the worker and to include him in the national life. The foremost contemporary

Mexican historian Daniel Cosío Villegas judged, "The present dignity which the Indian has achieved was worth the blood and destruction of the Revolution." What the Revolution meant to the people can be seen in the powerful murals of Diego Rivera, the daring architecture of the National University, the rhythmic movement of the Ballet Folklórico, or heard in the vibrant music of Carlos Chávez. Together they reveal the soul of a proud Mexico emancipated by a ferocious but necessary Revolution.

NATIONALISM AS A FORCE FOR CHANGE

Nationalism, perhaps more than any other single force, impels change in twentieth-century Latin America. Difficult to define precisely, nationalism in this text means a group consciousness that attributes great value to the nation-state, to which total loyalty is pledged. Members of the group agree to maintain the unity, independence, and sovereignty of the nation-state as well as to pursue certain broad and mutually acceptable goals. Two of those goals in the twentieth century have been modernization and economic independence. The nationalists have been in the vanguard of those promoting rapid development of Latin America, and thus they have served as eager agents propelling change.

Nationalism is not a novelty introduced by the twentieth century. It can trace its roots far back into the Latin American past. It evolved slowly over the centuries, at different times assuming different characteristics. During the colonial period, particularly during the eighteenth century, the local elite developed a literature praising their surroundings and extolling the beauty and purity of the New World. The intensifying conflict between the creoles and the mazombos on the one hand and the reinóis and peninsulares on the other sharpened the "nativism" of those born in the New World, consequently deepening their alienation from the Iberians. By such a psychological process the nation in the historical sense preceded the nation in the political sense. Indeed, Latin American historians affirm that the spiritual and emotional maturity of their countries predates political independence. Two Peruvians, Víctor Andrés Belaúnde and Jorge Basadre, speak of "colonial nationalism" and "conciencia de sí," a self-consciousness, evident in Peru in the eighteenth century—if not before. The Mexican Daniel Cosío Villegas concluded that Iberian colonial oppression encouraged a "nationalist sentiment and ardor" foreshadowing Latin American independence. Such native pride and growing self-consciousness had its inevitable triumph in the proclamations of independence. Transformed from bucolic nativists into ardent nationalists the elite created and defended their new nations.

The declarations and wars of independence gave a much sharper focus to nationalism. The rhetoric, symbols (flags, anthems, heroes), and battles infused enthusiasm and determination into many ranks of the Americans, particularly into the elite, intellectuals, and the urban dwellers. Wars, boundary disputes, and foreign threats helped to maintain or intensify that political nationalism throughout the nineteenth century. Juan Manuel de Rosas ably manipulated Argentine xenophobia to weld diverse and distrusting regions into a national union. In Brazil, the throne of the emperor provided a convenient focal point which rallied the loyalty of all regions and classes of the enormous, sprawling, and disconnected empire. As the nineteenth century waxed, internal trends buttressed the sporadic demonstrations of defensive nationalism. The races mixing at a fast rate obscured ethnic origins to create a homogeneous mestizo citizenry distinctive to the New World, and some of the racial combinations were unique to specific countries. As the nations became more conscious of their peculiar personalities, they developed a stronger sense of national identity. Railroads, telegraph lines, and steamships further unified each nation. Together they successfully combated the major threat to national unity: regionalism.

As the twentieth century opened, a wave of cultural nationalism swept the hemisphere. The intellectuals, long slavish imitators of European styles, turned their backs on their former mentors to seek the indigenous roots of national culture. They probed national psychology, questioned national motives, and reexamined the past. Scholars such as José Enrique Rodó in Uruguay, João Capistrano de Abreu and Euclydes da Cunha in Brazil, Ricardo Rojas in Argentina, José Vasconcelos in Mexico, and José Carlos Mariátegui in Peru offered novel introspective theories to explain national development (or lack of it) which relegated the usual emphasis on Europe to a secondary plane. In reinterpreting the past, historians paid greater attention to the influence of the interior, the hinterlands, and the frontier. Nowhere was that trend more evident than in Brazil. In a brilliant essay presented in 1889, Capistrano de Abreu was the first to point out the influence of the interior on the formation of Brazil. According to him, the interior was the true Brazil; the more heavily populated coast was just an extension of Europe. Only when the coastal inhabitants turned their backs to the sea and penetrated the interior did they shed their European ways and become Brazilianized. Da Cunha confirmed that thesis in his masterpiece *Os Sertões* (translated into English as *Rebellion in the Backlands*). From his perceptive study of the interior, he concluded that on the frontier, in the hinterland, he beheld the real Brazil and the true Brazilian. He spoke of the backwoodsmen as "the very core of our nationality, the bedrock of our race," and of their society as "the vigorous core of our national life." Rojas came to similar conclusions about the Argentine interior. Essays, poems, and novels on the gaucho, now perfectly romanticized as the frontier "type," were the vogue in the Platine region.

As the battle lines hardened between nationalism and foreign influences, Ricardo Rojas cried for the salvation of Argentine youth "from the foreign clergy, from foreign gold, and from foreign books." At the same time in Brazil, Ronald de Carvalho, one of the major exponents of the new cultural nationalism, exhorted his followers, "Let us forget the marble of the Acropolis and the towers of the Gothic cathedrals. We are the sons of the hills and the forests. Stop thinking of Europe. Think of America!" A Latin American renaissance in art, literature, music, and dance resulted from those proddings. It originated in Mexico, then appeared in Brazil, and spread thereafter—sometimes with less effect than others—to the rest of the republics. Its appearance coincided with the emergence of a new cultural medium, the film, which quickly reflected the new trends. The film industry used nationalism for its own purposes as was readily evident in Mexico. One of the first Mexican movies, "El Grito de Dolores" (The Cry of Dolores), 1910, glorified Father Hidalgo and his role a hundred years before in declaring Mexico's independence. "Cuauhtémoc," in 1918, paid homage to that last Indian emperor as a national hero. In the following year "Juan Soldado" (John Soldier) emphasized the exploits of the common soldier in the Revolution, the first of a long series of movies exalting the Revolution. The film provided the intellectuals with their most effective medium to address the populace. It proved to be highly useful in enlisting the support of the masses for the nationalist cause.

Strong political undercurrents swirled within the waters of cultural nationalism. The arts were not separate from politics; those participating in one often took part in the other, truer of the intellectuals than the politicians. The nationalists initiated a search for new indigenous solutions to old political problems. The Cuban José Martí set the tone in his plea:

> In order to govern well, one must pay attention to reality. The wise leader in America is not he who knows how the German or the Frenchman is governed, but he who knows of what elements his own country is composed and how he can guide them as a unity—by means of methods and institutions native to his own country—toward that desirable condition in which each man knows himself and exerts himself. . . . The government must be born of the country. The spirit of the government must be that of the country. The form of the government must adjust itself to the inherent structure of the country. Government is nothing more than the balance of the natural elements of the country.

The Mexican Constitution of 1917 was the first example of a constitutional document reflecting indigenous experiences and needs rather than merely copying the political ideologies of Western Europe and the United States.

The collapse of the international economy in 1929–30 and the prolonged depression which followed caused attention to shift to yet another form of nationalism: economic or developmental. The difficult years emphasized once again to the Latin Americans the dependency and vulnerability of their economies. Cuba's economy broke down: foreign trade in the early 1930s was 10 percent of the 1929 figure. Uruguay's exports dropped 80 percent in the early 1930s. Brazil's exports plummeted from US$445.9 million in 1929 to US$180.6 million in 1932, while Argentina sold 40 percent less in the 1930–34 period than in the previous five years. In short, by 1932, Latin America exported 65 percent less than it had in 1929, proving once again that foreign trade contributed mightily to the cyclical fluctuations of the Latin American economy. The nationalists demanded that steps be taken to increase the viability of the national economies and conversely to reduce their dependency on the gyrations of the international market caused by the buying whims of a few highly industrialized nations. Plans were made to increase economic diversification and to promote industrialization. Industrialization appealed to both common sense and pride. For one thing, it promised to diversify the economy; for another, it kept previous foreign exchange from being spent to import what could be manufactured at home. At the same time, an acute shortage of foreign currencies meant that either the nations manufactured their own goods or they did without.

The economic crisis motivated the governments to play an increasingly active role in the national economies. They introduced long-range economic planning, exerted new controls, and offered incentives. Devalued currency, import controls, and higher tariffs stimulated national industry, and all those measures received the support of the nationalists.

The wider participation of the governments in the economies and the mounting demands for faster development shifted the leadership of the nationalist movement from the intellectuals, who had long enjoyed a quasi-monopoly in directing it, to the governments themselves, which began to understand the potential power of the movement. At the same time the base of support of nationalism expanded to include, on occasion, the masses, or more specifically the urban working classes. They were told and they believed, rightly or wrongly, that the foreign investor exploited them, extracting huge profits from Latin

America while paying minimal wages. In other words, the foreigner perpetuated the local poverty. It was a simple argument with great emotional appeal.

Nationalism remained an amorphous sentiment, but passions could be brought to a boil over certain issues and none was more inflammable than oil. It symbolized economic nationalism, representative of the longing many Latin Americans felt to control their own natural resources. Nationalists argued that the discovery and exploitation of their own petroleum was not only economically desirable but the guarantee of real national independence and, in the case of several of the larger countries, of world-power status. "Whoever hands over petroleum to foreigners threatens our own independence," one Latin American nationalist leader warned. No acts in recent memory received more popular acclaim than the nationalization of foreign oil industries in Bolivia in 1937 and in Mexico in 1938. On the other hand, the alienation of a nation's petroleum through concessions to foreign companies has contributed to the fall of several recent Latin American governments as President Arturo Frondizi (1958–62) learned in Argentina and President Fernando Belaúnde Terry (1963–68) in Peru.

When the oil question is handled adroitly, it can become a strong prop buttressing a nationalist government. President Getúlio Vargas of Brazil (1930–45; 1951–54) ably used the oil issue to his advantage. Sensing the growing importance of oil, emotionally and economically, he created the National Petroleum Council in the 1930s to coordinate and intensify the search for oil. In 1939, the first successful well was drilled, and it brought forth oil from Brazil's soil. The excited nationalists at once called for the creation of a national oil industry. In a bid for wider popular support, Vargas urged the creation of a state oil monopoly to oversee exploration and to promote the development of petroleum resources. Its creation in 1953 followed a passionate national campaign and marked a major victory for the nationalists. They had triumphed over those who argued that it would be more economical for experienced foreign companies to drill for oil and pay Brazil a royalty on whatever was pumped out. The nationalists denounced that argument. After all, the issue was an emotional, not an economic, one. They wanted Brazil to retain control over one of its most precious and important resources. Their arguments convinced the masses that a national oil industry represented sovereignty, power, independence, and well-being. The masses responded with enthusiastic support, a demonstration of the power economic nationalism can muster.

In the decades after World War II, economic nationalism assumed four distinct characteristics. First, the political left took over much of the leadership, imposing their ideas and their vocabulary. As one result, contemporary nationalism relies heavily on the Marxist lexicon, a fact that exposes the movement to constant denunciations that the Communists dominate or direct it. The accusation is not only false but it vastly oversimplifies the complexity of nationalism and hinders efforts to better understand it. Second, the nationalists have increased the criticism of foreign economic penetration. They accuse the foreign investors and companies of perpetuating Latin America's underdevelopment by keeping the population poor, ignorant, feeble, and imbued with a feeling of inferiority. They harken to the warning of José Martí: "A people economically enslaved but politically free will end by losing all freedom, but a people economically free can go on to win its political independence." As a cruel irony, the figures seem to demonstrate that foreign investment aids the investor and debilitates the host nation, at least in Latin America. Former Foreign Minister Gabriel Valdes of Chile noted:

> We can assert that Latin America is contributing to finance the development of the United States and other affluent nations. Private investments have meant, and mean today for Latin America, that the amounts that leave our continent are many times higher than those that are invested in it. Our potential capital is diminishing, while the profits of invested capital grow and multiply at an enormous rate, not in our countries but abroad.

Figures released by the United Nations Economic Commission for Latin America verify his statement. During the years 1960–66, the flow of private investment into Latin America reached US$2.8 billion, while the repatriation of profits and income amounted to US$8.3 billion. A net loss of US$785 million per year in Latin America's balance of payments resulted. As one consequence, the rich, developed nations profited handsomely at the expense of impoverished, underdeveloped Latin American nations.

Third, the nationalists have mounted their most vitriolic attack against the United States. The reason is obvious: the United States is the largest single investor in Latin America. In 1970, the United States had invested over US$14 billion in Latin America, nearly three-quarters of which was concentrated in minerals, petroleum, and manufacturing industries. The presence of United States business is overwhelming, not just in the small Caribbean republics but in the major nations too: 15 of the 25 largest companies in Argentina are owned by North American companies and 6 of the 30 largest companies in Brazil are United States firms. Consequently, any campaign against foreign capital automatically assumes anti-Yankee tones. Then, too, the United States government and the major United States investors have become closely identified with the Latin American oligarchy and in the eyes of the nationalists with the preservation of the status quo. Action occasionally replaces accusation. The Peruvian government in 1968 seized the International Petroleum Company, a Jersey Standard subsidiary, and in 1969 expropriated W. R. Grace's rich sugar estates. In late 1969, the Bolivian government nationalized Gulf Oil's subsidiary. The most spectacular recent nationalization occurred in Chile in mid-1971. President Salvador Allende authorized the take over of the three major copper producers, Anaconda, Kennecott, and Cerro, promising the owners porper indemnity.

Finally, the nationalists pay ever greater attention to economic development in a desperate attempt to modernize their countries. Developmental nationalism continues to call for government control of natural resources, limitations of foreign capital, accelerated industrialization, and trade with all nations regardless of their political or economic ideologies. The developmental nationalists show a greater impatience with the ideologies of the past and more interest in experimenting with new ones. They are ready to try collective or cooperative forms of land and industrial use. In the words of Alberto Bailey, a Bolivian nationalist:

> We have many points in common with Cuba, but we're not Marxists. We don't have any Marxist base and we don't have a fixed ideology that explains everything. We believe that the nationalist revolution will reestablish the sovereignty of the nations. It will establish the basis for a more just society. It will probably end up in a form of socialism, but that may take a long time.

Whether Latin Americans are willing to wait much longer for their nation's development is another question. Indications are that patience wears rapidly thinner, as the appeal of economic nationalism grows. The Secretary-General of the Organization of American States, Galo Plaza, concluded, "One of the most powerful forces in Latin America today, and one of the least understood outside the region, is the upsurge of economic nationalism."

In the twentieth century, the thrust of nationalism has altered dramatically. While once the nationalists were absorbed in tracing the historic roots of their country and in glorifying the potential wealth and natural beauty of their land, now they are concerned with the future. They foresee a future in which the institutions and patterns of the twentieth century will replace those of the colonial past. To reach that future they must industrialize and modernize. Nationalism is the catalyst which promises to bring about much of the change.

CHANGING RACIAL ATTITUDES

The nationalists in the twentieth century came to appreciate a long neglected fact: the rich and varied racial heritage of Latin America accounted for the region's uniqueness and vitality. Unfortunately, although the Indian, African, and European contributed jointly to the formation of Latin American civilization, the three groups by no means enjoyed equality. The European and his New World descendants occupied the highest level of society, with the mestizos, mulattoes, Indians, and blacks relegated to lower rungs of the social ladder. Without the benevolent protection of the Iberian monarchs, the position of the Indians and blacks, if anything, deteriorated in the nineteenth century. Some intellectuals contributed to their misery as well as to national psychosis. In their eagerness to mouth European ideas, they read and circulated the specious racist doctrines so in vogue among Europeans in that century.

The wealth of biological thought in the nineteenth century, the popularity of Darwinism and Spencerianism, and the complex ethnic composition of Latin America aroused a lively interest in race and racial theories. Latin America's cultural mentor, France, offered a poisonous array of pseudoscientific books attesting to the superiority of the Northern European. Widely read by the end of the century was the social psychologist Gustave Le Bon, who methodically classified all mankind into superior and inferior races with the Europeans indisputably at the top. Among other things, he asserted that miscegenation produced an offspring inferior to either parent. Another champion of the Aryan, the anthropologist Georges Vacher de Lapouge, minced no words in his chief work, *L'Aryen, son Role Social*, to support the theory of racial significance in cultural development. In line with his thesis, he characterized Brazil as "an enormous Negro state on its way back to barbarism." Bombarded by such influence and inheritors of a sociopolitical system in which the European and his offspring ruled while the Indian, the African, and their offspring obeyed, most Latin Americans equated whiteness with beauty, intelligence, and ability. Conversely, the darker the people the less likelihood that they would possess those desired characteristics. Intellectuals such as Francisco Bulnes in Mexico, Carlos Octavio Bunge and José Ingenieros in Argentina, Alcides Argüeda in Bolivia, and Manuel Bonfim in Brazil, blamed miscegenation for the backwardness and anarchy of Latin America. In doing so, they condemned their peoples to a feeling of inferiority.

The rising tide of nationalism caused some Latin Americans to question those dreary racial concepts. To accept the European doctrines, they finally realized, would condemn Latin America perpetually to a secondary position. The nationalists concluded that the doctrines were simply another means devised by the Europeans to humiliate and subjugate Latin America. In due course, the Latin Americans rejected the foreign racist doctrines, and in so doing they took a major step toward freeing themselves from European cultural domination.

In the early twentieth century, the Latin Americans began to take a new interest in the Indians, cheated, robbed, overworked, suppressed, and massacred throughout the nineteenth century. Disturbed by the rapid decline of the Indian population as well as by the terrible tales of brutal exploitation of the natives by the rubber barons of the Amazon, the Brazilian government created the Indian Protection Service in 1910 to defend them and to incorporate their diminishing numbers into the national family. The *Aprista* movement appeared in Peru by the end of the second decade of the twentieth century and spread thereafter to other countries. Advocating an Indian renaissance, it strove to uplift the Indian and glorified America's indigenous past. In 1919, President Augusto Leguía of Peru declared the Indian community once again to be a legal corporation. The Indian benefited handsomely from the Mexican Revolution. Under the banner of Emiliano Zapata, he fought for the restitution of his lands. Eventually the Revolution did return his lands to him, as well as offer him an education and a place in the new Mexican society. Lázaro Cárdenas, more than any other Mexican president, served the Indians; in order to institutionalize his concern, he created the Department of Indian Affairs in 1936. Unjust biases against America's Indian past were finally uprooted, and Indian themes became respectable for art, literature, music, and dance. Men at last pointed with justifiable pride to their Indian past.

At the same time attitudes toward the black also underwent change. As the first step, it was necessary to end black slavery in Latin America. The Spanish-speaking republics abolished it between 1821 and 1854. The institution lingered on in Spain's Caribbean islands and in Brazil. Tremendous international pressures bore down on Spain and Brazil to free their slaves. After mid-century internal pressures welled up. Spain feared that to manumit the slaves would drive the insular landowners to declare their independence. Cautiously the Spanish government abolished slavery in Puerto Rico in 1873, freeing approximately 31,000 blacks. The process in Cuba was slower. The Moret Law, passed in 1870 but only published in Cuba in 1872, liberated children born of slaves after September 18, 1868, although subjecting the freeborn black to a system of tutelage until 18 years of age. In 1880, the government ended slavery but with proviso that former slaves had to continue to work for eight years for their former masters. Finally, in 1886, the crown abolished the tutelage system, freeing all blacks from compulsory labor.

The abolition movement in Brazil was even more protracted. No one seriously advocated an immediate end to slavery. The economy could not absorb the shock of so radical a move. The abolitionists therefore favored a gradual emancipation, to take place over a lengthy period of time. The emperor, too, counseled the gradual approach in order to avoid disturbing the economy and committed his prestige to such a course. The Conservative government headed by the Visconde do Rio-Branco enacted the Law of the Free Womb in 1871, which declared all children born to slave mothers to be free. At the time there were approximately 1.5 million slaves and a free population of 8.6 million. The law slowly doomed slavery in Brazil. Africa as a source of slaves had been closed since 1850; after 1871, the only other source, the womb, could bring forth no more slaves. However, patience with the slow results of the Rio-Branco Law wore thin. Before the end of the 1870s, the slavery question once again confronted the public. The concern for the welfare of the remaining slaves called forth some forceful spokesmen and prompted the formation of some active abolitionist societies.

Several highly articulate blacks contributed to the leadership of the abolitionist campaign: José Carlos do Patrocínio, a persuasive journalist, wrote ceaselessly for the cause and became a symbol of the campaign; André Rebouças organized abolitionist clubs and spoke and wrote profusely in support of abolition; and Luís Gonzaga de Pinto Gama spent his youth as a slave and later became a distinguished lawyer who specialized in defending slaves in court. He claimed credit for freeing 500 slaves through the courts. A fiery advocate of immediate abolition, he declared, "Every slave who kills his master, no matter what the circumstances may be, kills in self-defense." He also preached "the right of insurrection." Given to poetry, he began one of his better known verses, "My loves are beautiful, the color of night."

The slavery issue forced itself to the forefront of politics as one group after another favored the abolitionist cause until only the slave owners themselves were left as apologists of a discredited institution. Finally, on May 13, 1888, to cries of approval from those in attendance, the parliament passed the Golden Law liberating the remaining three-quarters of a million slaves. When Princess-Regent Isabel put her signature to the law, slavery finally disappeared from the Western Hemisphere. If the slave expected the Golden Law to transport him at once to a promised land, he became disillusioned quickly enough. Life continued to be hard for him, as he lamented in this popular verse:

> Everything in this world changes,
> Only the life of the Negro remains the same:
> He works to die of hunger,
> The 13 of May fooled him.

The battle for his freedom had ended, but he faced a second struggle, his psychological emancipation from the feeling of racial inferiority, derived from long centuries of slavery. The assumption of racial inferiority was by no means limited exclusively to the blacks. Whites, too, had to overcome ingrained prejudices to reevaluate the ability of the blacks and their role in the Americas.

During the early twentieth century interest in the black's new struggle as well as in his contributions to the New World grew. The new interest was most evident in those areas where the populations of African descent were largest, the Caribbean and Brazil. In Cuba, the prolific intellectual Fernando Ortiz began publishing his studies of the Negro as early as 1906. Together with the black Nicolás Guillen, the originator of the *negrismo* school of poetry, he founded the Society for Afro-Cuban Studies in 1926 and thereafter devoted himself with increasing fervor to the study of the Negro. In Haiti in the 1920s, Jean Price-Mars took up his pen to urge his fellow blacks to accept their African heritage and to use it as a cultural resource.

At the same time, the Brazilians looked with clearer vision on their African past. A contemporary of the racist Bonfim, Afonso Celso, refused to accept his colleague's negative predictions about Brazil's innate inferiority. In his blatantly nationalistic *Porque Me Ufano do Meu País* (Why I Am Proud of My Country), Celso proudly affirmed, "Today it is a generally accepted truth that three elements contributed to the formation of the Brazilian people: the American Indian, the African Negro, and the Portuguese. . . . Any one of those elements, or any combination of them, possesses qualities of which we should be proud." His book contained a chapter praising the heroic resistance of the blacks to slavery, in which he lavishly bestowed the adjectives "courageous" and "noble." The pioneer of anthropological studies of the Negro in Brazil, Dr. Raimundo Nina Rodrigues, worked in Bahia from 1890 to 1905. Although not totally free of the prejudices of his day, he felt a great sympathy toward the blacks and manifested a lively interest in their condition. He studied the African cultures in order to identify their survivals in Brazil, and in that manner was able to indicate more correctly than previously the contributions of various African civilizations to the formation of Brazil. For example, he disproved the long-accepted idea that the Bantu predominated among Brazilian blacks by pointing out the strong cultural presence of the Sudanese groups, particularly the Yoruba, in Bahia. A few years later, another scholar, Manuel Raimundo Querino, emerged in Bahia to write about the black, his religions, and his contribution to Brazilian history. Querino was of special interest and significance because he was Brazil's first black historian, and he has provided a unique and extremely valuable perspective on Brazilian history. His major historical essay "The Black Colonist as a Contributor to Brazilian Civilization" first reached print in 1918. In it, he concluded:

> Whoever takes a look at the history of this country will verify the value and contribution of the Negro to the defense of national territory, to agriculture, to mining, to the exploitation of the interior, to the movement for independence, to family life, and to the development of the nation through the many and varied tasks he performed. Upon his well-muscled back rested the social, cultural, and material development. . . .
>
> The black is still the principal producer of the nation's wealth, but many are the contributions of that long suffering and persecuted race which has left imperishable proofs of its singular valor. History in all its justice has to respect and praise the valuable service which the black has given to this nation for more than three centuries. In truth, it was the black who developed Brazil.

It was fitting that the intellectuals of Bahia—an area where the African always predominated—first discovered the Brazilian blacks and began to emphasize the heroic role they had played in Brazil's development.

Simultaneously the literati turned their attention to the same subject. Several novelists of the late nineteenth century, Aluísio Azevedo, in his *O Cortiço* (The Tenement), and Adolfo Caminha, in his *O Bom Crioulo* (The Good Negro), described at length the black as a member of the urban proletariat. In some of his best novels, Afonso Henriques Lima Barreto raised his voice to protest the discrimination against the Negro which manifested itself in Rio de Janeiro, described it in some of its ugliest aspects, and called for justice. Menotti del Picchia characterized the Brazilian as a mulatto in his lengthy poem "Juca Mulatto"; it was the first time in Brazilian poetry that a mulatto appeared as the hero. The more enlightened attitudes toward the races removed embarrassments which earlier had inhibited or confused the intellectuals. Thus freed, they became increasingly proud of the nation's racial amalgamation, which they began to view as an achievement, not a disgrace.

Gilberto Freyre helped to break the last chains binding the intellectuals to their racial uncertainties when he published *Casa Grande e Senzala* (*The Masters and the Slaves*) in 1933. The national and international acclaim which greeted his study freed the intellectuals from any remaining cultural complexes. Freyre's cogent discussion of the creation of a unique, multiracial civilization in Brazil opened vast new areas for research and study. In 1934 the first Afro-Brazilian Congress met in Recife, and two years later a second one convened in Salvador. The papers read during those sessions and the discussions which followed emphasized the revised opinion about the black and his newly assigned place within the Brazilian family.

The more realistic appraisal of the African presence improved the black's position in Brazilian society, but it would be quixotic to conclude, as is so often done, that Brazil knows no racial prejudice. The facts prove otherwise. Newspapers regularly run help-wanted advertisements seeking whites only. Until well after mid-twentieth century, both the diplomatic corps and the naval officer corps remained lilywhite. After World War II, it was necessary to promulgate a law to punish overt discrimination. In all fairness, though, it must be pointed out that Brazil probably has less racial tension and less racial prejudice than any other multiracial society, past or present. The races mix freely in public places. Interracial marriage is reasonably common. A more formidable barrier than race may well be class. Class membership depends on a wide variety of factors and their combination: income, family history and/or connections, education, social behavior, tastes in housing, food, and dress, as well as appearance, personality, and talent. Henry Koster noted during his residence in Brazil in the early nineteenth century, "The inferiority which the mulatto feels is more that which is produced by poverty than that which his color has caused, for he will be equally respectful of a person of his own caste who may happen to be rich." The observation is equally valid in the twentieth century, as the Brazilian sociologist Thales de Azevedo has pointed out in his studies. As it happens, the upper class traditionally has been and still remains mainly white, the lower class principally colored. The significant point, though, is that colored people can and do form a part, albeit a small part of the upper class, just as whites are by no means uncommon in the lower classes. Upward mobility exists and education promotes it. With effort, skill, and determination (plus a little luck), class barriers can be hurdled, but it is not easy.

There have always been movements afoot among the black community to improve the conditions of its members. Often those movements have stressed the value of education as the principal means of raising the social and economic position of the black, but on occasion the trend was to encourage a back-to-Africa migration, a movement noticeable during the last half of the nineteenth century. Rarely sounded is a note of militancy equal to that heard in the United States or in the Caribbean.

Black militancy has become increasingly a characteristic of the Caribbean, and there has been an interaction between such militancy there and in the United States as the biographies of Marcus Garvey and Stokely Carmichael, among others, testify. The Caribbean is overwhelmingly black, although in Trinidad, Guyana, and Surinam, there are also large numbers of Asians, particularly from India. Those areas still under European tutelage in the twentieth century protested vigorously, particularly from the 1930s onward, the social and economic injustices with their attendant de facto racial prejudice. In many cases those areas sought their independence. In 1962, after an unsuccessful attempt to federate, Jamaica and Trinidad and Tobago separated to become independent states. Barbados asserted its sovereignty in 1966, and in that same year, Guyana, after many difficulties, achieved its independence. Unfortunately independence or self-government seems to have solved few of the area's problems. In Jamaica, 1 percent of the farms occupy 56 percent of the total acreage, and unemployment among the impoverished and poorly educated masses can reach on occasion as high as 50 percent. An unbalanced distribution of wealth menaces social tranquility. Approximately 50 percent of the economy is controlled by only 1 percent of the population, and that small segment is not black but Chinese, Lebanese, American, Canadian, and British. Elsewhere in the Caribbean, as in Jamaica, foreign companies continue to dominate the region's primary industries: oil refining, sugar cane growing and processing, and bauxite mining. Relatively few of the Caribbean blacks have managed to reap much benefit from independence.

The disappointments arising from frustrations after independence helped to encourage the growth of the Black Power movement which reached its height in the Caribbean after black leaders replaced the whites. The years 1968, 1969, and 1970 witnessed Black Power demonstrations across the breadth of the Carribean from the Bahamas to Trinidad. The Black Power advocates called for radical solutions to the area's lingering problems of poverty, illiteracy, unemployment, underemployment, and exploitation, demanding a new order based on nationalism and populism. They extol as their principal goal local, black control of the economy, thus moving beyond nominal political independence to economic independence. That economic power still rests in the hands of nonblacks has become a source of deepening resentment in the area. In 1971, to the applause of the nationalists, Prime Minister Forbes Burnham of Guyana nationalized the big Canadian-owned Alcan bauxite operation, a move carefully studied by leaders throughout the Caribbean.

Perplexing economic problems do not characterize only the new black republics of the Caribbean. Haiti, independent since 1804, still has not resolved its major problems, and the situation looks more desperate than ever. In mid-1971, the United Nations singled out Haiti as the only Latin American nation among the 25 "least developed" nations of the world. Of its 4 million inhabitants, approximately 90 percent were illiterate. The annual per capita income hardly exceeded $40. Half of all children born there died before reaching their fifth birthday.

The question remains open as to what extent the Cuban Revolution has benefited the black. The Africans contributed heavily to the development of Cuba, and although figures vary about the racial composition of the population today, a reasonable estimate distributes it as 30 percent white, 20 percent mestizo, 49 percent Negroid, and 1 percent Oriental. In the past the white predominated in the upper strata of society and the blacks in the low. The Revolution claims to have eradicated racial prejudice and to have given an equal opportunity to all men regardless of color. Certainly the photographs and documentaries coming out of Cuba indicate a greater active participation of the black in national life. However, blacks from the United States who have visited Cuba in the 1960s differ in their interpretation. John Clytus, a black nationalist leader, lived in Cuba from 1964 to 1967 and reported his conclusions in *Black Man in Red Cuba*. The absence of blacks in leadership roles and the government's policy to discourage the creation of a sense of identity among Cuba's blacks disappointed Clytus who returned to the United States where he could protest against racial prejudice and advocate black nationalism. On the other hand, Elizabeth Sutherland, another black, visited Cuba in 1967 and related her impressions in *The Youngest Revolution: A Personal Report on Cuba*. She noted the continued presence of old racial prejudices and myths, but realistically commented that man—socialist or otherwise—sheds hoary prejudices slowly. What impressed her was the distinction that "where the previous society's institutions and authority had all stood behind racism, the [Cuban] Revolution stood against it." She noted some positive achievements of the Revolution which favored the black: the illiteracy rate, previously very high among blacks, had fallen to the remarkably low figure of 4 percent, housing for the blacks had improved, integration had become complete, and public forms of racial discrimination had been eliminated. She concluded that Cuba was moving as rapidly as was humanly possible toward racial harmony and justice. Obviously a final assessment still has to be made.

Racial attitudes in Cuba as elsewhere in the hemisphere have changed considerably during the twentieth century. The myth of racial inferiority or superiority has been destroyed. As one result the Indian and the black occupy a more favored position today than they did at the opening of the century. Everywhere important steps have been taken to eradicate racial prejudice. Although much has been accomplished, much still remains to be done.

seven

Development,
Democracy, and
Disillusionment

Workers Demonstrating in Front of the National Palace in Guatemala City

In the decades since 1945, Latin America developed rapidly and during part of that time the forces favoring democracy seemed to triumph. Aspirations for change mounted as greater numbers of the population were exposed to the benefits of a more modern society. Unfortunately those aspirations outpaced actual change. Too few enjoyed the benefits of what change took place, and too many of the age-old political, economic, and social structures and patterns remained to permit faster and more complete change. As the rate and extent of change failed to fulfill expectations, frustrations mounted. The frustrations increased societal tensions. In three countries, governments tried revolutionary experiments to expedite change and to solve old problems. In many others, the military, also victims of accelerating frustration, imposed its own solution which, more often than not, was a reaffirmation of older patterns, in short a reversion to the past. The failure to change and democratize at the speed and to the extent desired has created a widespread feeling of disillusion in contemporary Latin America.

THE ROCKY ROAD TO DEVELOPMENT

The modernization process continued apace in the twentieth century as some parts of Latin America adopted more recent techniques, methods, and ideas to replace the more time-honored but less effective ones. Modernism struggled with traditionalism in what was essentially a contest between the static countryside and the more dynamic cities. Certainly the process and effects of modernization revealed themselves more readily in and near the urban areas than elsewhere. Likewise, those effects continued to be more visible among the elite, middle class, and urban working class than among the peasants.

Various indicators pointed to a quickening movement of part of Latin America from a traditional to a modern society by mid-twentieth century. In some countries, such as Argentina, Brazil, Chile, Mexico, and Uruguay, the movement was quite noticeable; in others, such as Paraguay, Bolivia, Ecuador, Honduras, and Haiti, it would take a careful observer to discern much inclination toward modernization.

The following comments contrasting traditional with modern societies in mid-twentieth century Latin America are of an extremely general nature, applicable to some areas of some countries but questionable with regard to other areas of the same country or to other countries. The discussion aims to point out some indicators by which a Latin American country's progress toward modernization can be measured. Traditional societies are agrarian: they have as high as 80 percent of their work force engaged in agriculture, while modern societies can get by with as few as 10 percent on the farms. At mid-century, Latin America still had about 50 percent of its work force concentrated in agriculture, although that percentage had been steadily declining. Between 1945 and 1955, the percentage of the work force engaged in agriculture dropped from 57.4 percent to 51.6 percent. Not surprising, then, modern societies are urban and traditional societies tend to be rural. By 1950, Latin America stood on the threshold of becoming more urban than rural, a reflection of major population shifts in the previous half-century. A high degree of literacy characterizes the modern society, while illiteracy—with the exception of a well-educated elite—plagues the traditional. Approximately 50 percent of Latin America's population did not know how to read and write. Traditional society divides into a large peasantry and a small elite with sharp distinctions between the two. It is as difficult as it is rare to cross class lines. On the other hand, in the broadly stratified modern society, class distinctions become blurred, easing social mobility. Urban Latin America enjoyed far greater flexibility in its social structure than the rural area. Nonetheless, in both, there existed a well-defined elite whose ranks were difficult for outsiders to join. Traditional and modern societies revere different values. The traditional accepts the world as it exists, including of course the class and power structures. The traditional individual adapts to his surroundings. He is person-oriented. Individual relationships matter most to him and consequently he places primary emphasis on his dealing with people. Treatment in an impersonal way by doctors, lawyers, social workers, or governmental bureaucrats alienates him. He suspects any colleague who seeks to exert leadership or rise above the group. He refuses to make long-run plans. In contrast, the individual embracing the benefits of modernization becomes increasingly object-oriented. He has goals outside his group which often take precedence over personal relationships: education, a profession, a better standard of living, a different style of life. Change and flexibility constitute the keystones of modern societal values. The conflict between activism and fatalism continued in Latin America, but by and large the struggle over values took place in the cities. The peasantry submissively accepted its lowly status. Latin America had an extremely low level of technology, content with methods passed down from generation to generation. A modern society, to maintain and to accelerate its advance, innovates and invents freely, questioning past practices with the intention of improving them and in the process raises the level of technology. Finally, the traditional society has a subsistence economy which centers on local markets although it often furnishes one primary product for the international market. Conversely, in a modern nation a complex commercial network covers the breadth of the land, and its links with the outside world are many. As a consequence of intensive, efficient economic activity, the per capita income in a modern nation exceeds that of a more traditionally oriented one by many times. Whereas the average per capita income in the United States at mid-century approximated $3,000, in Latin America it was less than $400, ranging from a high of $800 in Venezuela to a low of $70 in Haiti. As might be expected, the income was badly distributed. In Argentina, Brazil, and Mexico, those in the top 10 percent income bracket received 40 percent of the national income, while those in the bottom 40 percent earned only 10 percent. In all of Latin America, 20 percent of the population received 60 percent of the national income. Over 70 percent suffered abject poverty.

It is evident that despite great advances made in the twentieth century few of the Latin American societies qualified in their entirety as modern. While the elite and middle classes enjoyed many of the benefits of a modern society, the fact remained that conditions for the masses had not improved. A majority of the population remained immersed in the past. Modern society had penetrated very insignificantly into rural Latin America, a fortress of traditionalism, where a majority of the Latin Americans lived.

The latifundia, more than any other institution, preserved the past. In 1960, 54 percent of the population lived in the countryside. Although the percentage dropped to 46 in 1970, the total rural population rose during that decade from 108 to 133 million. Consequently, change in Latin America, whether by reform or revolution, can be truly effectual only when it reaches the overwhelming number of landless peasants too. Land tenure has been the key to agriculture, indeed the key to the economy since agriculture has remained the economic basis for Latin America. During the 1960s, 52 percent of Latin America's total international earnings came from agriculture. Those exports have been extremely important because they determined the availability of foreign exchange for capital goods. True, during the twentieth century, the agricultural sector of the economy gradually reduced its contributions to the gross national product, but nonetheless it continued to play a decisive role in the economy.

Despite the fact that agriculture formed the basis for the area's economy, few nations tried to reform the centuries-old agrarian structure—Mexico being the sole exception until the 1950s—or to modernize agriculture. The landowning system in most of Latin America remained flagrantly unjust, based, at least in part, on the accumulation of huge tracts of land by means of force, chicanery, and dubious measures approved by the passage of time and the connivance of bureaucrats. In no other area of comparable size in the world did there exist a higher concentration of land in the hands of a few than in Latin America. As of 1950, 2 percent of the Argentine estates accounted for 60 percent of the land; in Brazil, 1.6 percent of the fazendas covered 50 percent of the land; in El Salvador, 1 percent of the haciendas included 50 percent of the land; in Paraguay, 11 haciendas controlled 35 percent of the land. The figures were comparable in most of the rest of the countries. And the general tendency in this century has been for the large properties to increase in both number and size. On the opposite end of the scale lay another problem: the minifundium, a property so small that often it failed to sustain its owner much less to contribute to the regional or national economies. That problem, too, was widespread. As of 1950, 42 percent of the farms in Argentina claimed only 1 percent of the land; in Brazil, 22 percent of the rural properties possessed only 0.5 percent of the land; in El Salvador, 80 percent of the farms had less than 12 acres each; in Paraguay, 44 percent of the farms were less than 12 acres each. Table 1 illustrates the plight of the minifundia and the dominance of the latifundia. Looking at the statistics available for the early 1960s, the researcher can conclude that 63 percent or 18 million adult farmers owned no land; another 5.5 million owned insufficient amounts of land; 1.9 million possessed sufficient land; and 100,000 owned too much land for the social and economic good of the area.

Latin Americans traditionally have farmed their land inefficiently. The large estates included much land their owners either did not cultivate or undercultivated. Experts estimated that Latin Americans in the mid-twentieth century farmed only about 10 percent of their agricultural holdings. In Brazil, Venezuela, and Colombia, approximately 80 percent of the farmland was unused or unproductively used for cattle raising at the end of the 1950s. The landowners held their property not to farm but for purposes of prestige and speculation. For those parcels of land under cultivation, the owners seldom took full advantage of the manpower available or used any but the most antiquated farming techniques. The slash-and-burn method remained the most popular means of clearing the land. The farmers rarely spread fertilizer or did so sparingly. Consequently the land eroded, became easily exhausted, and depleted quickly. Productivity, always low, fell. A man of routine and custom, the farmer used the hoe, unmodified for centuries. The plow was rare, the tractor even rarer. As late as 1930, tractors were practically unknown in Mexico. In Brazil, in 1940, only one in four farms boasted of a plow; one in 500 possessed a tractor. A major indictment of the agrarian structure and the farming methods has been that the Latin Americans were never able to feed themselves well and during the past few decades have been incapable of supplying their own food requirements. Chile, for example, shifted in the 1940s from being a net agricultural exporter to becoming a net agricultural importer. By the mid-1950s agricultural products accounted for 25 percent of Chile's total imports. In short, that nation was spending about 18 percent of

TABLE 1   Land Ownership in Latin America

Size of Farms in Hectares (1 hectare = 2.47 acres)	Percentage of Farms	Percentage of Land Area
0-20	72.6	3.7
20-100	18.0	8.4
100-1000	7.9	23.0
Over 1000	1.5	64.9

Source: Richard P. Schaedel, "Land Reform Studies," *Latin American Research Review*, I, No. 1 (Fall 1965), 85. Reproduced with the permission of the publisher.

its hard-earned foreign currency on food which all experts agreed Chile could grow itself, a tragedy by no means unique to Chile. By 1965, food-stuffs constituted 20 percent of Latin America's purchases abroad.

Agriculture in the twentieth century lost none of its speculative, reflexive nature so characteristic of the mercantilist and neomercan-tilist past. For its prosperity, it continued to rely heavily on a few ex-port commodities, always very vulnerable on the international market. Prices depended on the demands of a few industrialized nations. Fur-ther, new producers and substitutes appeared to challenge and under-sell them, thus increasing Latin America's economic vulnerability. Africa, in particular, emerged as a formidable competitor for inter-national markets. After World War II, the prices of agricultural prod-ucts gradually declined to the dismay of the Latin Americas (while at the same time the prices of imported capital goods spiraled upward). Still, the latifundia by and large followed their hoary practice of offer-ing one crop for sale. On a fair price for coffee alone, for example, de-pended the well-being of an alarming number of Latin Americans at the end of the 1950s: coffee composed 67 percent of Colombia's exports, 42 percent of El Salvador's, 41 percent of Brazil's, 38 percent of Haiti's, 34 percent of Guatemala's, and 31 percent of Costa Rica's. On the ex-port of sugar, bananas, cacao, wheat, beef, wool, and mutton depended other Latin American economies.

The economic inefficiency of the land structure was one matter, the human misery it perpetuated quite another. Rural society with its hereditary social position resisted change. The few landlords lived in comfort; the peasant masses existed in misery. The rural workers earned a pittance in wages—if, indeed, they received wages—and most probably were heavily in debt to their employer. Debt peonage was as common as it had been in the eighteenth and nineteenth centuries. The Brazilian Graciliano Ramos captured the pathos and hopelessness of the peasant in his novel *Barren Lives*, set in the drought-tortured Northeast. The peasant Fabiano realizes that everything conspires to prevent his es-cape from poverty.

> In the division of stock at the year's end, Fabiano received a fourth of the calves and a third of the kids, but as he grew no feed, but merely sowed a few handfuls of beans and corn on the river flat, living on what he bought at the market, he disposed of the animals, never seeing his brand on a calf or his mark on the ear of a kid.
>
> If he could only put something aside for a few months, he would be able to get his head up. Oh, he had made plans, but that was all foolish-ness. Ground creepers were never meant to climb. Once the beans had been eaten and the ears of corn gnawed, there was no place to go but to the boss's cash drawer. He would turn over the animals that had fallen to his lot for the lowest of prices, grumbling and protesting in distress,

trying to make his meager resources yield as much as possible. Arguing, he would choke and bite his tongue. Dealing with anyone else he would not let himself be so shamelessly robbed, but, as he was afraid of being put off the ranch, he would give in. He would take the cash and listen to the advice that accompanied it. He should give thought to the future, be more careful. . . .

Little by little the boss's brand was put on Fabiano's stock, and when he had nothing left to sell, the backlander went into debt. When time came for the division, he was in the hole, and when accounts were settled he received a mere nothing.

This time, as on other occasions, Fabiano first made a deal regarding the stock, then thought better of the matter, and, leaving the transaction only half agreed upon, he went to consult with his wife. Vitória sent the boys to play in the clay pit, sat down in the kitchen, and concentrated . . . adding and subtracting. The next day Fabiano went back to town, but on closing the deal he noted that, as usual, Vitória's figuring differed from that of the boss. He protested, and received the usual explanation: the difference represented interest.

He refused to accept the answer. There must be some mistake. . . . The mistake couldn't be found, and Fabiano lost his temper. Was he to take a beating like that his whole life long, giving up what belonged to him for nothing? Was that right? To work like a slave and never gain his freedom?

The boss became angry. He refused to hear such insolence. He thought it would be a good thing if the herdsman looked for another job.

At this point Fabiano got cold feet and began to back down. All right, all right. There was no need for a fuss. If he had said something wrong, he was sorry. He was ignorant; he had never had any learning. He knew his place; he wasn't the cheeky kind. He was just a half-breed. He wasn't going to get into any arguments with rich people. He wasn't bright, but he knew how to show people proper respect. . . . The boss calmed down and Fabiano backed out of the room, his hat dragging on the brick floor.[1]

The plight of Fabiano seemed typical of millions of other peasants. For them, housing was primitive, the diet inadequate, health and sanitary conditions abysmal, and education generally nonexistent, and where existent, substandard.

Josué de Castro entitled his study of the depressed agricultural region of northeastern Brazil *Death in the Northeast* and concluded, "The Northeast of Brazil remains a region of crisis where hunger and misery, instead of gradually subsiding, increase in intensity." In that huge region, scarcely 4 percent of the population owned most of the land. Poverty, hunger, social waste, illiteracy, and chronic illness predominated. Life expectancy barely reached 30 years, a child died every

[1]Graciliano Ramos, *Barren Lives* (Austin: University of Texas Press, 1969), pp. 93–95. Reprinted with the permission of the publisher.

42 seconds, 85 per hour, 2,040 per day. Even in more developed regions like the Central Valley of Chile, the peasant (known locally as the *inquilino*) led a marginal existence. He dwelt with his family in a one-room mud hut, with earthen floor and thatched roof, without sanitary facilities, running water, or heating. The *patrón* granted him use of a small plot for a garden, and from it came the meager rations for an always hungry family. The caloric intake barely sustained life; malnutrition predominated; death was expected momentarily. Obviously the peasant in Latin America existed rather than lived. The human plight staggered the imagination, but it failed to produce sufficient reforms. Only when it became all too apparent that the changeless countryside delayed modernization of the nation did reformers expand their customary urban perspective to contemplate the rural tragedy.

A modern city could not fully develop engulfed by the rural institutions of the colonial past. The city folks demanded more food at a lower price and the haciendas and fazendas proved their inability to comply. As part of the rural population migrated toward the city, farming needed to become increasingly efficient to feed the growing non-agrarian population. Failure to produce more efficiently necessitated the food imports mentioned above. At the same time, an industrial economy required expanding markets for the manufactured goods. The industrialists saw their capacity to produce far exceed the ability of their compatriots to purchase. The countryside offered little encouragement to the industrial process since the peasants earned little money and often the patrón paid the peasant in kind rather than in currency, a feudal vestige incompatible with modernization. To further expand industrialization required rural reforms. Hemispheric leaders meeting at Punta del Este, Uruguay, in 1961, finally voiced a concern with agrarian problems. They signed a declaration "to encourage . . . programs of comprehensive agrarian reform leading to the effective transformation, where required, of unjust structures and systems of land tenure. . . ." It proved easier to make that declaration than to carry it out.

The depressing reality of the inefficiency of the archaic agrarian sector prompted discussion favoring the reform of the land structure. Until the 1950s, Mexico remained the single nation which had broken the colonial land patterns and structures to experiment with the redistribution of land and with communal landholdings. Mexico made many errors, from which both the Mexicans and other Latin Americans learned. It became apparent that just to divide up the land worked to the disadvantage not only of the national economy but also of the peasant since it deprived him of some necessary services formerly provided by the patrón. The peasant to be transformed into an independent farmer required much more than just a piece of land; he needed advice, instruction, seeds, equipment, and credit, the absence of which doomed reform to failure. Nor was it desirable to split the estates into plots too small to be productive. Such a reform would simply substitute the problems of minifundia for those of latifundia. Mexico experimented and over the decades solved many of its agrarian problems. It became increasingly apparent to friend and foe alike of agrarian reform that after 1940 Mexico's experiment succeeded. Agricultural production rose. Also, and far more importantly, the Mexican peasants enjoyed a higher standard of living. They formed a new market for transistor radios, toothpaste, shoes, bicycles, wristwatches, and other products of the burgeoning consumer industries. Mortality rates among them fell. Life expectancy lengthened by as much as 50 percent. In some favored areas, the peasants enjoyed those social services previously reserved for urban dwellers.

Torn by many considerations, reformers proposed a variety of new solutions to the old land problem, not all of them germane. In those nations where land reform was actually taking place, the most common procedure was to divide the land into units considered economically viable and distribute them to the peasants. Mexico in many instances delivered individual land grants to the peasants but in others returned to the communal landholding patterns of its Indian past, the *ejido*. The government of Fidel Castro in Cuba refused to subdivide the land. The estates taken from individuals or companies were operated by the workers as cooperatives under government supervision. The land reform advocated by President Salvador Allende in Chile in 1971 favored the cooperative over individually owned units. Many of the reformers sidestepped the main issue—and thus avoided a direct confrontation with the entrenched landowner class—by proposing the resettlement of peasants in distant unused lands, often the jungles. Those cautious reformers failed to face honestly the question of why the unused lands had never been occupied. The reason was simple: they were marginal at best, of no value at worst. The lands either were a long distance from the markets or possessed low fertility of soil or suffered from bad weather or were plagued with an unhealthy climate or any combination of the above. In short, there were excellent reasons why the conquistadores, the Church, the landed aristocracy, or the government had never taken possession of those lands. To use scarce capital in opening up such marginal territory was questionable economics. Rather, it seemed wiser that first efforts and available capital should go toward making the high-potential land already accessible to ready markets produce more than it did. Latin America's rural problem, with few exceptions, has not been so much the need for more land as the necessity to exploit more intensely and productively the land already available.

Many factors delayed the process of land reform. Obviously the large landowners refused to consider any plan, automatically labeling such efforts as communist. Even the progressive middle class found it difficult to move from the splendid sounding theories of land reform to practice. The peasants themselves—at least through the 1940s and with the exception of Mexico—remained passive, inarticulate, and disorganized. Not until 1955 were the first Peasant Leagues founded in Northeastern Brazil. In truth, land reform was far too radical a process for many Latin Americans to embrace. In taking land from one group and bestowing it on another, the reform would give property to a new group, and of course status, prestige, and dignity would accompany ownership so that the new group would possess the potential for power, the potential to challenge other interest groups and iniquitous institutions. For that reason, those in power, with a few exceptions which will be examined later, have paid lip service on occasion to land reform but generally have shied away from actually enacting and implementing it.

Those who would change society continued to lavish their attention and energy on industrialization, regarded by ever increasing numbers of people as the key to modernization. The blow the Depression dealt agriculture in the 1930s made industrialization seem all the more desirable, even inevitable. The jolt cleared away much of the former resistance to industrialization. Falling prices and demands for primary products precipitated an acute balance of payments crisis. Latin America possessed scant funds to meet its foreign debts or interest payments abroad or to import the manufactured items to which it had become so accustomed. At that point, economic nationalists argued cogently that industrialization would diversify the economy, prevent scarce foreign exchange from being spent abroad for what could be produced at home, and raise national self-sufficiency. Sympathetic to those arguments and compelled to experiment, many of the governments enacted laws favorable to the encouragement of local industry: higher tariffs, multiple exchange rates, import controls, subsidies, tax privileges, etc. By reducing foreign competition, the governments made investment in local industry more profitable and hence more attractive. Industrial growth during the 1930s was impressive. In Argentina, between 1911 and 1935, some 31,000 industries were established—a third of that number in the 1931–35 period. Economists cite 1933 as the year in which the rhythm of Brazilian industrialization accelerated. In the five years thereafter, the volume of industrial production increased by approximately 40 percent and the value of industrial production, taking into account monetary devaluation, went up 44 percent, making industrial production some 60 percent greater in value than the combined output of livestock and agriculture. All statistics indicated that industry was growing at a much faster rate than agriculture.

Industrialization throughout Latin America shared a number of characteristics in common. It tended to concentrate in only a few cities in each of the countries. Most of the manufacturing was done in small plants employing only a few workers. The process depended heavily on hand labor. The level of capitalization remained low and so did the output, mainly because of the limited markets. The factories produced principally consumer items. In certain countries—notably Argentina, Brazil, and Mexico—the consumer industries became so well developed that it was no longer necessary to import those items. On the negative side, limited and well-protected local markets tended to encourage inefficiency in production. Although textiles and foodstuffs constituted the most important segment of the growing volume of manufacturing, a slight shift toward capital goods became noticeable in the largest countries by the late 1930s. As the national industries increasingly bought more local raw products and sold their finished goods in the local markets, it became apparent that the economy depended less on export than it had in the past. In short, the industrializing process was modifying the economic structure of the nation. Almost all manufacturing was done for the local market; few items were exported and manufactured goods still do not make a significant contribution to Latin America's exports. Unfortunately the Latin Americans never fully exploited their region's rich natural resources and sent many of their raw products abroad for processsing.

Required by the economic distress of the 1930s, the governments began to play a more active role in the economy. The state became a major economic decision-maker. Adopting the concept of long-range planning, the state increasingly supervised national development. Where necessary, the government directed, operated, or owned certain industries. Within less than a quarter of a century, the Brazilian government came to dominate the vital fields of oil, electricity, and steel. Steel, considered a key industry for serious industrialization, demonstrated the new attitude of the Latin American governments toward planning of and participation in the economy. President Getúlio Vargas of Brazil, encouraged by the military and the nationalists, ordered plans drawn up in 1940 for a steel mill—Brazil possessed the largest known iron reserves in the world, although the country was deficient in coal. He organized the National Steel Company the following year which at once initiated work on a steel plant at Volta Redonda, situated between Brazil's principal cities, São Paulo and Rio de Janeiro. The mill began to operate in 1946. By 1955, Volta Redonda was producing 646,000 tons of steel, an annual output doubled by 1963. At the same time, the Mexican government was in the process of expanding national production of steel by increasing the capacity of the mill at Monterrey and building a new plant at Monclova, which became the largest integrated iron and steel producer in Latin America. Argentina and Chile began to operate their own steel mills in the 1940s.

The period following World War II witnessed a surge of industrialization, particularly during the years 1945–57. The trend toward the production of capital goods increased, despite the continuing speculative nature of industrialization. Native capitalists continued to prefer quick and high profits over a definite and limited period of time rather than long-term, slow-growing investments, the type needed to really promote the production of capital goods. Partially for that reason, the governments became ever more involved in financing larger and more risky industries. Brazil amply illustrated the growing importance of industry within the economy. Whereas in 1939, the industrial sector provided 17.9 percent of the national income, it furnished 35.3 percent by 1963. The trends toward government planning of and participation in the economy became characteristic of Argentina after Juan D. Perón assumed the presidency in 1946. His first Quinquennial Plan aimed to accelerate industrialization and to promote greater economic independence. Hence, it fell well within the confines of the economic nationalism engulfing Latin America at the time. A National Economic Council oversaw the economic progress of the nation and a Trade Promotion Institute encouraged exports. The government began to take over banks, railroads, and the telephone and telegraph system. Traditional British influence over the economy waned. Table 2 indicates Argentina's progress toward industrialization during the Perón years.

All nations of Latin America did not participate equally in the industrial surge. Industrialization concentrated in a few favored geographical areas. At the end of the 1960s, three nations, Argentina, Brazil, and Mexico, accounted for 80 percent of Latin America's industrial production. In fact, more than 30 percent of the total factory production was squeezed into the metropolitan areas of Buenos Aires, Mexico City, and São Paulo. Five other nations, Chile, Colombia, Peru, Uruguay, and Venezuela, produced 17 percent of Latin America's industrial goods, leaving the remaining 3 percent of the manufacturing to the 12 other republics.

TABLE 2   Argentine Progress Toward Industrialization

	1946	1954
Number of industrial establishments	84,985	148,363
Number of workers	889,032	1,007,270
Wages and Salaries (in thousands of pesos)	2,462,742	13,713,769
Value of production (in thousands of pesos)	14,793,358	76,586,271

Following World War II, foreign investment in Latin America rose spectacularly, showing a decided preference for petroleum, manufacturing, mining, and public utilities. United States investments—by far the most predominate—reached their peak in 1963 at which time direct private investment totalled nearly $9 billion, while total United States assets in the area exceeded $15 billion. Foreign capital controlled a disproportionate share of the industries in each nation. For example, the extent of foreign investment in Brazilian industry in 1970 was substantial: approximately 22 percent of the capital of all industrial firms, or 32 percent of medium and large firms. The proportion of foreign ownership ranged from 100 percent in the automotive industry and 82 in pharmaceuticals to 55 percent in the production of machinery and chemicals and 32 percent in the processing of foodstuffs. Of the fifty-five largest companies operating in Brazil during the 1960s, thirty-one were foreign-owned. The attraction of course was high profits. Indeed, investors received more return than they could expect from similar investments in the United States, Canada, or Western Europe. United States investors earned 11.1 percent on the book value of their Brazilian operations in 1969, a drop from 12.1 percent earnings in 1968. Argentine industry likewise felt the influence of foreign capitalists. Of the ten principal industrial firms operating in Argentina in 1971, eight were owned by foreigners and the remaining two by the government. Foreigners owned more than half of the private banks in that country. In Mexico, too, foreign economic influences remained considerable. Well over $1 billion of United States direct investment concentrated in Mexico, and over two-thirds of that was in manufacturing. It has been asserted that in the early 1960s, foreign interests—predominantly those of the United States—controlled 28 percent of the 2,000 largest companies in Mexico. Furthermore, their influence was clearly evident in another 14 percent. Despite, then, impressive industrial growth and diversification in Latin America, the area still relied heavily on foreign interests and capital.

Industrialization has sown the seeds of new problems for Latin America. For one thing, it funneled wealth increasingly into the hands of a few. In Buenos Aires, for example, 0.2 percent of the industrial proprietors controlled 65 percent of the production and employed 50 percent of the workers at the end of the 1960s. Further, the ties between industrialists and large landowners seemed to be closer than most people either realized or cared to admit. It can be misleading to think of separate landowning and industrialist classes because in many instances —although it must be emphasized not in all—the two groups are one and the same or the overlapping of the two may be partial. Thus, one could observe—and this was as true in the larger and more prosperous nations such as Argentina and Brazil as it was in the smaller nations—

a growing industrial concentration in the hands of a few alongside a great concentration of land ownership, and very often, the same men playing the dual role of landowner and industrialist. Such an interrelation of interests confused efforts made in favor of reform.

One significant consequence of industrialization has been the growth of the better defined urban proletariat class. During the twentieth century the growing number of industrial workers struggled to organize and in some instances exerted political influence in the process. In a few cases they provided a power base for populist governments. A populist government in Latin America depended for its political support on the "popular" masses, most particularly on the urban, industrial proletariat. Modern communications—especially the radio—permitted the populist leaders to appeal directly to the masses.

Labor organization began in the nineteenth century. Possibly the first trade union in Latin America was the Printing Trades Workers' Union founded in Buenos Aires in 1853, more a mutual-aid society during its first decade than anything else. By the 1880s, the trade-union movement gained momentum in Argentina, and in 1890 the workers established their first central labor organization. At about the same time labor unrest stirred Chile, but it was not until 1909 that Chilean workers banded together to form the Chilean Workers' Federation, the country's first central labor group. The origins of the Mexican labor movement dated from the late 1860s, and the movement grew rapidly during the next two decades. Porfirio Díaz eventually viewed organized labor as a threat and made repeated efforts to thwart further growth. The government's bloody repression of the workers' strike in 1907 solidified labor's opposition to the aging caudillo. In that year, workers in the textile mills of Puebla struck for higher wages, fewer working hours, compensation for injuries, pensions, and an end to chit payments and wage discounts. Violence erupted, and Díaz dispatched troops to end the strike. They shot down hundreds of the workers, a few of the many workers sacrificed to the continuing struggle of labor to raise its voice and exert some power. Despite handicaps and hardships, by 1920, trade unions existed in most of Latin America.

The emergence of a conscious labor program of goals and the organization of the workers into unions encouraged new coalitions to challenge the traditional elite and in some cases to exercise power. In Uruguay, Batlle encouraged labor organization and favored the workers with some of the most advanced social legislation of the day. Labor, in turn, enthusiastically supported him. Irigoyen in Argentina, Alessandri in Chile, and Carranza in Mexico were also among the first Latin American presidents to court labor and to rely in part on labor for their support. In return, they conferred some benefits on the working man. Later, labor played even a more prominent role, particularly during the administrations of Getúlio Vargas (1930–45; 1951–54) in Brazil, Lázaro Cárdenas (1934–40) in Mexico, and Juan D. Perón (1946–55) in Argentina, all three of whom qualify, at least in part, as populist presidents. Vargas clearly understood the importance of the growing proletariat in Brazil. Almost at once after taking power in 1930, he created the Ministry of Labor which served as the means by which the government dealt with the workers. By careful maneuvering, he used the urban workers to help check the formerly overwhelming power of the traditional elite. The workers pledged their support to him in return for the benefits he granted them. With a highly paternalistic—and some say demagogic—flourish, Vargas conceded to the workers more benefits than they had previously obtained through their own organizations and strikes. A decree ordered the Ministry of Labor to organize the workers into new unions under governmental supervision. By 1944, there were about 800 unions with a membership exceeding half a million. The government prohibited strikes but did establish special courts and codes to protect the workers and to provide redress for their grievances. Under the government's watchful eye, the unions could and did bargain with management. Further, Vargas promulgated a wide variety of social legislation favoring the workers. He decreed retirement and pension plans, a minimum wage, a workweek limited to 48 hours, paid annual vacations, maternal benefits and child care, educational opportunities and literacy campaigns, safety and health standards for work, and job security. In short, Vargas offered to labor in less than a decade the advances and benefits which the proletariat of the industrialized nations had agitated for during the previous century. Little wonder, then, that the urban working class (for the benefits did not extend into the rural areas) rallied to support the president. In 1945, Vargas created the Brazilian Labor Party, which frankly and aggressively appealed to the urban worker. Small at its inception, the party grew impressively in size and strength during the following two decades, while the other two major parties declined in strength.

Simultaneously Cárdenas wooed the Mexican urban laborers in order to counteract the growing influence of the conservatives in the government. He won their endorsement for his revolutionary government. To strengthen labor, he advised the workers to organize into one monolithic confederation. To that end, he oversaw the establishment of such an organization which in 1936–37 included most of the nation's unionized labor. At the same time, he restructured the official governmental party so that it rested on four "sections" of support, one of which was labor. Organized labor thus encouraged and directed by the government, achieved an unprecedented importance in Mexico. Both sides benefited. The standard of living of the workers rose and so did their sense of dignity as active participants in the national government. The government intervened to settle most labor-management disputes in favor of labor. Further, the workers assumed management of the National Railways Company and cooperated in the management of the petroleum industry. With the encouragement of Cárdenas the labor movement reached its highest degree of organization, greatest prestige, and strongest influence. Cárdenas profited from the vigorous and loyal labor organization. Partially as a result of the strength labor lent him, he triumphed over party and political rivals, promulgated the revolutionary reforms he favored, and improved his position in bargaining with foreign economic interests and local industrialists.

Perón, too, based much of his political power on an alliance with labor. Previous Argentine governments had done little to favor the workers despite the industrial surge and the expansion of labor's ranks. Perón perceived the potential of the working class and utilized it after the military coup d'etat of 1943 to project himself into power. As Secretary of Labor in the new government he lavished attention in the form of wage increases and social legislation on the hitherto neglected workers, who responded with enthusiastic endorsement of their patron. During the two years Perón held the labor portfolio, the trade unions nearly quadrupled in size. Perón adroitly manipulated the labor movement so that only leaders and unions beholden to him were officially recognized. When military leaders, suspicious and resentful of the growing power of Perón, imprisoned him in October of 1945, workers from around the country angrily descended on the center of Buenos Aires and paralyzed the capital. The military, devoid of any visible popular support, immediately backed down and freed Perón. With the full backing of labor, he easily won the presidential elections of 1946 and his followers dominated the new Congress.

During his decade of government, Perón relied heavily on the approval and support of organized labor for his strength. His wife, Eva Duarte de Perón, handled at least in part the relations of the government with the workers. She was instrumental in making the labor unions subservient to the ambitions of her husband. However, it would be too simplistic to lament the demise of the union's freedom. In truth, they never had enjoyed much liberty—at best tolerance—under previous governments, and certainly prior to Perón they had gained few victories for their rank and file. The unions did compromise their liberty but they did so in return for undisputed advantages and for a greater feeling of participation in government than they had ever felt under the elitist leaders who had governed Argentina, with, of course, the notable exception of the middle-class government of Irigoyen. Perón's nationalist rhetoric cheered the workers, who identified more closely with his programs than those of any previous government. They rallied behind him to taunt the foreign and native capitalists who they believed had exploited them. Perón, like the other populist leaders of the time, exuded a charismatic charm. One North American visitor, G. S. Fraser, recounted his impression of Perón in the following terms:

> As the doors were flung open, the General came forward to greet us, shaking each of us heartily by the hand. He looks to be a man in his late thirties. . . . He is not tall, but very broad and strong. He has a very likeable, slightly shy smile. . . . His eyes are weary and tired. . . . He managed to put us at our ease, to build up a coherent case for himself, and as a man to capture our sympathy. He had a frank and open way with him and gave us an impression, new to us in our discussions of Argentina politics, of practical common sense. He has a certain disarming ordinariness, and knows how to make what he had been doing sound the natural thing to do. He is genial. One is aware of unusual energy and capacity, and also, after a time, of certain limitations. The limitations spring, I think, from the fact that he is a professional soldier, though with a political intelligence quite unusual in soldiers. But he thinks of the morale of the regiment; and he thinks of the citizen as existing for the state, as the soldier exists for the regiment. Again, his tactics are military rather than strictly political ones; he thinks of dividing and dispersing the opposition, not of finding some basis of agreement with it. He has no sympathy, that is to say, for what one calls in a wide sense the liberal attitude of life.

Perón never lost the support of the working class. His fall from power in 1955 resulted from certain economic errors he had made, a loss of Church approval, the firm and increasingly effective opposition of the traditional oligarchy, and—most importantly—the withdrawal by the military of its previous support. The middle class and the elite rejoiced in his fall; the event stunned great multitudes of the masses who had given their leader enthusiastic support in return for more benefits and dignity than they received from all the previous governments combined.

The faith of the working classes in the Peronist doctrines did not disappear. His supporters constituted for a decade and a half thereafter the single largest cohesive political group in Argentina. Despite all the handicaps subsequent governments imposed on them, they continued to make impressive showings at the polls. As late as 1965, the Peronists won more than a quarter of the seats in the Chamber of Deputies.

Obviously such populist governments as the Perón one so well represents found little favor among Latin America's elite, both the traditional elite and those who, thanks to greater social fluidity in the twentieth century, had recently achieved that exalted status. They resented any erosion of their power from below. Increasingly the middle class, as a group, seemed frightened by the prospects of populist government and consequently tended to align with the elite. Certainly the previous arrangements between urban labor and the middle class, noticeable in some instances during the first decades of the twentieth century, disintegrated as the middle class became apprehensive of a threat, real or imagined, to their status and ambitions from labor. By mid-twentieth century, identifying more with the elite against whom they had once struggled but whose life-style they incessantly aped, the middle class when forced to select between the masses and change and the elite and the status quo tended to opt for the latter.

The new power struggles took place in the cities, which were playing an ever more preponderant role in the development of Latin America. In the decades after World War II, the cities in Latin America grew at a faster rate than those in any other part of the world. Latin America became more urbanized than the world as a whole. During the decade 1945–55, the urban populations of seven countries—Brazil, Mexico, Bolivia, Peru, El Salvador, Panama, and the Dominican Republic—increased approximately 55 percent, while those in another four countries—Cuba, Chile, Venezuela, and Uruguay—went up nearly 45 percent. Since 1955, the rate of concentration of the population in the cities continued to climb rapidly. During the 1960s, the rate of urban growth averaged 4.5 percent annually—or three times the rate of urban growth in the United States. The population surge of Colombia's four major cities, indicated in Table 3, exemplified the broader trend throughout Latin America.

Uruguay, where more than 80 percent of the population lives in cities, has become the most urbanized Latin American republic. Three nations, Argentina, Chile, and Uruguay rank among the 15 most urbanized nations of the world. Much of the urban population concentrates in the capitals, which with few exceptions are disproportionately large. Fully one-half of Uruguay's population lives in Montevideo; one-third of all Argentines reside in metropolitan Buenos Aires; one-quarter of the Chileans, Cubans, and Panamanians inhabit their capital cities; in Peru, Venezuela, Paraguay, and Costa Rica, one-fifth of the populations live in the capitals. As of 1970, over 50 percent of Latin America's population lived in cities of 2,000 or more inhabitants. The countryside now depends on the cities, a complete reversal of historical roles.

TABLE 3   Growth of Colombia's Major Cities, 1951–70 (in thousands)

	1951	1964	1970
Bogotá	720	1,700	2,400
Medellín	360	770	1,030
Cali	280	640	870
Barranquilla	280	500	620

Urban population growth can be attributed in part to the continuing high birthrate. Between 1920 and 1960, Latin America witnessed a phenomenal demographic rise, an average of 2.9 percent per year, which amounted to a 126 percent increase. The figure becomes even more impressive when compared to Europe's population growth of only 23 percent for the same period. City and countryside did not share equally in the growth. Better health care and medical facilities in the city meant infant mortality rates were lower and life expectancy higher there than in rural areas. Further, faster urban growth could still be explained in terms of the push exerted by grinding rural poverty on the peasant to move into the city to seek a better life, as well as of the pull exercised by the industries, glitter, and promise of the city. Thus, the statistics for Mexico revealed that between 1930 and 1968, the urban population grew at the rate of 4.5 to 5 percent per year, while the rural population increased by only 1.5 percent per year. That pattern seemed representative of much of Latin America.

As the cities grew in size so did the ranks of the middle class and proletariat. Though always a minority within the total population, those two groups were highly articulate. Their concentration near the seat of government afforded them power disproportionate to their numbers, and they did not hesitate to wield it to aggressively push their goals. At some times and in some countries, those two urban classes had the strength to propel into the presidency men who favored their ambitions. Little wonder then that political power focused ever more sharply on the cities.

For some, taking advantage of the more broadly stratified urban society with the blurred distinctions between classes, the city facilitated social and economic mobility and thus fulfilled its promise of hope. However, for the illiterate, inexperienced, and technically untrained, the city offered little more than misery. Unsuitable for employment in a modern city, they had difficulty finding jobs. Unemployment rates were high. In 1970, Lima had 16 percent of its working-age, male population unemployed; the figure for Barranquilla, Colombia, was 19 percent. Those figures do not take into account underemployment which prevails throughout the area. Many of those who were fortunate enough to find jobs soon discovered that they paid so little that it was a struggle to keep families housed and fed on the pittance. Many became the scavengers of society. An urban family of average income spent 50 percent of its earnings on food, 10 percent on clothing, and 10 percent on transportation, leaving little to be divided among housing, education, medicine, and other necessities. Little wonder then that slums developed and squatter hovels sprang up in all major Latin American cities. The squatter settlements, known as *villas miserias* in Argentina, *favelas* in

Brazil, *callampas* in Chile, *barriadas* in Peru, and *ranchos* in Venezuela, were conglomerations of one-room shanties, where Latin America's most precious resource, its people, wasted away with bloated bellies,
underdeveloped bodies, dysentery, fever, and myriad diseases. In 1970,
more than one-third of Latin America's urban population lived in sub-
marginal housing. On the average, 40 percent of the inhabitants of the
capital cities lived in "spontaneous settlements," a euphemism for
squatters' shacks. Contemporary Caracas offers a sobering example: of
its 2 million inhabitants 800,000 inhabit *ranchos* (shanties). Oscar Lewis
described the miserable existence of the urban poor in several of his
books. Depicting life in one slum of Mexico City, he wrote:

> The *Panaderos vecindad* where she [Guadalupe] lived consisted of a
> row of fourteen one-room adobe huts about 10 by 15 feet, built along the
> left side and across the back of a thirty-foot wide bare lot. The rentals
> for the huts were from $1.60 to $2.40 a month. The average monthly
> income in the *vecindad* was $8.40. Guadalupe and her first husband,
> Ignacio, were among the very poorest, with a combined monthly income
> of only $5.20. When she died, Guadalupe's worldly possessions were worth
> only $121.13.
>   The empty lot was enclosed on two sides by the walls of adjacent
> brick buildings and in front by a recently built brick wall with a narrow
> open entrance that leads to the courtyard. The only pavement in the
> yard was a walk of rough stone slabs laid by the tenants themselves, in
> front of the apartments. Five of the dwellings had makeshift sheds, con-
> structed by setting up two poles and extending the kitchen roofs of tar-
> paper, tin, and corrugated metal over the low front doorway. The sheds
> were built to provide a dry, shady place for the artisans who lived and
> worked there. Piles of equipment, tin, bundles of waste, steel strips, wire,
> nails and tools, kept on old tables and benches cluttered the covered
> space. Toward the rear of the yard, two large cement water troughs, each
> with a faucet, were the sole source of water for the eighty-four inhabitants.
> Here the women washed their dishes and laundry and bathed their chil-
> dren. In the back of the lot two broken-down stinking toilets, half cur-
> tained by pieces of torn burlap and flushed by pails of water, served all
> the tenants.
>   The rest of the lot, strewn with stones and filled with unexpected
> holes, was criss-crossed by clotheslines held up by forked poles. In the
> daytime, the lot was filled with children in ragged clothing and ill-fitting
> shoes, or barefoot, playing marbles or running between the lines of
> laundry, heedless of the warning shouts of the women. Children, barely
> able to walk and still untrained, sat or crawled in the dirt, often half-
> naked, while their mothers watched them from where they were working.
> In the rainy season the yard became muddy and full of water so that it
> sometimes flooded the low dwellings.[2]

[2]Oscar Lewis, "A Special Supplement: A Death in the Sanchez Family," *The
New York Review of Books,* September 11, 1969, p. 31. Reprinted with the permission of Random House, Inc.

In such misery lived tens of millions of Latin Americans who drew little satisfaction from the industrialization and modernization altering certain aspects of the life of their nations. Those impoverished masses witnessed the unfolding of history but still did not exercise their potential to shape it.

A FLIRTATION WITH DEMOCRACY

The rhetoric to which the United States marched into World War II wafted throughout the rest of the hemisphere. The Latin Americans in general supported the effort of the United States in the struggle against the Axis powers. At a special conference in Rio de Janeiro in January of 1942, the representatives of the various republics voted to recommend that their governments break diplomatic relations with the Axis nations. All complied, although Chile delayed any action until January of 1943 and Argentina until March of 1945. Brazil dispatched troops to fight in the Italian campaign and Mexico sent an air squadron to the Pacific. The war brought Latin America and the United States into even closer contact than previously. Trade with Europe being difficult if not impossible during the war years, the economies of North and South America meshed more intimately than ever before.

The Allies' march to victory in Europe in 1944 marked democracy's triumph over dictatorship and the consequences shook Latin America. Questioning why they should support the struggle for democracy in Europe and yet suffer the constraints of dictatorship at home, many Latin Americans rallied to reform their own political structures. A group of prominent Brazilians opposed to the continuation of the Vargas dictatorship mused publicly, "If we fight against fascism at the side of the United Nations so that liberty and democracy may be restored to all people, certainly we are not asking too much in demanding for ourselves such rights and guarantees." The times favored the demise of dictatorship in Latin America. In 1944, Fulgencio Batista fell in Cuba, Hernández Martínez abandoned office in El Salvador, and Jorge Ubico fled Guatemala; in 1945, four strongmen, Alfonso López Pusmarejo of Colombia, Manuel Prado of Peru, Isaías Medina of Venezuela, and Getúlio Vargas of Brazil, were forced from office. A wave of freedom of speech, press, and assembly engulfed much of Latin America. New political parties emerged to represent broader segments of the population. Democracy, always a fragile plant anywhere, seemed ready to blossom throughout Latin America. Certainly nowhere for the previous century and a half had more homage been paid to the virtues and trappings of democracy than in Latin America, and, yet, the reality had seldom been realized. A functional democracy was difficult in a

society which had still not integrated all its members. Even of those included in the mainstream of national life, few could vote. In the presidential elections of Brazil prior to 1930, never more than 3 percent of
the population cast a ballot. Prior to World War II few women and
few illiterates voted. Power struggles among the elite took little account
of the desires of the masses. Democratic experience and tradition were
limited. The patterns of authoritarian rule and change of government
by coup d'etat, once set, were difficult to alter. But for about two decades after World War II, there seemed to be a genuine movement toward the democratization of Latin America. Brazil provided an interesting case study which in its broadest interpretation typifies the fate
of the democratization process in much of contemporary Latin America.

The Brazilian military quietly removed Vargas from office in 1945
and guaranteed free elections. Three major, national political parties
formed representative roughly of left, center, and right. A constituent
assembly prepared a new constitution, promulgated in 1946, which provided all the safeguards for a democratic republic. Although the military did intervene in politics between 1946 and 1964, in 1954, 1955, and
1961, the officers retired at once, leaving the government in the hands
of civilians, and the democratic process continued. The elections of
1945, 1950, 1955, and 1960 were totally free. Different parties won the
presidency and there was a peaceful, democratic transfer of power. All
regarded the elections as generally honest. An elaborate system of electoral courts removed the control of the elections from those in power
and guaranteed the voters complete freedom at the polls and an accurate tabulation of the votes cast. The electorate steadily increased in
size. Illiterates were still excluded from the voting rolls, disenfranchis-
ing at least half the population over 18 years of age. Nonetheless, the
percentage of the population registered to vote increased from 16 percent in 1945 to 25 percent in 1962. The number of voters climbed
rather steadily during that period at approximately 20 percent every
four years. Two new groups, the urban proletariat and the industrial
middle class, took important positions in the political spectrum. The
vocal urban groups created a lively public opinion which the governments increasingly heeded. Further, the judicial system as it evolved
under the Constitution of 1946 provided another bulwark for nascent
Brazilian democracy. Elaborate constitutional safeguards promoted a
judicial independence unique in Latin America. The Federal Supreme
Court had jurisdiction to rule on the constitutionality of all legislation,
federal, state, or local. Although the bench never exercised the power
of its counterpart in the United States, it did inhibit, check, and reverse
arbitrary actions of the executive and legislature. All indications were
that Brazil's experiment with democracy was succeeding.

Throughout Latin America, the democratization process, in general terms, followed a similar pattern. Two crucial tests for democracy were whether the elections were free and whether the president left office at the end of his constitutionally prescribed term. Although the presidents continued to wield considerable power, they were limited to a definite period of office, a maximum of six years, and seldom permitted to run for immediate reelection. In a surprising number of cases —Ecuador provided a pleasant example in the 1950s—the constitutional mechanism functioned more effectively than it had in the past. Peaceful and honest elections were held and the results acknowledged by all candidates. In many cases, presidents quietly turned over their sashes of office after serving their legal terms of office.

The number of electors increased. Only Brazil, Chile, Colombia, and Peru continued to exclude illiterates. As the democratization process widened the base of political participation, it counted on the more active participation of women, first in the elections and soon thereafter in the government. The woman played a major, albeit unsung, role in the development of Latin America. For centuries, women of the lower classes worked side by side with men in the field, tended shop, bartered in the markets, and handled the minor duties of commerce. They bore primary responsibility for raising children. The more privileged households offered their women greater opportunity for education and a fuller social life. Still, they dedicated much of their time to directing the management of the home and caring for the children. The stories of the seclusion of Latin American women may be overly exaggerated. In the pages of her diary, Frances Calderón de la Barca frequently mentioned the presence and participation of upper-class Mexican women at the social events in the early 1840s. Generally she regarded them as charming, elegantly dressed, and well educated. She lauded the family life of the Mexican elite as exemplary. Sir Horace Rumbold, an English resident of Buenos Aires in 1880–81, observed that Argentine women of each succeeding generation in the nineteenth century received a better education. At parties, dances, and dinners, the younger women entered fully into the conversation, exhibiting wit, intelligence, and humor, a contrast to the older women present. Sir Horace concluded, "The women of the higher classes here certainly strike one at once as decidedly superior to the men."

Women participated in most facets of Latin American life. Sor Juana Inez de la Cruz, the Mexican poetess of the seventeenth century, is still considered to be one of the major voices of poetry in the Spanish language, a position she shares with the twentieth-century Chilean poetess Gabriela Mistral. The independence movements boasted of their heroines, such as Maria Dolores Bedoya de Molina of Guatemala and

Josefa Ortiz of Mexico. Paraguayan women shared in the hardships and struggles of the War of the Triple Alliance. For several generations after the tragic war, which nearly decimated the male population (probably less than 28,000 adult males survived the war), Paraguay depended upon the women to keep the nation developing. The absence of men in Asunción astounded an English visitor in the 1880s who saw only women buying and selling in the huge municipal market. When the Chilean males marched off to fight in the War of the Pacific (1879–83), women occupied many jobs formerly held by men. For example, they became the streetcar conductors in the major cities. The *soldaderas* accompanied the armies of the Mexican Revolution and played significant roles in that bloody struggle. On occasion women managed the huge estates and plantations. In his masterpiece *Doña Bárbara* (1929), the Venezuelan novelist Rómulo Gallegos created such a female farmer as the chief protagonist. Strong in character, determined, she managed a large ranch on the plains north of the Orinoco.

The woman took her first steps toward social and political equality with men in the cities where the traditional patriarchal families dissolved. Women took jobs in factories and offices and entered the professions. Teaching was the first profession conquered by Latin American women. By the end of the nineteenth century, it was common to find them in charge of the classroom. Pioneer feminist fighters, such as Carmela Horne de Burmeister and Julieta Lanteri of Argentina and Paulina Luisi of Uruguay, proclaimed the cause of equality for women. A distinguished physician, Dr. Luisi campaigned during the second decade of the twentieth century for social reforms, including political suffrage. In 1916, Dr. Lanteri, one of Argentina's first women physicians, wrote, "A hope begins to shine on the dark horizon; the awareness of her own value begins to awaken in woman." Brazilian feminists were active too. In 1923, Bertha Lutz founded the Brazilian Federation for Feminine Progress (Federação Brasileira pelo Progresso Feminino), one of the largest women's organizations in Latin America.

Years passed before women received the right to vote. Ecuador in 1929 made voting obligatory for men and voluntary for women. The women of Brazil in 1932, Argentina in 1947, Chile in 1949, and Mexico in 1953 were enfranchised. By the mid-1950s, with a few exceptions such as Paraguay and Nicaragua, women in most of Latin America voted. They soon entered public office. In 1956, for example, Argentina had 7 female senators and 24 female deputies; Brazil had 2 deputies; Chile 2 deputies; Costa Rica 3 deputies; and Cuba 1 senator; while in the United States Congress, there were 1 female senator and 16 female representatives. In 1970, one woman judge sat on the Argentine Supreme Court. The Feminist Party of Uruguay nominated Celica Guerrero de

Chiappa, a professor of education, as its candidate for the presidency in the 1971 elections. Clearly the role of the woman was broadening, although she still encountered ingrained prejudices. For example, in 1970, although 1.6 million Argentine women held jobs, only one out of every 100 had a supervisory or executive position.

Public opinion strengthened, and governments consulted and heeded it more than they had in the past. More often than not, large elements of the working class, middle class, intellectuals, and students advocated and defended democracy. Representatives of those groups formed new political parties whose platforms called for many needed reforms. Two such parties which attracted considerable attention were the Democratic Action Party of Venezuela and the Christian Democratic Party of Chile.

The Christian Democratic Party in Chile, as elsewhere in Latin America, advocated an ideology based on the humanistic writings of the French philosopher Jacques Maritain. Stressing Christian values, the party sought to modernize society and improve the conditions of man. It emphasized reform. Running on the Christian Democratic platform, Eduardo Frei swept into the Chilean presidency in 1964. Advocating democratic and evolutionary change, Frei warned, "Democracy will not be saved by those who, praising it as it now exists, petrify its abuses." His government, meeting with strong opposition in congress, moved by necessity slowly, apparently too slowly. Instead of resettling 100,000 families on land of their own, his goal, Frei managed to bestow farms on only 11,200. He failed to reach his other goals. The inability of the Christian Democrats to fulfill their promises opened the presidential palace to Salvador Allende in 1970, the world's first popularly elected Marxist president.

The Democratic Action Party of Venezuela under the forceful leadership of Rómulo Betancourt was democratic in conviction and mildly leftist in action. It advocated land reform and declared the government's right to expropriate oil properties, both of which, if carried out, promised considerable change for Venezuela. In the elections of 1958, Betancourt won the presidency. Two years later, he promulgated the Agrarian Reform Law. Exempting productive farms up to 370 acres, it expropriated large estates after indemnifying the owners and distributed them among the landless with the goal of making Venezuela self-sufficient in foodstuffs. Thus far, Venezuela is the only Latin American nation to carry out a significant land reform without the accompanying violent revolution. The Democratic Action Party held the presidency through 1968, first under Betancourt and then under Raúl Leoni. In the elections of late 1968, the Christian Democrats triumphed.

The Roman Catholic Church, at some times and in some places, raised an influential voice in favor of democracy and reform. The hierarchy on occasion condemned dictatorship. From the pulpit came some appeals for reform. In 1962 and again in 1963, the National Conference of Brazilian Bishops recommended basic land reforms. Bishops in Colombia, Chile, Peru, Bolivia, and Ecuador also advocated land reforms, as did the Latin American Bishops Conference. Speaking for the reform-minded wing of the Roman Catholic Church in Latin America, Archbishop Mark McGrath of Panama concluded in 1970:

> Their [Latin America's poor] tragedy is not only that they do not have enough to eat, not only that they do not have roofs over their heads, toilet facilities, or enough clothing, or that they are diseased. The tragedy is that they have not been living as full human beings. It is their dignity as human beings which is the heart of the problem.

That the Church intended to do more than just talk was indicated in 1971 in Ecuador. There the hierarchy announced their decision to turn over to 2,000 peasant families about 250,000 acres of the Church's arable land as a demonstration of support for land reform.

Together the forces favoring democratization wielded considerable strength. They needed to since they faced innumerable obstacles, not least of which were unemployment, underemployment, hunger, undernourishment, illiteracy, lethargy, and a legacy of institutions which in no way favored democracy. Democracy faced serious challenges in fragmented societies. The activities of certain groups, totalitarian political parties, ambitious politicians, and the military further retarded and then reversed the democratization process. The democratic experiments which characterized Latin America after World War II reached their apogee in 1959. In that year only four military governments held sway in Latin America, a record low. However, throughout the decade of the 1960s democratic government was challenged and the previous trend reversed as much of Latin America returned to military rule. In the brief span between 1962 and 1964, eight countries fell victim to military takeovers.

Once again it is instructive to look at Brazil as an illustration of how that reversal occurred. Just as the action of the Brazilian military in 1945 had opened the way for the experiment with democracy, so it was the military in 1964 which terminated the experiment. The constitutional ascendancy of Vice-President João Goulart to the presidency in 1961 seemed to signal the triumph of public opinion and the democratization process in Brazil. After a momentary intervention, the military were forced by public opinion to step aside and turn the presidency over to the constitutional authority. Following the populist leadership ideology initiated by his mentor, Vargas, President Goulart promised broad reforms. He loosened Brazil's ties with the United States in a bid for leadership in the Third World. Dedicated to a highly nationalistic program, he persuaded Congress to enact a law limiting profit remittances abroad by foreign companies and encouraged the building of hydroelectric dams in order to challenge foreign control over Brazil's electrical power. He attempted to reform the land structure. Labor unrest, strikes, and inflation disturbed the middle class, which felt its security and well-being were threatened. At that point the middle class allied with the traditional elite in complaint over Goulart's policies. Then, the president made a grave tactical error by appealing to the enlisted men of the armed forces for their support over the heads of their officers. The move alienated the officers who decided to remove the president. The military, cheered on by the elite and the middle class, marched against Goulart and unseated him on April 1, 1964. The generals who have controlled Brazil since then reduced congress and the courts to pliant tools, ruled by decree, purged all their political adversaries, abolished elections, substituted two sterile "approved" political parties for those which had developed in the 1945–64 period, established censorship of all the media, and filled the jails with political prisoners. Brazil's experiment with democracy ended, replaced by an old-fashioned military dictatorship which enjoys the support of a large part of the upper and middle classes.

The whim of the military remains as one of the major threats to democracy in all of Latin America. A highly privileged group, the officers receive excellent salaries and fast promotions, enjoy good housing and free medical care, divert themselves in handsome clubs, and in general partake of a wide variety of benefits. Most of them come from the lower and middle classes, and probably a majority have urban backgrounds. The military provides a splendid means of social mobility. On frequent occasions it has been the avenue from obscurity to the presidency. Although proportionately the size of armed forces in Latin America is small, they are expensive. The military absorbs, on the average, 25 percent of the national budgets, a hefty figure when one realizes that none of them fights a foreign war.

By tradition, the military considers itself the guardian of nationality. Whenever the senior officers agree that the well-being of the nation is threatened, they intervene in politics to eradicate the threat and to control the government for as long as they feel it necessary. Those military interventions can be frequent. One authority on military behavior in Latin America estimated that between 1930 and 1965 the officers staged 44 coups d'etat. Generally the officers see the political left as more dangerous to the nation and intervene most often when radical reforms are imminent. Thus, they tend to favor the status quo over change. On the other hand, there are examples of the military intervening to rescue democracy and to depose dictatorships. Recently some of the ranking military—certainly those in control of Peru and Bolivia in 1970 would be an example—have been mouthing reformist, even revolutionary, rhetoric.

By 1970, the military governed most of Latin America. They held sway in Argentina, Brazil, Bolivia, Paraguay, Peru, Panama, Honduras, Guatemala, and El Salvador. The democratic experiment continued in Costa Rica, Uruguay, Chile, Mexico (countries with a relatively long democratic experience), Colombia, and Venezuela. Under seige, Latin American democracy was receiving very little support from the major democracy in the hemisphere. In outlining United States policy for the 1970s, President Richard Nixon stated with regard to Latin America, "The United States has a long political interest in maintaining cooperation with our neighbors regardless of their domestic viewpoints. We deal with governments as they are." (With the convenient exception of Cuba of course.) The policy was in reality just a continuation of the doctrine followed during the Johnson administration, when the State Department declared in early 1964 that it would not distinguish between dictatorship and democracy.

The inevitable conclusion emerges that democracy has not been a great success in Latin America during the past century and a half. Perhaps democracy's difficulty has been its preoccupation with political formalities and formulas. With that emphasis, the democrats and the democracies they encourage and manage have failed to provide solutions for most of Latin America's major economic and social problems. The democrats have seemed content to apply a veneer of political democracy over institutions unsuitable to a democratic society. They have failed to create social and economic institutions compatible with a political democracy. Overconcern with form and lack of sufficient concern with reform have made most of Latin America's democracies, even when they are functioning at their best, sterile.

THE REVOLUTIONARY OPTION

Much of the change produced by democratization, nationalism, urbanization, industrialization, and modernization proved to be superficial: it affected only a small part of the life of the nations or it touched only a minority of the populations. Often the capital cities took on a veneer of change which did not extend to the rest of the country. In most nations and for major segments of the populations, reforms came too slowly and too ineffectively, if, indeed, they came at all. On four occasions thus far in the twentieth century, Latin Americans dispairing of evolutionary change and reform opted for revolution as a quicker and surer path to change. The Mexican experience has been related; it remains to look at the more recent experiences of Guatemala, Bolivia, and Cuba.

Guatemala, in many respects a microcosm of the problems besetting Latin America in the 1940s, had a population of three million of whom three-quarters were Indian (many did not speak Spanish) and the rest were mestizo. The illiteracy rate topped 75 percent and surpassed 90 percent in some areas. The per capita income was meager, life expectancy low, and nutrition substandard. The few who owned most of the land farmed it inefficiently and allowed much of it to lie fallow. Guatemala exported a few agricultural products, principally bananas and coffee, and remained at the mercy of an international market over which it had no influence, much less control. The taxes rested lightly on the wealthy—property and income taxes provided less than 10 percent of the tax revenue—but heavily on the masses since most of the governmental revenue came from taxes on consumer goods.

A desire to change some of the institutions and patterns which perpetuated the national misery pervaded the small, heterogeneous middle groups within Guatemala City. Intellectuals, the lower ranks of the civil service, students, labor, and young army officers were the principal elements which rose up to throw General Jorge Ubico out of office in 1944 and to terminate the harsh rule he had exercised over the country for 13 years. The new, provisional government encouraged the formation of political parties and guaranteed an honest election. Indeed, Guatemala witnessed one of the first free elections in its history, when in December of 1944, the voters selected by a six to one majority a 42-year-old professor, Juan José Arévalo, the candidate of the National Renovation Party (*Renovación Nacional,* or RN). He looked past the foreign interests and traditional oligarchy which had buttressed the Ubico regime to a new power coalition of peasants and workers, particularly the latter. In promising the nation a change, he categorized his government as one of "spiritual socialism." He announced:

> Guatemala has stopped being a democratic masquerade in order to convert itself into a democracy. Thus, with this new social reality and with this new moral investiture, we can continue without blushing or being abashed. . . . The government of Guatemala is aware of certain prejudices of the social order. The workers and the peasants are seen with distrust, perhaps even with scorn. . . . There has been a fundamental lack of sympathy for the workers. Now we are going to install a period of sympathy for the man who works in the fields, the factories, the shops, and commerce. We are going to re-evaluate civically and legally all the men of the Republic.

A new constitution, promulgated in 1945, regulated Guatemala's experiment with democracy and change. It owed much of its inspiration to the Mexican document of 1917. Like its model, it authorized a land reform and many new rights for labor.

Dependent upon the support of labor, Arévalo lavished attention on the workers. He abolished the discredited forced labor system used by Ubico, created a Social Security Institute, and promulgated an advanced Labor Code. On the books at any rate, the Guatemalan workers enjoyed many of those social benefits which their contemporaries had elsewhere in the world. With the encouragement of Arévalo, labor rapidly unionized, and the president consistently supported the unions in their struggles with the management of the United Fruit Company, the largest foreign company and the most powerful business in Guatemala. Arévalo skillfully used those disputes to stir nationalistic sentiment among Guatemalans, who were quite willing to endorse the charges of foreign exploitation hurled against the American-owned company. The preponderant presence of the foreign concern provided a convenient focal point for nationalist ire, which the leadership of the RN knew how to use for political purposes. Education, too, occupied much of the attention of the government which launched an intensive literacy campaign. During his five years in office, Arévalo headed a government which can be characterized as leftist, progressive, non-Communist, and highly nationalistic.

A mysterious and brutal assassination eliminated Francisco Arana, the most popular candidate to succeed Arévalo in the presidency, and opened the door to power for Colonel Jacobo Arbenz. Leading the RN Party, he received 65 percent of the vote and when Arévalo handed him the sash of office in 1951, Guatemalans witnessed one of the rare instances in their history of the peaceful and legal transfer of presidential power. Arbenz entered the presidency with one major nationalistic goal: to convert Guatemala from a dependent nation with a semi-colonial economy to an economically and thus politically independent nation. His goal harmonized perfectly with that of nationalists then and thereafter throughout Latin America.

As his first step, he sought to transform Guatemala's inefficient, semifeudal economy into a modern, efficient one. To do so required a far-reaching land reform. That step brought him into direct conflict with the powerful landowning oligarchy and the United Fruit Company. Arbenz had a firm legal base for the reform he intended. The Constitution of 1945 declared large estates to be illegal and conferred on the government the power to expropriate and redistribute land. The Agrarian Reform Law of 1952 declared that uncultivated land on estates over

220 acres where less than two-thirds of the estate was under cultivation was subject to expropriation and redistribution. The law provided compensation for expropriated estates. It affected only uncultivated land. The landowning elite immediately and vociferously charged that the reform was communistic. In their eyes, the Arbenz government had become a puppet of Moscow.

In Washington, the State Department watched apprehensively but said nothing until in 1953 the Guatemalan government seized 233,973 acres of unused land claimed by the United Fruit Company, a figure later raised to 413,573. As it had maintained consistently throughout, the Guatemalan government said it intended to put all uncultivated land into use and would make no exceptions, neither for nationals nor for foreigners. The United Fruit Company argued that it needed reserve lands for future use and in case of the destruction of any of its present plantations by a banana disease. The United Fruit had operated in Guatemala for many decades. It received its first concession from the Guatemalan government in 1906, and banana production climbed steadily thereafter. In 1947, Guatemala was the second largest producer of bananas in the world. During that time the economic power of the company multiplied. Not only was it the largest single agricultural enterprise in the country but it owned and controlled the principal railroad and the facilities in the major port, Puerto Barrios. The company had brought many benefits. Its workers enjoyed better housing and medical care than the average Guatemalan laborer. It paid its workers twice the wages of the coffee workers, but then the banana worker produced two or three times the wealth of his counterpart on the coffee plantation. Regardless of any benefits the company might have provided, it was extremely unpopular among the nationalists and vulnerable because it was foreign and exercised too powerful an influence over an economy being challenged as semifeudal and exploitative. As a matter of record, the company paid the Guatemalan government in duties and taxes about 10 percent of its annual profits, a sum regarded by indignant nationalists as far too low.

The State Department rushed to support the claims of the United Fruit Company against the Guatemalan government on the basis that the compensation offered the company was insufficient. Yet, the sum offered equaled the value of the lands declared by the company for tax purposes. At that point, the State Department began to charge that the Guatemalan government was infiltrated with, if not controlled by, Communists. Some critics of United States foreign policy wondered at the motivations of the United States government. They pointed out the close connections between CIA Director Allen Dulles and Secretary of

State John Foster Dulles and the United Fruit Company, a relationship which might have suggested some conflict of interests. The law office of John Foster Dulles had written the drafts of the United Fruit Company's 1930 and 1936 agreements with the Guatemalan government. Allen Dulles had served as president of the United Fruit Company. For that matter, the family of John Moors Cabot, then Assistant Secretary of State for Inter-American Affairs, owned stock in the banana company. As the verbal attacks of the State Department on Guatemala mounted, it became difficult, indeed, nearly impossible, to distinguish its charges from those of the United Fruit Company and both of them sounded remarkably similar to the statements of the native oligarchy. All three manifested a preoccupation with the Communist "menace," but none of them seemed concerned with the abysmal misery on which communism might well feed in Guatemala and other underdeveloped nations in the hemisphere.

Despite the mounting pressure, Arbenz pushed ahead with his program to decrease Guatemala's dependency. He announced the government's attention to build a highway from Guatemala City to the Atlantic coast and thereby end the transportation monopoly of the International Railways of Central America, owned and operated by the United Fruit Company. Further, he decided to construct a national hydroelectric plant. Until that time, foreigners produced Guatemala's electrical power, and the rates charged were among the highest in Latin America.

Nationalist and leftist rhetoric adorned the plans and pronouncements of Arbenz and his political supporters. By 1953, anti-Yankee sentiments proved very popular in governmental circles as well. Local and foreign Communists signified their approval and identified with the Guatemalan goals, but the sentiment for change, nationalist pride, and distrust of the United States were too genuine and too popular to bear out the claim that the Guatemalan people blindly followed Communist leadership. Nonetheless, critics of President Arbenz, principally from the native oligarchy, the United Fruit Company, and the State Department, intensified their accusations that his government had succumbed to Communist pressures. Actually the Guatemalans were enjoying a freedom of speech, assembly, and press to a degree which they rarely had in the century before 1944. Opposition parties thrived. The social legislation of the Arévalo-Arbenz period was not nearly so radical as that enacted in the United States during President Franklin Roosevelt's New Deal or in England under the Labor governments.

The Agrarian Reform Law figured as a major argument in the

charge of communism. However, time has more than exonerated that misquoted law. Opined Thomas F. Carrol of the Food and Agricultural Organization some years later, "Degree 900, the agrarian reform, which had its roots in the Constitution of 1945, is a remarkably mild and a fairly sound piece of legislation." Even the State Department—in 1961 —had to own up to the fact that the law was pretty mild, and what had been labeled "communistic" in 1954 became one of the models approved by the Alliance for Progress in 1961.

By late 1953, the Arbenz government feared intervention from the United States. Pressures and retaliations from the United States had plunged the Guatemalan economy into a tailspin. The State Department embargoed arms sales to Guatemala. Arbenz repeatedly requested arms since he felt his more conservative neighbors, Honduras and El Salvador, were encouraging exiles to prepare an attack on his country. Unable to equip the army with matériel from the United States, the president turned to a source only too eager to comply with the request. On May 17, 1954, a shipment of arms arrived from Poland. To the State Department, its arrival served as final proof that Guatemala had fallen under Communist control. The United States Air Force at once ferried military supplies to Tegucigalpa in order to equip a small army under the command of a Guatemalan army exile, Colonel Carlos Castillo Armas. On June 18, 1954, Armas and approximately 150 men crossed the border into Guatemala. They penetrated about 25 miles and engaged in no significant action. They did not need to. The Arbenz government fell because the army refused to act and the workers were not armed. A series of air attacks on the unarmed capital terrorized the population and broke the morale of the people. Those attacks caused more psychological than physical damage. The planes were furnished by the CIA and flown by United States pilots, as former President Dwight D. Eisenhower revealed in a publicly recorded interview on October 14, 1965. U.S. Ambassador John Peurifoy handled the changing of the government and with the enthusiastic endorsement of Washington installed Castillo Armas in the presidency. In a yes-or-no plebiscite, exactly as Ubico had done before him, Castillo Armas confirmed himself in power. The oligarchy hailed the new chief of state as a national hero. The United Fruit Company rejoiced too. After all, from the hands of the new leader the company received back its formerly confiscated lands. The State Department also approved. In a radio address on June 30, 1954, John Foster Dulles informed the American people of the changes in the Guatemalan government, which prompted him to declare, "The events of recent months and days add a new and glorious chapter to the already great tradition of the American States."

One cannot be sure if the statement was a master stroke of cynicism or satire.

Castillo Armas eradicated whatever traces of communism could be found but in the process also did away with democracy and reform. Guatemala had made an effort to change its institutions inherited from the past. It began with the most tenacious of them: the land structure. But Castillo Armas returned to the former landowners about 1.5 million acres of land which under the 1952 Agrarian Reform Law had been confiscated as idle and distributed to approximately 100,000 peasants—the only case of the reversal of a major land redistribution in Latin America. The experiment with change failed. Under the direction of Castillo Armas and similarly inclined successive chiefs of state, Guatemala returned after 1954 to the patterns of the past. Illiteracy, social injustice, unemployment, a one-crop economy, undernourishment, a large Indian population living outside the control of effective national government, latifundia, a restless military—indeed, the whole catalog of ills of Latin America—characterize the Guatemala of the early 1970s. But Guatemala's urban groups have grown in size; their frustration mounts. Guerrilla attacks on the government and the oligarchy in the city and in the countryside are daily events. In the decade ending in 1971, the undeclared civil war killed between 8,000 and 10,000 persons of every political persuasion. Change is the demand of the new urban generations. If the recent governments, which proudly label themselves democratic, cannot bring change, then a disillusioned generation may well turn to other means to effect it. A reporter from the *Christian Science Monitor* asked one student at the University of San Carlos, "Are you afraid of what communism would do to your country?" The student replied, "Just what would it do? Would it make conditions any worse than they are for 95 percent of the people? Would it take away the few schools we have? Would it make housing worse? I think it would not, and anyway I do not see how conditions could be much worse."

At the same time as Guatemala struggled with revolutionary change, Bolivia, too, chose to experiment with some radical solutions to old problems. Although Bolivia is ten times larger than Guatemala (Bolivia includes 424,163 square miles), they had in the early 1950s approximately the same population. The similarity did not end there. Approximately three-fourths of the Bolivians were Indians, most of whom did not speak Spanish; the rest of the population was mestizo. Illiteracy, undernourishment, sickness, low per capita income, and short life expectancy characterized the population. Starvation was one of the major causes of death. The majority of the population were peasants.

In the cities, particularly the capital, La Paz, dwelt the middle groups and industrial workers, both of which classes were small. Bolivia's political record had been particularly chaotic: during the first century and a quarter of independence something like 125 presidents had sat in the governmental palace. During that period, the economic and social structures continued practically unchanged since the colonial era. Like Guatemala, Bolivia depended on one major export, but unlike the Central American Republic, Bolivia's export was mineral, tin, rather than agricultural.

Bolivia's defeat at the hands of smaller and more impoverished Paraguay in the Chaco War, 1932–35, the major Latin American conflict of the twentieth century, jolted Bolivia from its colonial lethargy. Both nations claimed the Chaco, Bolivia as part of the colonial territory from which it was formed and Paraguay by right of possession. They bickered over it for a century, but when those hinterlands promised to produce oil, the arguments heated up into armed clashes. In the three-year war which followed, the Paraguayans soundly routed their larger foe. The defeat stunned Bolivia, which in its history had surrendered territory to all its neighbors. The humiliation of losing land to its smallest and weakest neighbor sobered the nation and caused anguished soul-searching. The disillusioned middle groups, young army officers, students, and intellectuals turned to socialism and Marxist ideology in hope of discovering some solution to national problems. They laid the blame for the war on international oil companies, claiming that two rival companies pushed Bolivia and Paraguay into war with the hope of obtaining favorable exploitation agreements from the victor. To show its ire, Bolivia confiscated the property of the Standard Oil Company of Bolivia on March 13, 1937, an action antedating Cárdenas' exploitation by a year. The government claimed and proved that Standard Oil had defrauded the state by illegally exporting oil. Colonel David Toro, the president who signed the expropriation order indicated the connection between the Chaco War and the new thought among frustrated Bolivians:

> The political situation and the social and economic problems arising after the Chaco War, whose solution was impossible within the traditional political situations, made necessary the intervention of the Army in defense of the interests and rights of the working class and ex-combatants.
>
> The social doctrine of the new government has been born in the sands of the Chaco, in the trenches where the civilians and military men have shed their blood for the Fatherland, putting at its service the maximum sum of their energies and sacrifices. It is there where such ideology crys-

tallized which today is realized in a revolutionary movement which must not enthrone civilian or military caudillos, but which carries the proposition of demanding the just renovating proposals of social justice.

Bolivian politics took many a turn before those sentiments could be acted upon. Those proposing change found it easier to expropriate a foreign company than to alter national institutions. When Toro attempted to impose a higher tax on the "tin barons" of Bolivia, he found himself bounced from the presidency.

Urban intellectuals under the leadership of Víctor Paz Estenssoro organized the National Revolutionary Movement (Movimiento Nacional Revolucionario, or MNR) in 1941, whose two primary goals were to nationalize the tin mines and to combat international imperialism. The decade of the 1940s was unusually chaotic, even for Bolivia. During those ten years, eight revolutions disturbed the nation and seven different presidents held office. In one four-year period, there were 18 ministers of labor; in another eight-month period, there were eight ministers of finance. The elite on the wildly whirling political carrousel seemed oblivious to the restless discontent welling up in the peasants and workers.

In the presidential election of 1951, as was customary, the government controlled the electoral machinery and the suffrage remained restricted to literate males, about 7 percent of the population. Despite those handicaps, an opposition party, in this case the MNR, won a resounding victory. The government evinced no intention of letting the winner, Paz Estenssoro, take office, and the army seconded that decision. A bloody struggle erupted in April of 1952 in which the MNR seized power by force and placed Paz Estenssoro, the winner at the polls, in office.

President Paz Estenssoro moved at once to implement the first goal of the MNR: to nationalize the tin mines, primary source of Bolivia's wealth. Three Bolivian families owned the mines: Patiño, Hochschild, and Aramayo. Patiño controlled most of the mining. His annual income exceeded that of the national government during any year. In fact, the annual allowance of one of his sons was greater than the government's budget for education. They took most of the profits from mining out of Bolivia in order to live opulently in Europe. Clearly, the mining companies exercised greater power than the government, and no previous government had dared undertake any project or make any major decision without the approval of the Patiños, Hochschilds, and Aramayos, a fact ex-President Toro could attest to. Because nearly the entire population opposed the arrogant power of the three families the expropriation decree proved to be very popular. The government took over the mines without giving any remuneration to the owners. Unfortunately, the price of tin on the world market fell—partially due to the huge quantities of tin the Soviet Union dumped. To guarantee the support of the well-organized and armed miners' unions, the government raised wages and benefits, moves which further threatened the fragile national economy. Not until 1966 did the mines report a profit for the first time since 1952.

Peasant agitation forced the government to turn its attention to land reform, a demand the MNR had been unprepared to meet. If "feudalism" could be a proper adjective to describe rural life in Latin America, it was nowhere more applicable than in Bolivia whose huge rural estates had changed little, if at all, since the sixteenth century. In 1952, 6 percent of the farm owners controlled 92 percent of the land. In that year, the Indian peasants threatened an uprising to seize the land. The specter of a civil war of extermination between the rural masses and the "whites" haunted the new government. Forced to act, Paz Estenssoro promulgated a land reform act in August of 1953, designed to end the extreme concentration of land ownership. Article 30 of the law abolished latifundia, but Article 35 exempted from expropriation large farms on which the owner had made substantial capital investments, used modern farming methods, and personally worked the land. The former owners received virtually no compensation. The government handed out land titles to almost 60,000 heads of family by 1960.

As one immediate result of the reform, the index of agricultural production fell. The period of adjustment with its general confusion, as the Mexican case also proved, is not always beneficial for the economy in the short run. Students of agrarian reform point out that the peasants tend to sell less of their product because they are able for the first time to eat better. Cold statistics also ignore the immeasurable psychological results and benefits for the nation. Land ownership turns peasants into responsible citizens; it bestows dignity reflected in the peasants new pride in self and country. It redistributes power. Fortunately, in Bolivia, the agricultural production index began to rise slowly in the late 1950s and by the mid-1960s had equaled and even surpassed the pre-reform levels.

The MNR turned upon the army, the political arbiter since independence. The senior officers had employed force in an effort to prevent the MNR from legally taking office in 1952. Paz Estenssoro distributed arms to the workers and peasants, whose militias gave the government the force it needed to impose its will. Then the government reduced the military to near oblivion, where it remained throughout most of the 1950s. The military proved its resilience, however, and slowly regained its strength, so much so that it was able to expel the MNR from office in 1964.

After serving his four-year term, Paz Estenssoro turned over the presidency to another MNR stalwart, Hernán Siles, who won the elections of 1956. A term out of office permitted Paz Estenssoro to run again for the presidency in 1960, and the voters enthusiastically endorsed his new bid for office. The free elections and peaceful transfers of power from one president to the next, each of whom served his full legal term, were phenomena novel to Bolivian political life. Unfortunately when election time came around again in 1964, President Paz Estenssoro made the error of tampering with the constitution to permit himself to be reelected, a genuinely unpopular maneuver. The army stepped in, a reversion to its prerevolutionary role, and took the reins of power. Although reform rhetoric has not been lacking in the years thereafter, revolutionary activity has been minimal. The most radical-sounding military government of recent vintage seized power under the leadership of General Juan José Torres in 1970–71. He claimed support from four sectors, the peasants, the workers, the students, and the armed forces, and promised "a popular nationalist government." In May of 1971, President Torres convened a "Popular Parliament," an assembly composed of delegates representing labor organizations, farmers, and leftist parties. His rhetoric favoring change remained unmatched by action. In short, the authentic revolution which the MNR initiated in 1952 went askew with the military coup d'etat in 1964, and for the time being there seems little chance of regaining the former revolutionary momentum. The military overthrow of the 10-month-old regime of Torres in August of 1971 definitely heralded a return to more traditional policies.

The varying reaction of the United States to the two revolutions seems paradoxical. While opposing the course of events in Guatemala and contributing to the overthrow of the Arbenz government, Washington lavished funds, technical aid, and support on the MNR governments of Bolivia. When Paz Estenssoro reached power by revolution in 1952, the State Department cautiously waited three months before extending recognition. President Eisenhower sent his brother Milton on a mission to Bolivia in 1953, a visit which proved to be the turning point in the relations between Washington and the MNR. Showing an unusual flexibility during the John Foster Dulles years, the State Department made the distinction that although the Bolivian revolution might be Marxist, it was not Communist, a distinction which, alas, the State Department has rarely been able to repeat. In short, to Washington officialdom, Paz Estenssoro seemed to offer the only viable alternative to communism in Bolivia, and on that basis, the United

States government granted aid on a generous scale. More U.S. dollars per capita have gone to Bolivia than to any other Latin American nation. During one year, the United States provided up to one-third of the national budget.

The apparent contradiction between United States attitudes towards Guatemala and Bolivia baffles the observer even more when he realizes that the Bolivian solutions were more radical than the Guatemalan. However, Guatemala had the temerity to expropriate property belonging to North American investors, while Bolivia, until seizing the property of the Gulf Oil Company in 1968, confiscated mainly the property of nationals. (North American investments in Bolivian tin and land had been minimal.) Geographically, Guatemala fell within the sphere of immediate United States interest and concern. The proximity of the United States limited Guatemala's options and facilitated intervention. Bolivia, on the other hand, is far removed from the United States, and its isolation complicates intervention, even of the indirect variety. Partially for those reasons, the United States found itself condemning as Communist the reform-minded government of Guatemala, while supporting financially a similar, if not more radical, government in Bolivia.

In 1959, Cuba became the fourth Latin American nation in the twentieth century to choose revolution as the means of changing inflexible patterns inherited from the past. The Cuban situation differed considerably from that of Guatemala and Bolivia. By Latin American standards, Cubans enjoyed a high literacy rate and a very high per capita income. It was an urbanized nation with a large middle class. Nonetheless, Cuba suffered from a number of serious problems. Proximity to the United States—the famous 90 miles—meant that Washington dominated Cuba. Economically, even politically, Cuba depended on the United States, and Washington showed a preference for governments in Havana which complemented international trade rather than instituted reforms at home. Cuba depended on a one-crop export, sugar, for its prosperity, and, as the Depression amply proved, the Cuban economy was as vulnerable as that of Bolivia. Corruption flourished in Havana, often on a spectacular scale. The nation's wealth concentrated in the lively capital and failed to trickle down to the impoverished provinces. Finally, years of dictatorship—Fulgencio Batista had controlled the government firmly but efficiently from 1933 to 1944; his second exercise of power, 1952–59, proved to be more brutal and less efficient—aroused a genuine and deep yearning among the Cubans for liberty.

Fidel Castro, a brash young representative of middle-class students and intellectuals, audaciously challenged the powerful Batista dictatorship, first in his quixotic 1953 attack on an army barracks and then after his "invasion" of 1956 as a very effective guerrilla fighter in the Sierra Maestra Mountains. Castro visualized a reformed Cuba, but in reality offered his compatriots little that was new. His social and economic programs can be traced back to the rhetoric and promises of other reformers in the 1930s and probably before. He said his struggle was to end the latifundia, limit foreign ownership, establish cooperatives, nationalize public services, enact social legislation, spread education, and industrialize the nation. Those programs appealed to broad segments of the Cuban population and stirred the island's nationalism. They echoed the basis upon which Grau San Martín rested his middle-class party in 1935: "nationalism, socialism, anti-imperialism."

What startled both Cubans and the rest of the world was that Castro, after the collapse of Batista on January 1, 1959, carried out his promises. Unlike his predecessors, he mixed action with talk. As a symbol of reform, Castro rode into power on a wave of unprecedented popularity, not only in Cuba but throughout Latin America. He seemed to represent purity over corruption, change over status quo. He captured the imagination of the masses with his panache, his intensity, and his concern with their plight. His nationalism and anti-imperialism immediately brought him into open conflict with the United States. When he felt that the government and businesses of the United States were trying to impede Cuba's revolution, he confiscated approximately $1 billion in North American property and investments and broke relations with Washington. In doing so, Castro ended the direct control of the economy by foreign-owned monopolies. Realizing that his small nation of only seven million inhabitants handicapped with a vulnerable sugar economy could not defy its colossal neighbor alone, Castro turned to the one nation, the Soviet Union, capable of and willing to stand up to the United States and provide Cuba with protection. Moscow was only too delighted to find an ally in the Western Hemisphere. Castro's daring defiance of the United States won for him and the Cuban Revolution admirers among many Latin Americans who found in his charges that "Yankee imperialism" perpetuated the status quo in Latin America enough truth to make them applaud his frankness and boldness.

It became abundantly clear after he assumed power that Castro intended to alter Cuba radically. He announced:

> The only thing that can resolve the problems of hunger and misery in the underdeveloped countries is revolution—revolutions that really change social structures, that wipe out social bonds, that put an end to unnecessary costs and expenditures, the squandering of resources; revolutions which allow people to devote themselves to planned and peaceful work.

He regarded education as one key to the new future. Teacher-training institutes sprang up; in a decade the number of teachers tripled; the number of schools quintupled; young, eager volunteers fanned out into the remotest corners of the island to teach reading and writing. Within a few years illiteracy virtually disappeared. By 1971, nearly one-quarter of the country's eight million inhabitants were in school. Education was free from nursery school through the university. Hospitals were built in remote cities and doctors became available in the countryside for the first time. The health of the nation improved and life expectancy increased. Public housing received attention from the government, and the living conditions of the masses were better than ever before. The government encouraged the arts and painting, dance, literature, cinema, and music flourished. Within the first months in office, Castro focused his attention on the land structure, and in June of 1959 promulgated the Agrarian Reform Law. As it turned out, the confiscated estates, for which no indemnity was paid, were not divided and turned over to the peasants but were worked by the peasants as cooperatives under the management of the omnipotent National Institute of Agrarian Reform.

The traditional power of the old oligarchy, military, and Church vanished; the state, that is, the popular dictatorship of Fidel Castro, filled the vacuum. Eschewing the sterile forms of the democratic farce which had previously characterized Cuban government, Castro claimed his government to be one of the people. To prove his confidence in popular support, he distributed arms to the peasants and workers to defend their new government—and they did. He frequently convoked the people to mass meetings where he sought—and received—their approval. It is all too easy for the sophisticated to scoff at those hectic mass rallies, but to the peasants and workers, neglected or exploited in the past, they provided a participation in the governing process which they previously had not known. It brought them closer to the source of power than they had ever been. In short, most of them were able to identify with the aims and methods of the Castro government. Most of the elite and middle class abhorred the changes which divested them of influence, prestige, and property. They fled Cuba in large numbers to escape the popular socialism which was rapidly changing the Cuba from which they had benefited so much.

Since the Castro experiment remains unfinished, any judgment of it would be premature. Within the larger confines of the development of Latin America, one might make the preliminary assessment that this Revolution is one more attempt by Latin Americans to challenge and change the institutions of the past in an effort to accelerate modernization, to unchain themselves from a colonial heritage and propel themselves into the twentieth century. Certainly it is the most radical experiment with change to date. In assessing the significance of the regime of Fidel Castro, the Swiss economist Pierre Goetschin concluded, "You may think what you like about Cuba, but there is no doubt that the revolution of Fidel Castro was a clear sign that the old order is degenerating and that there is a tremendous desire for change. This is the most notable fact about Latin America today."

Four nations, Mexico, Guatemala, Bolivia, and Cuba, underwent violent revolutions in the twentieth century and tried extreme solutions for nagging national problems. Similarities characterize the four revolutions (although notable differences also distinguish one from the other). All four of the revolutions had in common a desire to modify or eradicate hoary institutions considered incompatible with the drive for modernization. All recognized the importance of land reform in the restructuring of society and set about to radically change the ownership patterns. All were manifestations of intense nationalism. All involved the participation of the masses. All accelerated efforts to educate the masses. All favored one or another form of socialism. All hoped to increase their economic viability and the independence of action of their nations. All favored greater industrialization. All removed from power—at least temporarily—representatives of the old oligarchy.

The fates of the four revolutions varied. The Mexican Revolution succeeded and over the decades became institutionalized. The Guatemalan Revolution was first halted and then reversed. The Bolivian Revolution accomplished much but military intervention after 1964 seems to have slowed or impeded its course. The Cuban Revolution continues.

The United States reacted unsympathetically to three of the four revolutions. It took nearly three decades for Washington to reconcile itself to the new turn of events in Mexico. Washington steadfastly opposed the Guatemalan and Cuban revolutions. In alliance with Guatemalan dissidents, the CIA succeeded in ending the Guatemalan experiment, and in cooperation with Cuban exiles, the CIA—perhaps with its Central American success in mind—later tried (at least once) to remove Castro and blunt the Cuban Revolution. Thus far, its efforts have failed. Only the Bolivian Revolution enjoyed the support of the United States. Geographical isolation of and limited United States investment in that Andean nation probably permitted the State Department a greater latitude of action and flexibility than was possible in the three other cases. At any rate, in that single instance, the United States generously contributed to the cause of change in twentieth-century Latin America.

DISILLUSIONMENT

As has been obvious from the preceding discussions, change in twentieth-century Latin America has been erratic; progress has not always been visible; institutions inherited from the colonial and neo-colonial past have demonstrated a remarkable resiliency. Today's statistics can paint a depressing picture of the region: about two-thirds of a population of 270 million, which increases at the rate of nearly 3 percent per year, are physically undernourished; about one-half of the population are concentrated in 40 urban areas whose slums grow at an awesome rate; the overall illiteracy rate almost reaches 50 percent; about one-half the population suffer from infectious or deficiency diseases; about one-third of the working population remain outside the economic, social, and cultural pale of the Latin American community; the work force grows at a faster rate than the creation of new jobs; roughly 90 percent of the land belongs to 10 percent of the owners, a degree of concentration far greater than that in any other world region of comparable size; annual per capita income remains low, about one-tenth that of the United States. More such statistics could be marshalled, but the point is abundantly clear: Latin America is an area beset with serious social and economic problems. Frustrating is the fact that distressing backwardness persists despite the area's promising potential. Obviously the traditional institutions have done little to solve the problems, while, on the other hand, the change and modernization which have occurred in the last century have had a minimal effect, certainly so on the masses.

The major attempts to bring about change violently, as in Mexico, or peacefully, as in Uruguay, have been at best only partially successful. It is quite correct that the middle class has grown impressively in size and affluence, but at the same time the ranks of the impoverished lower classes have ballooned and their lot is little better than that of their forefathers. It is estimated that approximately two-thirds of the Mexicans do not share in the benefits of economic development. About 1 percent of the gainfully employed population of Mexico receives 66 percent of the national income, while most of the workers receive an income insufficient to satisfy minimal needs. There, as in Uruguay, the actual purchasing power of the workers declined during the decade of the 1960s.

Since past blueprints for change have provided less than satisfactory results, the Latin Americans concerned with change have sought new solutions. Some of the directions that search has taken can be seen in the Guatemalan, Bolivian, and Cuban revolutions. Indeed, the desire for change has appeared and reappeared as the constant leitmotiv of contemporary Latin America. The significance of Fidel Castro is that he represents the most recent and most radical experiment with change. He represents hope for the tens of millions of Latin Americans who were hopeless.

The fervor of the Castro Revolution in Cuba and the popular response it received from millions of Latin Americans awoke the government of President John F. Kennedy to the reality that the majority of the Latin Americans wanted change. Fearful that the formula they might choose would be communistic, Kennedy and his advisors devised an imaginative plan to encourage change and to channel it along a democratic path. In March of 1961, President Kennedy, always extremely popular among Latin Americans of all political suasions and socioeconomic levels, launched his Alliance for Progress, a program to encourage economic developments, to promote the growth of democracy, and to urge social justice. It was an optimistic program which if carried out would have altered much of Latin America. Unfortunately it failed, for the traditional oligarchy had no intention of its own free will to give away or sell its lands, to tax itself more heavily, or to share power with a broader base of the population. A decade after its pronouncement, there were more military dictatorships and less evidence of democracy than at any time in recent memory. In a ten-year span, military rule replaced 13 constitutional governments, and the United States continues to support lavishly the military in Latin America. In truth, over two-thirds of Alliance for Progress funds went to military dictators or to military-controlled civilian governments despite the intention that funds would be used to buttress democracy. The economic condition of the area is certainly more precarious today than it was in 1961. The rate of economic growth per capita over the decade averaged a pitiful 1.8 percent, lower than it was in the years before the Alliance for Progress and far from the minimal goal of 2.5 percent set by the Alliance. In November of 1968, President Richard Nixon concluded that the Alliance has "done nothing to reduce the ominous difference which exists between North and South America." Disappointment, almost disbelief, in the meager results of the Alliance after funneling nearly $10 billion into Latin America was widespread both in Latin America and in the United States. Senator Frank Church, Chairman of the Senate's Subcommittee on Western Hemisphere Affairs, voiced that dismay when he mused, "We thought we were seeding the resurgence of democratic governments; instead, we have seen a relentless slide toward militarism.

We thought we could remodel Latin societies, but the reforms we prescribed have largely eluded us." On March 13, 1971, the tenth anniversary of the Alliance for Progress passed unnoticed, unmentioned in Washington.

All indications point to a major economic reverse for Latin America during the decade of the 1960s. Foreign debt increased, world trade declined, and unemployment rose. External debt doubled during the decade to reach close to $20 billion. In 1959, 25 percent of Latin America's export income went to pay profits and interest to foreign investors and lenders. By 1968, the figure had risen to 36 percent. Apparently payments for foreign technology in the form of royalties, licensing agreements, and patent fees rose spectacularly during the same period. In Brazil, certainly an alarming example of such increases, those payments jumped from $6.4 million in 1963 to $70 million in 1968, the last year for which such figures are available. Between 1950 and 1968, Latin America's exports increased by only 3 percent per year, compared to a 7 percent figure for the rest of the world, which meant that Latin America's share of world trade fell in that period from 11 to 5.1 percent. During the 1960s, Latin America's share of the United States market dropped from 21 to 13 percent. During the decade, the number of unemployed between the ages of 15 and 65 rose from 18 to 23 million in a work force of approximately 83 million. The annual per capita income of about two-thirds of the agricultural population averaged less than $90 in 1970, a figure probably lower than it was a decade earlier. Both industrial and agricultural output were unable to keep up with population growth in the 1960s. Most distressing was the realization that much of Latin America is unable to feed itself; and without some immediate and far-reaching change, future prospects look even leaner. Juan Felipe Yriart, Assistant Director General of the United Nation's Food and Agricultural Organization warned regional representatives in 1970 that Latin American agricultural and cattle raising productivity during the previous 20 years was a cause for "deep concern" because statistics revealed "a persistent decline in the rhythm of growth in agriculture and livestock." He concluded, "The panorama of Latin America's farming industry is discouraging." Figures released by the Colombian government in mid-1971 revealed that with the exception of wheat, the production of all other agricultural products had dropped markedly. Imports of foodstuffs into Latin America during the decade of the 1960s rose, and a country like Bolivia imported in some years as much as 50 percent of its food supplies. A special report prepared in mid-1971 by the Organization of American States predicted "severe shortages" of food in the 1970s unless agricultural productivity rose dramatically and then noted that most Latin Americans only consumed minimal quantities of calories and protein. As causes of the dismal agricultural performance, the report pointed out that the governments emphasized industrialization to the neglect of agriculture, that laws and policies originally intended to spur agriculture had worked in reality to discourage it, and that the iniquitous land-owning system kept most of the arable land fallow.

While the rate of industrialization and modernization in Western Europe and the United States quickens, Latin America falls farther behind. In 1965, Latin America's gross income reached $60 billion, the exact sum the United States *added* to its own gross national product that year over the previous year. Failure to even keep up with the fast pace of progress elsewhere disturbs the Latin Americans and creates a state of constant tension. Not only have the old institutions failed them, but the realization grows that their experiments with democracy have in most cases been more frustrating than successful.

Democracy in Latin America has proven to be very fragile and ineffectual. Democratic government (or for that matter the authoritarian governments of the past) has demonstrated scant capacity to develop Latin America, to alter the traditional patterns of the past, or to propel Latin America into the future. One of the most striking characteristics of the 1960s was a growing disillusionment with democracy. Right and left and many with political preferences between the two extremes have despaired of seeing their nation's problems solved through the democratic process. Brazil's military rulers since 1964 have regularly blamed democracy for the nation's ills. In 1970, Minister of Education Jarbas Passarinho asked, "How can we speak of democracy when four out of five of our people are practically outside the economy?" Indeed, who can read Josué de Castro's moving *Death in the Northeast* and conclude that democracy has ever worked in Brazil? The author affirmed that democracy has served to preserve "abstract principles and existing systems of advantages"; it has not provided "the basic domestic reforms," most needed of which would be land reform. Another group in another region of Latin America, the Guatemalan guerrillas, espoused a political position favoring extreme socialist revolution and refused to participate in any democratic process of elections or compromises with the government. The failure of democracy to solve Guatemala's pressing problems has embittered the youth. Guerrilla movements have sprung up throughout Latin America angrily demanding the reforms which democracy has never enacted. Colombia, a nation with a reasonably good democratic record in the past 40 years, has been the scene of guerrilla warfare for the same period of time. In 1930–31, armed groups appeared in the mountains demanding an agrarian reform. The most popular guerrilla leader in modern Colombia, a priest named Camilo Torres, advocated in 1965 an extremely radical program: the nationalization of all natural resources, the expropriation without indemnification of all large estates, higher wages for the workers, and a popular government.

Probably one of the most surprising converts from democracy in recent times was Juan Bosch, long a favorite of the liberal democrats. He ranked as one of the leading intellectuals fighting the brutal regime of General Rafael Trujillo, who terrorized the Dominican Republic for 31 years, and advocating democratic government for the progress and well-being of his country. In 1962, following the assassination of Trujillo, he ran for the presidency and won, becoming the first democratically elected president to take office in his country in over three decades. The Kennedy administration welcomed the new government as "Democracy in the Caribbean." Seven months after Bosch's inauguration, the old-line Trujillo military overthrew him, revealing a not uncommon and quite convenient confusion in the minds of the oligarchy of "democracy" and "communism." At the time the United States took no action. However, three years later, when civilian and military supporters tried force to return Bosch to power, President Lyndon Johnson, labeling as "communism" what his predecessor had termed "Democracy in the Caribbean," dispatched 23,000 troops to that unhappy country. The intervention facilitated the rise to power of Joaquín Balaguer, longtime aid and confidant of the discredited Trujillo. The maneuvers showed Bosch "the real face of the United States," to use his own words.

Returning to his homeland in 1969, after four years in exile, Bosch was no longer the democrat he had always been. Apparently bitter experience and deeper reflection had brought him to new conclusions. He stated,

> Representative democracy cannot work in a country such as the Dominican Republic. It has served to maintain the privileges of a minority of property and wealth, and it has not provided the stability, personal safety, health care, and education that the majority want.

> Representative democracy has been a failure in Latin America for more than 150 years. It cannot guarantee true equality for all men, since it is a fundamentally unjust sociopolitical system which is organized and sustained by the principle that there are men who have a right to exploit and that there are others whose duty it is to allow themselves to be exploited.

In the place of the democracy he once had supported so enthusiastically, he advocates a "dictatorship with popular support," one with a socialist orientation. He sees a popular dictatorship as the only way to destroy some formidable institutions which he believes have prohibited Latin America's development. His popular dictatorship would reform the landowning structure by breaking up large, idle estates, draft and implement a master plan for development through diversification of the economy and industrialization, and nationalize all large companies whether foreign or domestic. He foresees support for such a popular dictatorship from the impoverished masses, the bourgeoisie which has more to gain from such a government than from association with the traditional oligarchy, the part of the hierarchy of the Roman Catholic Church increasingly concerned with the plight of the poor, and those military officers who desire to see their nation reformed and strengthened. Much of Latin America has been receptive to Bosch's ideas. His conversion from a reform-oriented democracy to radical change by means of a populist dictatorship indicates a trend among large numbers of Latin Americans disturbed by the dilatory nature of their democracies and eager for economic development and independence, agrarian reform, state ownership of natural resources, popular government, and the greater valorization of man.

To many Latin Americans, the democratic reformers have proven their inability to change colonial or neocolonial institutions, structures, or patterns. New groups entering the political struggles—the farmers, the workers, the students, for example—are not willing to accept old institutions, structures, and patterns which they not only had no hand in creating but which they feel have repressed them. The extreme right and left are offering radical solutions which are enticing greater numbers of supporters with the resultant political polarization of much of Latin America, a process noticeable by the mid-1960s, and accelerating thereafter. By 1970, well over half of Latin America's nations and population were living under authoritarian governments, either of the far right as in Argentina and Brazil or of the far left as in Cuba. The extremes are trying to offer new solutions to old problems, something which the more traditional parties and politicians have been reluctant to do. The leader of Uruguay's Christian Democratic Party, Juan Pablo Terra, concluded, "Traditional parties are not prepared to face today's problems. They work as a voting cooperative that is strong enough to gain power but not strong enough to govern." Many contend for power: the large landowners, the industrialists, the army, the Church, the middle class, the intellectuals, and the labor unions. None is powerful enough to rule but each is sufficiently strong to keep the others from ruling. The result is a political stalemate which fosters social, political, and economic stagnation. The extremists feel they can break that old stalemate. In doing so, they hope to accelerate the pace of change in

Latin America as the struggle goes forward to break the ties with the past. Meanwhile, Latin America manifests all the signs of an under-developed area: low per capita income, unequal distributions of wealth, economic dependency, high birth and death rates, endemic diseases, un-dernourishment, and illiteracy. These are old problems never satis-factorily resolved in Latin America. Today they beg new solutions. If reform fails to provide the solutions and to effect the changes desired by the majority, then revolution becomes inevitable in Latin America.

Statistical

Tables

TABLE 1   Fact Sheet on the Nations of Latin America and the Caribbean

Country	Area (Sq. Miles)	Population (1970)	Capital	Principal Products
Argentina	1,072,749	24,300,000	Buenos Aires	Meats, grains, wool, hides, dairy, meat by-products, minerals
Barbados	166	300,000	Bridgetown	Sugar, molasses, rum
Bolivia	424,163	4,600,000	La Paz	Tin, tungsten, lead, zinc
Brazil	3,287,195	93,000,000	Brasília	Coffee, cotton, cacao, beans, manganese, iron ore
Chile	286,396	9,800,000	Santiago	Copper, nitrate, wheat, iron, wines
Colombia	439,519	21,400,000	Bogotá	Coffee, petroleum, cattle, bananas, rice, cacao
Costa Rica	19,575	1,800,000	San José	Coffee, cacao, bananas
Cuba	44,218	8,400,000	Havana	Tobacco, sugar, nickel, other minerals
Dominican Republic	18,703	4,300,000	Santo Domingo	Cacao, sugar, coffee, bananas, rice
Ecuador	104,506	6,100,000	Quito	Bananas, cacao, coffee, gold, balsa wood
El Salvador	8,061	3,400,000	San Salvador	Coffee, cotton, oils, balsam
Guatemala	42,042	5,100,000	Guatemala City	Coffee, bananas, chicle, cotton
Guyana	83,000	800,000	Georgetown	Bauxite, sugar, rice, coconuts
Haiti	10,714	5,200,000	Port-au-Prince	Sisal, sugar, textiles
Honduras	44,480	2,700,000	Tegucigalpa	Bananas, coffee, lumber, silver, gold
Jamaica	4,411	2,000,000	Kingston	Bauxite, alumina, sugar, bananas, mineral fuels, rum, citrus fruits
Mexico	760,337	50,700,000	Mexico, D.F.	Cotton, petroleum, coffee, lead, zinc, corn, silver
Nicaragua	54,864	2,000,000	Managua	Coffee, cotton, corn
Panama	28,753	1,500,000	Panama City	Bananas, abaca, cacao, fish
Paraguay	157,047	2,400,000	Asunción	Lumber, tannin, livestock
Peru	496,223	13,600,000	Lima	Cotton, sugar, lead, copper, petroleum, gold
Trinidad and Tobago	1,980	1,100,000	Port of Spain	Petroleum, sugar, asphalt, rum, cacao, coffee, citrus fruits, cement
Uruguay	72,172	2,900,000	Montevideo	Wool, meat, hides
Venezuela	352,146	10,800,000	Caracas	Petroleum, iron ore, canned fish

Source: *Introduction to the Latin American Nations* (Washington, D.C.: General Secretariat of the Organization of American States, 1970).

TABLE 2   National Censuses of Latin American Republics: 1774–1970

Mexico		1867	257 000
1970	48 313 438	1778	106 926
1960	34 923 129		
1950	25 791 017	*Panama*	
1940	19 653 552	1970	1 414 737
1930	16 552 722	1960	1 075 541
1921	14 334 780	1950	756 631
1910	15 160 369	1940	566 589
1900	13 607 259	1930	428 021
1895	12 632 427	1920	263 712
		1911	289 538
Costa Rica			
1963	1 336 274	*Barbados*	
1950	800 875	1960	232 327
1927	471 524	1946	192 800
1892	243 205	1921	156 774
1883	182 073	1911	171 983
1864	120 499		
		Cuba	
El Salvador		1967	7 937 000
1961	2 510 984	1953	5 829 029
1950	1 855 917	1943	4 778 583
1930	1 434 361	1931	3 962 344
		1919	2 889 004
Guatemala		1907	2 048 980
1964	4 284 473	1899	1 572 797
1950	2 790 686	1887	1 631 687
1940	2 383 209	1877	1 509 291
1921	2 004 900	1861	1 396 530
1893	1 364 678	1841	1 007 624
1880	1 224 602	1827	704 487
		1817	572 363
Honduras		1792	272 300
1961	1 884 765	1774	171 620
1950	1 368 605		
1945	1 200 542	*Dominican Republic*	
1940	1 107 859	1970	4 011 589
1935	962 000	1960	3 047 070
1930	854 184	1950	2 135 872
1926	700 811	1935	1 479 417
1916	605 997	1920	894 665
1910	553 446		
1887	331 917	*Haiti*	
1881	307 289	1968 (Estimate)	4 674 000
1801	130 000	1950	3 097 220
1791	93 505	1918 and 1919	1 631 260
Nicaragua		*Jamaica*	
1963	1 535 588	1960	1 609 814
1950	1 057 023	1953	1 486 723
1940	835 686	1943	1 237 063
1920	638 119	1921	858 118
1906	505 377	1911	831 383

Trinidad and Tobago

1960	827 957
1946	557 970
1931	412 783
1921	365 913
1911	333 552
1901	255 148

Argentina

1960	20 010 539
1947	15 897 127
1914	7 885 237
1895	3 954 911
1869	1 737 076

Bolivia

1965 (Estimate)	3 698 000
1960	3 019 031
1900	1 696 400
1882	1 097 600
1854	1 544 300
1845	1 031 500
1835	992 700
1831	1 018 900

Brazil

1960	70 119 071
1950	51 944 397
1940	41 236 315
1920	30 635 605
1900	17 318 556
1890	14 333 915
1872	10 112 061

Chile

1970	8 836 223
1960	7 374 115
1952	5 932 995
1940	5 023 539
1930	4 287 445
1920	3 730 235
1907	3 231 022
1895	2 695 625
1885	2 507 005
1875	2 075 971
1865	1 819 223
1854	1 439 120
1843	1 083 801
1835	1 010 336

Colombia

1964	17 484 508
1951	11 548 172

1938	8 701 816
1928	7 851 000
1918	5 855 077
1912	5 072 604
1905	4 143 632
1870	2 391 984
1864	2 694 487
1851	2 243 730
1843	1 955 264
1835	1 686 038
1825	1 223 598

Ecuador

1962	4 649 684
1950	3 202 757

Guyana

1960	560 330
1946	369 678
1931	310 933
1921	297 691
1911	296 041

Paraguay

1962	1 819 103
1950	1 328 452
1936	931 799

Peru

1961	9 906 746
1940	7 023 111
1876	2 651 840
1862	2 460 684
1850	2 001 203
1836	1 373 736

Uruguay

1963	2 595 510
1908	1 042 686
1880	229 480
1852	131 969

Venezuela

1961	7 523 999
1950	5 034 838
1941	3 850 771
1936	3 491 159
1926	3 026 878
1920	2 411 952
1891	2 323 527
1881	2 075 545
1873	1 784 194

Source: Kenneth Ruddle and Mukhtar Hamour, eds., *Statistical Abstract of Latin America 1969* (Los Angeles: Latin American Center, UCLA, 1970), p. 67.

TABLE 3   Distribution of Populations by Urban/Rural Residences By Percentage

Country	Date of Information	Urban Residents	Rural Residents
Argentina	—	—	—
Barbados	1960	4.9	95.1
Bolivia	—	—	—
Brazil	1960	46.3	53.7
Chile	1960	68.2	31.8
Colombia	1964	52.8	47.2
Costa Rica	1963	34.5	65.5
Cuba	1967	53.4	46.6
Dominican Republic	1960	30.3	69.7
Ecuador	1962	36.0	64.0
El Salvador	1961	38.5	61.5
Guatemala	1964	33.6	66.4
Guyana	1960	15.5	84.5
Haiti	—	—	—
Honduras	1961	23.2	76.8
Jamaica	1960	23.4	76.6
Mexico	1960	50.7	49.3
Nicaragua	1963	40.9	59.1
Panama	1960	41.5	58.5
Paraguay	1962	35.8	64.2
Peru	1961	47.4	52.6
Trinidad and Tobago	—	—	—
Uruguay	1963	80.8	19.2
Venezuela	1961	67.4	32.6

Source: Statistics extracted from tables in Kenneth Ruddle and Mukhtar Hamour, eds., *Statistical Abstract of Latin America 1969* (Los Angeles: Latin American Center, UCLA, 1970), pp. 74–75.

TABLE 4   Transportation and Communication

Country	Year/Railroad length (miles)		Year/Road length (kilometers)		Year/Civil Aviation (kilometers flown in thousands)	
Argentina	1965	24,966	1968	136,690	1968	48,070
Barbados	—	—	1961	1,184	—	—
Bolivia	1968	2,189	1961	24,769	1968	3,650
Brazil	1968	19,917	1968	826,425	1968	88,650
Chile	1967	6,298	1969	54,610	1968	15,759
Colombia	1966	2,134	1968	46,000	1968	44,755
Costa Rica	1967	600	1968	18,931	1968	3,748
Cuba	1963	3,233	—	—	1968	6,459
Dominican Republic	1966	347	1968	10,268	1968	1,480
Ecuador	1964	717	1969	20,595	1968	8,920
El Salvador	1966	318	1968	8,641	1968	3,430
Guatemala	1965	595	1969	12,308	1968	3,751
Guyana	1968	78	1969	1,193	1968	600
Haiti	1964	157	1969	3,150	1968	520
Honduras	1967	624	1969	4,640	1968	7,832
Jamaica	1967	205	—	—	1968	3,470
Mexico	1968	12,271	1961	194,298	1968	45,579
Nicaragua	1964	250	1968	10,091	1968	1,570
Panama	1966	403	1969	6,721	1968	3,360
Paraguay	1969	274	1968	15,956	1968	1,720
Peru	1966	1,628	1969	41,184	1968	15,949
Trinidad and Tobago	1967	8	1968	7,258	1968	7,659
Uruguay	1966	1,716	1961	37,800	1968	3,310
Venezuela	1964	300	1969	51,102	1968	26,226

Source: Statistics extracted from tables in Kenneth Ruddle and Mukhtar Hamour, eds., *Statistical Abstract of Latin America 1969* (Los Angeles: Latin American Center, UCLA, 1970), pp. 226, 231, 239.

TABLE 5   Exports and Imports Value of Trade (Millions of U.S. Dollars)

Country	Exports		Imports	
	Year	Value	Year	Value
Argentina	1970	1,691	1970	1,494
Barbados	1968	37	1969	91
Bolivia	1970	199	1970	156
Brazil	1969	2,311	1969	2,242
Chile	1969	1,071	1969	907
Colombia	1969	608	1969	686
Costa Rica	1970	223	1970	268
Cuba	1967	717	1967	1,001
Dominican Republic	1970	260	1970	238
Ecuador	1970	92	1970	245
El Salvador	1970	254	1970	199
Guatemala	1968	222	1968	247
Guyana	1970	92	1970	119
Haiti	1969	38	1968	38
Honduras	1968	181	1969	184
Jamaica	1970	283	1970	463
Mexico	1970	1,501	1970	2,202
Nicaragua	1969	155	1969	177
Panama	1970	114	1970	304
Paraguay	1970	54	1970	73
Peru	1970	1,062	1970	667
Trinidad and Tobago	1970	487	1970	511
Uruguay	1970	175	1970	224
Venezuela	1969	2,892	1969	1,752

Source: Statistics extracted from tables in Kenneth Ruddle and Mukhtar Hamour, eds., *Statistical Abstract of Latin America 1969* (Los Angeles: Latin American Center, UCLA, 1970), pp. 268–69.

Glossary

Adelantado   An individual in colonial Spanish America authorized by the crown to explore, conquer, and hold new territory. He pushed back the frontier and extended Spanish claims and control of the New World.

Alcaldes mayores   In colonial Spanish America, appointed officials who held administrative and judicial responsibility on a local or district level.

Aldeia   An Indian village or settlement in Portuguese America administered by the religious orders until the mid-eighteenth century and then by secular officials thereafter.

Audiencia   The highest royal court and consultative council in colonial Spanish America.

Ayllu   A communal unit in the Incan empire which worked the land in common, part for themselves and part for the Incan ruler and priestly elite.

Bandeirante   Particularly active during the 1650–1750 period, an individual who penetrated the interior of Brazil to explore, to capture Indian slaves, or to search for gold.

Barriados   Squatter settlements in Peru.

Cabildo   The municipal government in Spanish America.

Cabildo abierto   The municipal council in Spanish America expanded under special circumstances to include most of the principal citizens of the municipality.

Callampos   Squatter settlements in Chile.

Capitão-mor (plural, *capitães-mor*)   A military rank given to commanders of the local militia in colonial Portuguese America.

Capitulación   A contract between monarch and *adelantado* stating the duties and rewards of the latter.

Casa da Suplicação   The highest court in the Portuguese empire and therefore the supreme court for judicial disputes in colonial Brazil.

Casa de Contratación   The House of Trade established in Spain in 1503 to organize, regulate, and develop trade with the New World.

Caudillo (Portuguese, *caudilho*)   A strong leader who wields complete power over his subordinates.

Cédula   A royal edict from the Spanish monarch.

Científico   A high administrator in the government of President Porfirio Díaz of Mexico (1876–1911) infused with Positivist ideas, who believed national problems could be solved by scientific solutions. Such men were prominent during the last two decades of his administration.

Compadrio   A godparent relationship.

Composición   A Spanish legal device for claiming land through surveys.

Comunero   A participant in the Comunero Revolt which occurred in New Granada in 1781.

Congregación   The Spanish policy of concentrating Indians into villages.

Consejo de las Indias   The Council of the Indies established in Spain in 1524 to advise the monarch on American affairs.

Conselho geral   In Portuguese America, a municipal council expanded under special circumstances to include most of the principal citizens of the municipality.

Conselho Ultramarino   The Overseas Council established in Lisbon in 1642 to advise the crown on matters relating to the empire and its administration.

Consulado   In colonial Spanish America, a guild of merchants acting as a sort of chamber of commerce.

Coronel (plural, *coroneis*)   A civilian political boss of a Brazilian municipality. The system of political control founded on the local bosses came to be known as *coronelismo*.

Corregidor   An official in colonial Spanish America who was assigned to Spanish as well as Indian communities as tax collector, policeman, magistrate, and administrator.

Creole   A white born in the Spanish-American empire.

Cumbe   A settlement of runaway slaves in Spanish America.

Ejido   The common land held by Indian communities and used for agriculture in Mexico.

Encomendero   The person who received an *encomienda*.

Encomienda   A tribute institution used in Spanish America in the sixteenth century. The Spaniard received Indians as an entrustment, *encomienda*, to protect and to Christianize, but in return he could demand tribute including labor.

Favela   Squatter settlement in Brazil.

Fazenda   A large estate or plantation in Brazil.

Fazendeiro   The owner of a large estate or plantation in Brazil.

Fuero militar   A special military privilege in Spanish America which exempted officers from civil legal jurisdiction.

Gaucho   The cowboy of the Pampas.

Hacendado   The owner of a large estate in Spanish America.

Hacienda   A large estate in Spanish America.

Homens bons   In Portuguese, literally the "good men," those who belonged to the upper echelon of Brazilian colonial society. They voted for members of the municipal council.

Inquilino   A Chilean peasant.

Jefe   Chief or leader. In Spanish America, it is often used as synonymous with *caudillo*.

Mazombo   In Portuguese America, a white born in the New World.

Mestizo   A person of mixed parentage. Usually it refers to a European-Indian mixture.

Mita   A forced labor system in which the Indian was required to labor for the state. It is most often associated with Indian labor in the Andean mines.

Oidor   A judge on the *audiencias* of Spanish America.

Palenque   A settlment of runaway slaves in Spanish America.

Patrón   In Spanish America, the owner or boss or one in a superior position.

Peninsular   In Spanish America, a white born in Europe who later came to the New World.

Porfiristas   Those in Mexico who supported Porfirio Díaz or his policies.

Porteño   An inhabitant of the city of Buenos Aires.

Presidencia   A subdivision of the viceroyalties of Spanish America, having a president as the chief executive officer.

Quilombo   A settlement of runaway slaves in Portuguese America.

Ranchos   Squatter settlements in Venezuela.

Regidor   Municipal councilman in Spanish America.

Reinol (plural, *reinóis*)   In Portuguese America, a white born in Europe who later came to the New World.

Relação   The high court in Portuguese America.

Repartimiento   A labor institution in colonial Spanish America in which a temporary allotment of Indians was made by a royal judge for a given task.

Residencia   In both the Spanish and Portuguese American empires, a formal inquiry into the conduct of a public official at the end of his term of office.

Sambo   A person of mixed Indian and African parentage.

Senado da Câmara   In Brazil, the municipal government, in particular the town council.

Sertão   The interior, backlands, or hinterlands of Brazil. The term refers particularly to the hinterland region of northeastern Brazil.

Sesmaria   A land grant in colonial Brazil.

Soldadera   During the Mexican Revolution, a woman who was attached to a soldier. The *soldaderas* cooked for the soldiers, tended the ill and wounded, and fought.

Tenente   In Brazil, an army lieutenant. The word is often used to denote those junior army officers during the 1920s and early 1930s who favored social, economic, and political reforms.

Vecindad   Literally "neighborhood" in Spanish, but in Mexico City it can refer to a "tenement" dwelling.

Villas miserias   Squatter settlements in Argentina.

Visita   In both the Spanish and Portuguese-American empires, an on-the-spot administrative investigation of a public employee ordered by the monarch.

Visitador   In colonial Spanish and Portuguese America, an official in charge of making a special investigation for the monarch in the New World.

A Guide

to the

Paperback Literature

in English

Beginning in the early 1960s, the publishing houses began to issue an ever larger number of excellent and relatively inexpensive paperback books on Latin America. Some of them were now soft-cover editions of former hard-cover books; others were original paperback editions. For the first time the student and general educated public interested in better understanding Latin America could select from a wide variety of titles those which most struck their fancy or aroused their curiosity.

The following guide to the paperback literature on or about Latin American history in English is divided into two parts. The first indicates some of the best works which complement and expand the various topics discussed in this brief history. In it, listed under the chapter and section headings used in the book, the reader will find appropriate books in print which will give greater detail or other viewpoints on the subject discussed in this text. Some of these recommended books conceivably could fit under several sections. In such cases, I arbitrarily listed the book under the section to which I thought it most closely related. For some chapters and sections, either appropriate paperbacks were already out of print and therefore not included or I could find no paperback to recommend. Varied and growing as the paperback library is, it still neglects several eras (the nineteenth century for example), several areas (Chile would be a pertinent example), and many subjects (modernization would certainly be an important oversight). Some hardcover monographs could be mentioned which treat some of those neglected eras, areas, and subjects. However, since those monographs are not readily available and can be quite expensive, I purposely excluded them from this guide. For those who might wish to acquaint themselves with a long and inclusive guide to the hard-cover works, as well as essays and articles, on Latin American history, I recommend that they consult Charles C. Griffin, ed., *Latin America: A Guide to Historical Literature* (Austin: University of Texas Press, 1971).

I. THE ORIGINS OF A MULTIRACIAL SOCIETY

MAGNUS MORNER, *Race Mixture in the History of Latin America* (Boston: Little, Brown, 1967).

    A. The Land

IRMGARD POHL and JOSEPH ZEPP (Kempton E. Webb, ed.) *Latin America: A Geographical Commentary* (New York: Dutton, 1967).

    B. The Indian

HAROLD E. DRIVER, ed., *The Americas on the Eve of Discovery* (Englewood Cliffs, N.J.: Prentice-Hall, 1964).

ALVIN M. JOSEPHY, JR., *The Indian Heritage of America* (New York: Bantam, 1969).

ROBERT WAUCHOPE, ed., *The Indian Background of Latin American History* (New York: Knopf, 1970).

    C. The European

WILLIAM C. ATKINSON, *A History of Spain and Portugal* (Baltimore: Penguin, 1960).

HAROLD B. JOHNSON, ed., *From Reconquest to Empire: The Iberian Background to Latin American History* (New York: Knopf, 1970).

    D. Confrontation and Conquest

IRWIN R. BLACKER, *The Portable Prescott. The Rise and Decline of the Spanish Empire* (New York: Viking, 1966).

C. R. BOXER, *Four Centuries of Portuguese Expansion, 1415–1825. A Succinct Survey* (Berkeley: University of California Press, 1969).

BERNAL DÍAZ, *The Conquest of New Spain* (Baltimore: Penguin, 1967).

LEWIS HANKE, *Aristotle and the American Indians: A Study in Race Prejudice in the Modern World* (Bloomington: Indiana University Press, 1970).

———, *The Spanish Struggle for Justice in the Conquest of America* (Boston: Little, Brown, 1965).

F. A. KIRKPATRICK, *The Spanish Conquistadores* (New York: World Publishing, 1962).

WILLIAM H. PRESCOTT, *The History of the Conquest of Mexico* (Chicago: University of Chicago Press, 1966).

———, *The Conquest of Peru* (New York: Mentor, 1961).

E. The African
GILBERTO FREYRE, *The Masters and the Slaves* (New York: Knopf, 1964).

II. THE INSTITUTIONS OF EMPIRE

C. R. BOXER, *The Golden Age of Brazil* (Berkeley: University of California Press, 1969).

CHARLES GIBSON, *Spain in America* (New York: Harper & Row, 1966).

CAIO PRADO, JR., *The Colonial Background of Modern Brazil* (Berkeley: University of California Press, 1969).

STANLEY J. STEIN and BARBARA H. STEIN, *The Colonial Heritage of Latin America* (New York: Oxford University Press, 1970).

A. Land and Labor
FRANÇOIS CHEVALIER, *Land and Society in Colonial Mexico. The Great Hacienda* (Berkeley: University of California Press, 1970).

LAURA FONER and EUGENE GENOVESE, eds., *Slavery in the New World. A Reader in Comparative History* (Englewood Cliffs, N.J.: Prentice-Hall, 1969).

FRANK TANNENBAUM, *Slave and Citizen: The Negro in the Americas* (New York: Random House, 1963).

B. The State
C. H. HARING, *The Spanish Empire in America* (New York: Harcourt Brace Jovanovich, 1963).

CHARLES GIBSON, ed., *The Spanish Tradition in America* (New York: Harper & Row, 1968).

C. The Church
RICHARD E. GREENLEAF, ed., *The Roman Catholic Church in Colonial Latin America* (New York: Knopf, 1971).

III. INDEPENDENCE

R. A. HUMPHREYS and JOHN LYNCH, eds., *The Origins of the Latin American Revolutions* (New York: Knopf, 1965).

A. A Changing Mentality Begets New Attitudes and Action
ARTHUR P. WHITAKER, ed., *Latin America and the Enlightenment* (Ithaca, N.Y.: Cornell University Press, 1965).

B. The Slaves Declare Haiti's Independence
HUBERT COLE, *Christophe, King of Haiti* (New York: Viking, 1970).

CYRIL L. JAMES, *Black Jocobins: Toussaint L'Ouverture and the San Domingo Revolution* (New York: Random House, 1963).

C. An Unsuccessful Popular Revolution in Mexico
D. Elitist Revolts
DAVID BUSHNELL, ed., *The Liberator: Simón Bolívar* (New York: Knopf, 1970).

JOHN J. JOHNSON, *Simón Bolívar and Spanish American Independence, 1783–1830* (Princeton, N.J.: Van Nostrand Reinhold, 1968).

WILLIAM SPENCE ROBERTSON, *The Rise of the Spanish-American Republics as Told in the Lives of their Liberators* (New York: Free Press, 1965).

J. B. TREND, *Bolívar and the Independence of Spanish America* (New York: Harper & Row, 1968).

IV. NATIONAL CONSOLIDATION

A. The Transfer and Legitimization of Power
HUGH M. HAMILL, JR., *Dictatorship in Spanish America* (New York: Knopf, 1965).

B. The Tense Societies

Domingo F. Sarmiento, *Life in the Argentine Republic in the Days of the Tyrants, or Civilization and Barbarism* (New York: Hafner, 1960).
　　C. *Economic Stagnation*
V. THE EMERGENCE OF THE MODERN STATE
　　A. *Political Stability*
Clarence H. Haring, *Empire in Brazil: A New World Experiment with Monarchy* (New York: Norton, 1968).
　　B. *Modernization*
Euclydes da Cunha, *Rebellion in the Backlands* (Chicago: University of Chicago Press, 1970).
Paul Friedrich, *Agrarian Revolt in a Mexican Village* (Englewood Cliffs, N.J.: Prentice-Hall, 1970).
　　C. *Economic Prosperity*
　　D. *The Social Milieu*
Norman S. Hayner, *New Patterns in Old Mexico: A Study of Town and Metropolis* (New Haven, Conn.: College and University Press, 1966).
Andrew H. Whiteford, *Two Cities of Latin America, A Comparative Description of Social Classes* (Garden City, N.Y.: Doubleday, 1964).
　　E. *Continuity and Change*
Philip D. Curtin, *Two Jamaicas, The Role of Ideas in a Tropical Colony, 1830–1865* (New York: Atheneum, 1970).
Stanley J. Stein, *Vassouras, A Brazilian Coffee County, 1850–1900. The Role of Planter and Slave in a Changing Plantation Society* (New York: Atheneum, 1970).
　　F. *The Presence of the United States*
Neill Macauley, *The Sandino Affair* (Chicago: Quadrangle, 1971).
Dexter Perkins, *A History of the Monroe Doctrine* (Boston: Little, Brown, 1963).
Julius W. Pratt, *Expansionists of 1898* (Chicago: Quadrangle, 1964).
Armin Rappaport, *The Monroe Doctrine* (N.Y.: Holt, Rinehart & Winston, 1964).
Arthur P. Whitaker, *The United States and the Independence of Latin America, 1800–1830* (N.Y.: Norton, 1964).

VI. THE PAST REPUDIATED

Richard N. Adams et al., *Social Change in Latin America Today: Its Implications for United States Policy* (New York: Random House, 1960).
Jean Franco, *The Modern Culture of Latin America. Society and the Artists* (Baltimore: Penguin, 1970).
　　A. *The Middle Sectors in Politics*
John J. Johnson, *Political Change in Latin America: The Emergence of the Middle Sectors* (Stanford: Stanford University Press, 1969).
　　B. *Mexico's Violent Response to the Past*
Howard F. Cline, *Mexico: Revolution to Evolution, 1940–1960* (New York: Oxford University Press, 1963).
Stanley R. Ross, *Is the Mexican Revolution Dead?* (New York: Knopf, 1966).
Frank Tannenbaum, *Peace by Revolution, Mexico after 1910* (New York: Columbia University Press, 1966).
James W. Wilkie, *Mexican Revolution: Federal Expenditure and Social Change Since 1910* (Berkeley: University of California Press, 1970).

James W. Wilkie and Albert L. Michaels, eds., *Revolution in Mexico: Years of Upheaval, 1910–1940* (New York: Knopf, 1969).

John Womack, Jr., *Zapata and the Mexican Revolution* (New York: Random House, 1970).

   C. Nationalism as a Force for Change

Samuel L. Baily, ed., *Nationalism in Latin America* (New York: Knopf, 1970).

E. Bradford Burns, *Nationalism in Brazil, A Historical Survey* (New York: Praeger, 1967).

Frederick C. Turner, *The Dynamics of Mexican Nationalism* (Chapel Hill: University of North Carolina Press, 1970).

   D. Changing Racial Attitudes

Carl N. Degler, *Neither Black Nor White, Slavery and Race Relations in Brazil and the United States* (New York: Macmillan, 1971).

Charles Wagley, ed., *Race and Class in Rural Brazil* (New York: UNESCO, 1963).

VII. DEVELOPMENT, DEMOCRACY, AND DISILLUSIONMENT

Richard Bourne, *Political Leaders of Latin America* (Baltimore: Pelican, 1969).

Irving L. Horowitz, ed., *Masses in Latin America* (New York: Oxford University Press, 1970).

John J. Johnson, ed., *Continuity and Change in Latin America* (Stanford, Calif.: Stanford University Press, 1967).

————, *Military and Society in Latin America* (Stanford, Calif.: Stanford University Press, 1967).

Martin C. Needler, *Political Development in Latin America: Instability, Violence, and Evolutionary Change* (New York: Random House, 1968).

Peter Ranis, *Five Latin American Nations, a Comparative Political Study* (New York: Macmillan, 1971).

Karl M. Schmitt and David D. Burks, *Latin American Government and Politics* (New York: Praeger, 1963).

Paul E. Sigmund, ed., *Models of Political Change in Latin America* (New York: Praeger, 1970).

   A. The Rocky Road to Development

Charles W. Anderson, *Politics and Economic Change in Latin America* (Princeton, N.J.: Van Nostrand Reinhold, 1967).

Joseph R. Barager, *Why Perón Came to Power* (New York: Knopf, 1968).

Andre G. Frank, *Latin America: Underdevelopment or Revolution* (New York: Monthly Review, 1969).

Celso Furtado, *Obstacles to Development in Latin America* (Garden City, N.Y.: Doubleday, 1970).

José Luis de Imaz, *Los Que Mandan (Those Who Rule)* (Albany: State University of New York, 1970).

Claudio Veliz, ed., *The Politics of Conformity in Latin America* (New York: Oxford University Press, 1970).

   B. A Flirtation with Democracy

John Friedmann, *Venezuela, From Doctrine to Dialogue* (Syracuse, N.Y.: Syracuse University Press, 1965).

   C. The Revolutionary Option

Luis E. Aguilar, ed., *Marxism in Latin America* (New York: Knopf, 1969).

Regis Debray, *Strategy for Revolution: Essays on Latin America* (New York: Monthly Review, 1970).

Eduardo Galeano, *Guatemala: Occupied Country* (New York: Monthly Review, 1969).

John Gerassi, ed., *Revolutionary Priest. The Complete Writings and Messages of Camilo Torres* (New York: Random House, 1971).

Daniel James, ed., *Complete Bolivian Diaries of Che Guevara and Other Captured Documents* (New York: Stein and Day, 1969).

George Lavan, *Che Guevara Speaks, Selected Speeches and Writings* (New York: Grove Press, 1968).

Lee Lockwood, *Castro's Cuba, Cuba's Fidel* (New York: Random House, 1969).

James Petras and Maurice Zeitlin, eds., *Latin America, Reform or Revolution* (New York: Fawcett, 1968).

T. Lynn Smith, ed., *Agrarian Reform in Latin America* (New York: Knopf, 1965).

Rodolfo Stavenhagen, ed., *Agrarian Problems and Peasant Movements in Latin America* (New York: Doubleday, 1970).

　　D. Disillusionment

Josué de Castro, *Death in the Northeast, Poverty and Revolution in the Northeast of Brazil* (New York: Random House, 1969).

John Gerassi, *The Great Fear in Latin America* (New York: Crowell Collier and Macmillan, 1965).

Carolina Maria de Jesus, *Child of the Dark. The Diary of Carolina Maria de Jesus* (New York: New American Library, 1963).

C. Neale Ronning, ed., *Intervention in Latin America* (New York: Knopf, 1970).

The second part of this guide refers the reader to general paperback books on Latin America as well as to a few of the growing numbers of novels by Latin American writers, now translated and in paperback editions, which provide still another means of understanding Latin America. These works cut across the chapters and sections delineated in this text and for that reason did not fit well into the first listing.

1. Interpretive Studies

Gilberto Freyre, *New World in the Tropics: The Culture of Modern Brazil* (New York: Random House, 1963).

Jacques Lambert, *Latin America, Social Structures and Political Institutions* (Berkeley: University of California Press, 1969).

Octavio Paz, *The Labyrinth of Solitude: Life and Thought in Mexico* (New York: Grove Press, 1961).

Samuel Ramos, *Profile of Man and Culture in Mexico* (New York: McGraw-Hill, 1963).

Julius Rivera, *Latin America, a Sociocultural Interpretation* (New York: Appleton-Century-Crofts, 1971).

William L. Schurz, *This New World: The Civilization of Latin America* (New York: Dutton, 1964).

Frank Tannenbaum, *Ten Keys to Latin America* (New York: Random House, 1966).

2. Readings and Problems Books

Harold A. Bierck, ed., *Latin American Civilization: Readings and Essays* (Boston: Allyn & Bacon, 1967).

LEWIS HANKE, ed., *History of Latin American Civilization. Sources and Inter-pretation.* Vol. I, *The Colonial Experience,* Vol. II, *The Modern Age* (Boston: Little, Brown, 1967).

_____, *Readings in Latin American History,* Vol. I, *To 1810,* Vol. II, *Since 1810* (New York: Crowell Collier and Macmillan, 1966).

BENJAMIN KEEN, ed., *Readings in Latin American Civilization, 1492 to the Present* (Boston: Houghton Mifflin, 1967).

FREDERICK B. PIKE, ed., *Latin American History: Select Problems. Identity, Integration, and Nationhood* (New York: Harcourt Brace Jovanovich, 1969).

RAMÓN E. RUIZ, ed., *Interpreting Latin American History From Independence to Today* (New York: Holt, Rinehart & Winston, 1970).

3. Regional and National Histories

Argentina

THOMAS F. MCGANN, *Argentina: The Divided Land* (Princeton, N.J.: Van Nostrand Reinhold, 1966).

JAMES R. SCOBIE, *Argentina, A City and A Nation* (New York: Oxford University Press, 1964).

ARTHUR P. WHITAKER, *Argentina* (Englewood Cliffs, N.J.: Prentice-Hall, 1964).

Brazil

E. BRADFORD BURNS, ed., *A Documentary History of Brazil* (New York: Knopf, 1966).

ROLLE E. POPPINO, *Brazil. Land and People* (New York: Oxford, 1968).

CHARLES WAGLEY, *An Introduction to Brazil* (New York: Columbia University Press, 1971).

The Caribbean

JOHN E. FAGG, *Cuba, Haiti, and the Dominican Republic* (Englewood Cliffs, N.J.: Prentice-Hall, 1965).

JAMES G. LEYBURN, *The Haitian People* (New Haven, Conn.: Yale University Press, 1966).

WYATT MACGAFFEY and CLIFFORD R. BARNETT, *Twentieth Century Cuba. The Background of the Castro Revolution* (Garden City, N.Y.: Doubleday, 1965).

J. H. PARRY and P. M. SHERLOCK, *A Short History of the West Indies* (New York: St. Martin's, 1968).

ERIC WILLIAMS, *History of the People of Trinidad and Tobago* (London: Deutsch, 1964).

Central America

MÁRIO RODRÍGUES, *Central America* (Englewood Cliffs, N.J.: Prentice-Hall, 1965).

Chile

FEDERICO GIL, *The Political System of Chile* (Boston: Houghton Mifflin, 1966).

KALMAN H. SILVERT, *Chile, Yesterday and Today* (New York: Holt, Rinehart & Winston, 1965).

Colombia

HARRY BERNSTEIN, *Venezuela and Colombia* (Englewood Cliffs, N.J.: Prentice-Hall, 1964).

ROBERT H. DIX, *Colombia: The Political Dimensions of Change* (New Haven, Conn.: Yale University Press, 1969).

Mexico

C. C. Cumberland, *Mexico: The Struggle for Modernity* (New York: Oxford University Press, 1968).

Justo Sierra, *The Political Evolution of the Mexican People* (Austin: University of Texas Press, 1969).

Lesley Byrd Simpson, *Many Mexicos* (Berkeley: University of California Press, 1967).

Eric Wolf, *Sons of the Shaking Earth: The People of Mexico and Guatemala; Their Land, History, and Culture* (Chicago: University of Chicago Press, 1970).

Venezuela

Harry Bernstein, *Venezuela and Colombia* (Englewood Cliffs, N.J.: Prentice-Hall, 1964).

4. U.S.-Latin American Relations and Inter-American Relations

Donald M. Dozer, ed., *The Monroe Doctrine, Its Modern Significance* (New York: Knopf, 1965).

Earl T. Glauert and Lester D. Langley, eds., *The United States and Latin America* (Reading, Mass.: Addison-Wesley, 1971).

Edwin Lieuwen, *U.S. Policy in Latin America* (New York: Praeger, 1965).

Herbert L. Mathews, ed., *The United States and Latin America* (Englewood Cliffs, N.J.: Prentice-Hall, 1963).

O. Carlos Stoetzer, *The Organization of American States, An Introduction* (New York: Praeger, 1965).

Bryce Wood, *The Making of the Good Neighbor Policy* (New York: Norton, 1967).

5. The Novel

Ciro Alegría, *The Golden Serpent* (New York: New American Library, 1963). Peru.

Jorge Amado, *Gabriela, Clove and Cinamon* (New York: Fawcett, 1964). Brazil.

Mariano Azuela, *The Underdogs: A Novel of the Mexican Revolution* (New York: New American Library, 1963).

Carlos Fuentes, *The Death of Artemio Cruz* (New York: Noonday, 1966). Mexico.

Machado de Assis, *The Psychiatrist and Other Stories* (Berkeley: University of California Press, 1963). Brazil.

Index

Abreu, João Capistrano de, 4, 9, 169
Academies, in colonial Brazil, 70, 71
Aconcagua, 5
Adelantado, 13, 16, 17, 29, 35, 42, 52, 55
Afonso, Martim, 35
Africa, 6, 12, 13, 20–23, 60, 112, 177, 178,
    181, 192
Afro-Brazilian Congress, 180
Agrarian reform, see Land reform
Agriculture, 18, 134, 190, 194, 195, 223,
    231–32
    in colonial Brazil, 51
    desire to ease restrictions on, 71–72
    in early Spanish America, 15–16
    increasing inability of Latin America to
        feed itself, 231–32
    inefficiency of, 191–92
    the large estate, 112–15
    pre-Colombian, 9, 10, 11
    production in twentieth-century Mexico,
        165
    the source of wealth in colonial Latin
        America, 37–38, 55
    status during first half of nineteenth
        century, 112

Alamán, Lucas, 103, 104
Alberdi, Juan B., 127
Aldeia, 33, 48, 59
Alencar, José de, 138
Alessandri, Arturo, 156, 157, 200
Allende, Salvador, 174, 195, 211
Alliance for Progress, 219, 230–31
Amazon River, 5, 6, 17, 47, 50, 51, 60, 100
    introduction of steamships on, 109
Anchieta, José de, 33, 59, 61
Andes, 5, 6, 8, 17, 50, 82, 130
Angola, 60
Aprista, 176
Arana, Francisco, 216
Araucanian, 7
Arbenz, Jacobo, 216, 217, 218, 219, 224
Arévalo, Juan José, 215, 216
Argentina, 6, 57, 81, 82, 83, 94, 97, 99, 102,
    103, 119, 125, 127, 129, 130, 131, 134,
    135, 140, 142, 152, 157, 168, 170, 171,
    172, 173, 188, 189, 197, 198, 199, 200,
    205, 207, 214
    economic boom in late nineteenth
        century, 132–33
    education in nineteenth century, 139

Argentina (*cont.*)
  growing industrialization, 196
  growth of banking, 133
  immigration prior to 1914, 140–41
  industrialization, 1870–1914, 135
  landowning structure, 190
  Perón government, 202–3
  political development in nineteenth
    century, 124
  role of middle sectors, 1892–1930,
    155–56
  under Rosas, 94–95
  unions, 200
  urban growth, 137
  women, 209, 210, 211
Argüeda, Alcides, 175
Armas, Carlos Castillo, 219, 220
Army, *see* Military
Asia, 6, 7, 11, 14, 16
Assis, Machado de, 123
Asunción, 18, 53, 57, 210
Audiencia, 52
Austria, 98
Avellaneda, Nicolás, 139
Ayacucho, 76, 82
Azevedo, Aluísio, 179
Azevedo, Thales, de, 180
Aztecs, 7, 10
  civilization of, 8
  conquest of, 16–17

Bahamas, 181
Bahian Conspiracy, 74–75
Balaguer, Joaquín, 233
Balboa, Vasco Núñez de, 15
Balbuena, Bernardo de, 68
Bananas, 217, 218
Bandeirantes, 50
Banks, 158
  creation of in nineteenth century, 133–34
Bantu, 179
Barbados, 181
Barbosa, Ruy, 154
Barca, Frances Calderón de la, 100,
    113–14, 209
Barreto, Afonso Henriques Lima, 179
Barrios, Justo Rufino, 139
Basadre, Jorge, 168
Batista, Fulgencio, 207, 225, 226
Batlle, José, 157–59, 200
Belaúnde, Víctor, Andrés, 168
Belgrano, Manuel, 69, 70
Benalcázar, Sebastián de, 17
Betancourt, Rómulo, 211
Beveridge, Albert J., 145–46

Birthrate, 205
Black militancy, 181–82
Black power, 181–82
Blacks:
  attention from Brazil's literati, 179–80
  Brazil's first black historian, 179
  changing attitudes toward, 176–83
  contributions to the New World, 21–23
  participation in the conquest of the
    New World, 21
  struggle for psychological emancipation,
    178–80
  studies of, in Brazil, 178–79
Blaine, James G., 145
Blanco-Fombona, Rufino, 147
Board of Conscience and Religious Orders,
    45
Board of Revenue, 47
Bogotá, 5, 18, 146
Bolívar, Simón, 70, 72, 75, 81, 82, 87, 92, 95
Bolivia, 7, 82, 94, 101, 102, 112, 125, 132,
    174, 188, 204, 214, 231
  the Bolivian Revolution, 220–25, 228,
    230
Bonfim, Manuel, 175, 178
Bonifácio, José, 70, 83
Books:
  books popular in eighteenth century, 69
  early book trade, 69
Bosch, Juan, 233–34
Boundaries, source of controversy, 102–3
Bourbon reforms, 53–55
Brandão, Ambrósio Fernandes, 68
Brazil, 3, 6, 7, 10, 15, 18, 19, 20, 21, 23, 27,
    33, 35, 38, 39, 41, 51, 68, 81, 94, 95,
    97, 102, 103, 107, 109, 119, 120, 121,
    125, 126, 127, 128, 129, 130, 131, 132,
    134, 135, 140, 142, 152, 157, 168, 169–
    70, 171, 173, 188, 189, 191, 192, 196,
    197, 198, 199, 204, 205, 207, 208, 209,
    214, 232
  abolition of slavery, 176–78
  British economic dominance, 110
  colonial government, 44–50
  colonial landowning structure, 36, 37
  declares independence, 83
  democratic experiment ends, 1964,
    212–13
  democratization process, 1945–1964, 208
  diplomatic attention to U.S., 147
  discovery of, 14
  early evidences of nativism, 68
  early labor systems, 33–34
  early trade, 15
  easy transfer and legitimization of
    power, 89–91

Brazil (*cont.*)
  education in nineteenth century, 139
  end of slave trade, 112
  growing industrialization, 196, 198
  growing interest in black culture, 178–80
  growth of banking, 133
  Indian Protection Service, 176
  industrialization at end of nineteenth
    century, 135
  immigration prior to World War I, 139
  landowning structure, 190
  maintenance of unity, 101
  and Monroe Doctrine, 98
  political development in nineteenth
    century, 121–23
  poverty in Northeast, 193–94
  question of racial prejudice, 180
  role of middle sectors, 1889–1930,
    153–55
  steel industry, 197
  urban growth, 137
  Vargas government, 201
  women, 210
Brazilian Highlands, 5
Brazilwood, 15, 29, 41
Brinton, Crane, 75
Brito, João Rodrigues de, 71, 72
Buenos Aires:
  city of, 18, 40, 46, 53, 55, 57–58, 69, 99,
    101, 110, 124, 129, 137, 141, 156, 198,
    199, 200, 202, 204
  province of, 6, 57, 94, 124, 135
Bulnes, Francisco, 175
Bulnes, Manuel, 134
Bunge, Carlos Octavio, 175
Burgos, Laws of, 31
Burmeister, Carmela, Horne de, 210
Burnham, Forbes, 182

Cabildo, 53
Cabildo abierto, 53
Cabot, John Moors, 218
Cabral, Pedro Alvares, 14, 15
Calderón, Francisco García, 81
California, 101, 106, 143, 144
Calles, Plutarco Elías, 161, 162, 164
Caminha, Adolfo, 179
Caminha, Pero Vaz de, 11
Camoes, Luís de, 14
Cano, Juan Sebastián del, 16
Cape Horn, 3
Capitalism, 108, 130
Capitão-mor, 49–50
Capitulación, 16
Captaincy, 47–48, 52

Cárdenas, Juan de, 68
Cárdenas Lázaro, 162, 165–66, 167, 176,
    200, 201–2, 221
Carib, 7
Caribbean, 7, 20, 21, 29, 35, 38, 72, 77, 143,
    144, 146, 173, 181, 182
  black militancy in, 181
  growing interest in black culture, 178
  introduction of steamships into, 109
Carillo, José Baquíjano y, 69, 74
Carranza, Venustiano, 161–62, 163, 167, 200
Carvalho, Ronald de, 170
Casa da Suplicação, 45, 47
Casa de Contratación, 16, 40, 51, 53, 55
Casas, Bartolomé de las, 32, 59
Castillo, Bernal Díaz del, 9
Castro, Fidel, 195, 225, 226, 227, 228, 230
Castro, Josué de, 193, 232
Caudillo (Portuguese, Caudilho), 50, 120,
    133
  characteristics of nineteenth-century
    caudillos, 93–96
Celso, Afonso, 178
Central America, 5, 7, 17, 81, 98, 101, 103,
    144
Central and South American Cable
    Company, 129
Chaco War, 221
Charles III, 53, 54, 62
Charles V, 17, 31, 52
Chávez, Carlos, 164, 168
Chibcha, 7, 17
Chile, 6, 7, 8, 17, 54, 82, 95, 97, 101, 102,
    108, 109, 119, 120, 121, 125, 126, 127,
    128, 130, 131, 135, 140, 142, 144, 152,
    173, 174, 188, 195, 198, 200, 204, 206,
    207, 209, 214
  bombardment of Valparaiso, 98
  condition of the peasants, 194
  education in nineteenth century, 139
  immigration prior to 1914, 141
  need to import food, 191–92
  political development in nineteenth
    century, 123–24
  role of middle sectors, 1918–1925,
    156–57
  role of military in nineteenth century,
    96
  unions in, 200
  urban growth, 137–38
  women's votes, 210
Christian Democratic Party:
  in Chile, 211
  in Venezuela, 211
Christophe, Henri, 78
Church, Frank, 230–31

Church, Roman Catholic, 27, 142, 234
  and caudillos, 95
  in the colonial period, 58–63
  conflicts with the State, 105–7
  conflict with the Brazilian government, 122–23
  controversy over patronage, 104
  criticism of Church, 104
  and democracy and reform, 212
  dependency of Catholic Church in Portuguese Africa on Brazil, 60
  and the Indians, 30–32, 33–34
  influence of blacks on, 22–23
  and Mexican Revolution, 163, 164, 166, 167
  opposed to reform in nineteenth century, 96
  and patriarchy, 113
  and Pombal, 48
  relations with new nations, 103–7
  relations with the State during the colonial period, 42
  role of colonial education, 61–62
  role in education, 104
  role in Iberian expansion, 12, 13
  separation of Church and State in Uruguay, 159
  and unification of Spain, 13
  Vatican recognition of the new nations, 105
  wealth in nineteenth century, 103
  wealth of, 62–63
CIA, 219, 228
Cisplatine War, 102
Cities, as focal point for independence agitation, 80–81
Clayton-Bulwer Treaty, 144, 146
Clytus, John, 182
Code Noir, 77
Coffee, 51, 126, 132, 192
  coffee interests in Brazilian politics, 153–54
Colombia, 7, 17, 39, 82, 92, 121, 146, 191, 192, 198, 204, 207, 209, 214, 231, 232–33
Colônia do Sacramento, 46, 57
Colonization, early Spanish, 15, 17–18
Columbus, Christopher, 7, 13, 14, 15, 18, 35, 52, 58
Communications, physical difficulties of, 100–101
Communism, 173, 196, 217, 218, 219, 220, 224, 230, 233
Compadrio, 50
Comte, Auguste, 129, 130
Comunero Revolt, 74

Comuneros, 74
Conquest of the New World, 16–17, 18
Conselho Geral, 49
Conservatism:
  as a political philosophy in the nineteenth century, 105, 120
  in Uruguayan politics, 157
Constitutions:
  Argentina, 1853, 97
  Brazil, 1824, 90–91, 97
  Brazil, 1891, 123
  Brazil, 1946, 208
  Chile, 1833, 97, 123, 157
  Chile, 1925, 157
  Colombia, 1858, 92
  Guatemala, 1945, 216, 219
  increasing respect for, 120
  Mexico, 1857, 97, 106, 125
  Mexico, 1917, 162–63, 167, 171, 216
  in monarchical Mexico, 92
  in the nineteenth century, 96–97
  Uruguay, 1919, 158–59
Consulado, 40, 57
  Real Consulado de Caracas, 73
Córdoba, Francisco Hernández de, 15
Coroneis, 50
Cortés, Hernán, 9, 16, 17, 31
Costa Rica, 100, 129, 132, 134, 152, 192, 204, 210, 214
  report on industrialization, 134–35
Council of the Indies, 51–52, 53
Cousiño, Isadora, 137–38
Coutinho, José Joaquim da Cunha de Azeredo, 71
Creole, 53, 67, 73, 74, 75, 78, 79, 80, 82, 91, 102, 115, 140, 141, 142, 162
Cruz, Anselmo de la, 72
Cruz, Sor Juan Inez de la, 209
Cuba, 21, 23, 54, 127, 129, 131, 144, 146, 171, 195, 204, 207, 210, 214
  abolition of slavery, 76–77
  black studies, 178
  Cuban Revolution, 225–29, 230
  Cuban Revolution and the black, 182–83
Cunha, Euclydes da, 169–70
Cuzco, 8

Darío, Rubén, 138
Debt peonage, 35, 112, 120, 192
  example of, 192–93
DeForest, David Curtis, 69
Democracy, 156, 159, 160, 207, 211, 212, 213, 214, 216, 232

Democracy (*cont.*)
 disillusionment with, 232–34
 obstacles to, 212
Democratic Action Party, 211
Democratization, 207–14
Depression of the 1930s, 171, 196, 197
Dessalines, Jean-Jacques, 78
Development, 174
 a goal of nationalism, 168
Dias, Bartolomeu, 13
Díaz, Porfirio, 124–25, 127, 130, 133, 143,
 160, 161, 200
Dictatorship, 207, 213
 popular, 233–34
Dominican Republic, 99, 102, 144, 146,
 204, 233–34
Dominicans, 30, 32, 59
Dulles, Allen, 217
Dulles, John Foster, 218, 219–20, 224

Economic planning, 171–72, 197–98
Economic Societies of the Friends of the
 Country, 70, 71
Ecuador, 7, 8, 17, 82, 101, 130, 188, 209,
 210, 212
Education, 156
 and the Cuban Revolution, 227
 and the Guatemalan Revolution, 216
 and the Mexican Revolution, 163–64
 in nineteenth-century Uruguay, 139, 157
 as a privilege of the elite in the
 nineteenth century, 139
 role of the Church in colonial
 education, 61–62
Eisenhower, Dwight D., 219, 224
Ejido, 106, 163, 195
Electrical power, 166, 213, 218
Elites, 152, 153, 154, 160, 168, 188, 203, 213,
 222, 227
El Salvador, 3, 192, 204, 207, 214, 219
 landowning structure, 190
Encomienda, 29–32, 35
England, 39
 interest in trade with colonial Latin
 America, 72, 73
 investment in Latin America by 1914,
 134
 protection to the Braganzas, 76
 see also Great Britain
Enlightenment, 61, 68–71, 75, 78, 91, 96,
 104
 economic influence of on new nations,
 111
 influence on lower classes, 74–75
Estenssoro, Víctor Paz, 222, 223, 224

Europe, 6, 129, 133, 140, 169, 170, 207
European expansion, 11, 12
Exports, 196, 231
 attention to export sector of economy,
 133
 rise of, in last half of nineteenth
 century, 131

Farías, Valentín Gómez, 95, 105, 106
Fazenda, 36
 description of in nineteenth century,
 113–15
Federalism, 91, 101, 122, 124
 in Brazil, 90, 91, 121
 clash between federalism and centralism
 in Argentina, 94–95
 debates over its merits in Spanish
 America, 92
Ferdinand of Aragon, 13, 16, 31, 32
Ferdinand VII, 76, 79, 99, 105
Feudalism, 29, 37, 134, 142, 223
 vestiges of in early twentieth-century
 Mexico, 160
Film industry and Mexican nationalism,
 170
First Republic, 154
Flores, Edmundo, 165
Fonseca, Deodoro da, 123, 153
France, 144
 cultural dependence on, 87
 circulation of French racist doctrines,
 175
 French architectural influence, 138
 French investment in Latin America by
 1914, 134
 and the Haitian slave rebellion, 77–78
 interventions in nineteenth century, 99,
 107
 and the recognition of Haiti, 99
Francia, José Gaspar Rodríguez de, 94
Franciscans, 59
Frei, Eduardo, 211
Freyre, Gilberto, 22, 180
Frondizi, Arturo, 172
Frontier, 169
 as an explanation of Brazilian unity,
 102, 169–70
 influence on Argentine development, 170
Fuero militar, 54

Gallegos, Rómulo, 210
Gálvez, José de, 75
Gálvez, Matías de, 41
Gama, Luís Gonzaga de Pinto, 177

Gama, Vasco de, 14
Gante, Pedro de, 59
Gaucho, 94, 139, 170
Germany, 127
  German investment by 1914, 134
Gold, 15, 16, 18, 22, 27, 33, 38, 39, 44, 50, 51
Golden Law, 177, 178
Goulart, João, 212–13
Government, 142, 227
  early imperial concepts of, 41–43
  functioning of government during
    colonial period, 43–56
Great Britain, 98
  declining influence, 147
  dominant economic position in
    nineteenth-century Latin America,
    110, 111
  interventions in nineteenth-century
    Latin America, 99
  Latin America's economic dependence
    on, 87
  Presence in nineteenth century, 143,
    144
  and railroads, 127
  see also England
Greater Antilles, 5
Grijalva, Juan de, 15
Guanabara Bay, 5
Guaraní, 7
Guatemala, 8, 101, 128, 192, 207, 214, 221,
  232
  education in nineteenth century, 139
  Guatemalan Revolution, 215–20, 224–25,
    228, 230
Guatemala City, 5, 215
Guerrillas, 220, 232
Guiana Highlands, 5
Guillen, Nicolás, 178
Guipúzcoa Company (Caracas Company),
  40, 72–73
Guyana, 181, 182
Guyaquil, 130

Hacienda, 36, 37, 141, 165
  descriptions of in nineteenth century,
    113–15
  size in early twentieth-century Mexico,
    160
Haiti, 3, 22, 23, 67, 76, 102, 146, 182, 188,
  189, 192
  French recognition of, 99
  reevaluation of African past, 178
  struggle for independence, 77–78
Havana, 18, 55, 225
Hay-Pauncefote Treaty, 146

Hernández, José, 139
Hidalgo, Miguel, 78–79, 80, 159, 170
High Court (Relação), 46–47, 52
Hispaniola, 15, 16, 60, 76
Holy Alliance, 98, 105
Honduras, 99, 188, 214, 219
Huerta, Victoriano, 161, 166
Huitzilopochtli, 8
Humboldt, Baron von, 55, 59, 68, 69, 103

Immigration, 51, 119
  contribution to urban growth, 136,
    140–41, 152
Imperialism, 101, 103, 222
  intellectuals denounce U.S. imperialism,
    147
Inca, 7, 11, 17
  civilization, 8–9
  conquest of, 17
Indian cultures:
  early study of, 61
  general characteristics, 7
  similarities among the high cultures,
    9–10
Indians, 35, 160, 168, 175, 220
  Christianization of, 58–61
  divesting the Indian of land, 36
  end to Indian tribute, 111
  European dependence upon, 19–20
  renewed interest in Indian during early
    twentieth century, 176
  role in Mexican independence
    movement, 78–79
  as source of labor, 20, 29–35, 56
  Tupac Amaru Revolt, 74
Industrialization, 39, 136, 141, 153, 155,
  166, 171, 194, 228, 232
  characteristics of, 197
  colonial restrictions on, 41
  early call for, 70
  early economic policies unfavorable
    toward, 111, 112
  effect of railroads on, 128
  growth of working class and labor
    politics, 200–204
  increasing pace of, 196, 198
  in the nineteenth century, 134–36
  problems resulting from, 199
  regarded as the key to change, 196–97
Inflation, 213
Ingenieros, José, 175
Inquisition, 13, 61
Intendency system, 54
Inter-American Conference, First, 145

Intervention, 98–100, 103, 107, 143, 144, 166–67
Investments, 131, 166, 173, 231
  British investments in early nineteenth century, 110, 111
  extent and characteristics of foreign investments by 1914, 134
  mounting foreign investments during the last half of nineteenth century, 133
  rise after 1945, 199
  rise of U.S. investments, 145, 147
Iriberri, José de Cos, 72, 108
Irigoyen, Hipólito, 155–56, 200, 202
Isaacs, Jorge, 138
Isabel, 13, 29
Isabel, Princess of Brazil, 177
Iturbide, Agustín de, 79–80, 81, 92

Jamaica, 181
Jesuits (Company of Jesus), 33, 34, 48, 58, 59, 60, 62
  as educators, 62
John III, 34, 42
John IV, 45
John V, 48
John VI, 45, 76, 83, 89, 91
Johnson, Lyndon, 233
Joseph I, 48
Juárez, Benito, 99, 106, 107

Kennedy, John F., 230, 233
Kidder, Daniel F., 114–15, 121

Labor:
  as basis for populist governments, 201–4
  Blacks as laborers, 21
  changes in labor system in nineteenth century, 111–12
  colonial labor institutions, 29–35
  Indians as laborers, 20
  organization of, 200
Landowning systems, 35–37, 50, 142, 190
  as a cause of misery, 108
  Church ownership of land, 103
  increase in size of estates, 112
  keeps land fallow, 232
  in Mexico, early twentieth century, 160
  related to industrialization, 199
Land reform, 79, 96, 106, 156, 161, 194, 213, 228
  in Bolivia, 223

  in Chile, 211
  and the Church, 212
  in Cuba, 227
  efforts at 194–95
  failure of Batlle to reform Uruguay's land structure, 158
  in Guatemala, 216–20
  in Mexico, 163, 165
  tardiness of, 190–91, 195–96
  in Venezuela, 211
Lanteri, Julieta, 210
La Plata River (and region), 5, 6, 15, 17, 18, 46, 50, 57–58, 60, 94, 100, 103, 110
Lapouge, Georges Vacher de, 175
Latifundia, 36, 120, 142, 190, 192, 195, 223
Lavradio, Marquis of, 36, 41, 46
Law Codes, 43–44
Law of the Free Womb, 177
Le Bon, Gustave, 175
Leguía, Augusto, 176
Leo XII, 104–5
León, Cieza de, 9
León, Juan Ponce de, 15
Leoni, Raúl, 211
Levene, Ricardo, 124
Lewis, Oscar, 206
Ley Juárez, 106
Ley Lerdo, 106
Liberal Alliance, 156
Liberalism:
  goals of nineteenth-century Chilean liberalism, 124
  as a political philosophy in nineteenth century, 105, 120
  in Uruguayan politics, 157
Lima, 15, 21, 55, 57, 61
Lisbon, 44, 45, 46, 47, 49, 83
Literary sources for history, 95, 123, 192–93, 210
  for black history, 179–80
Livestock, 16, 18, 51
Lodge, Henry Cabot, 145
L'Ouverture, Toussaint, 77, 78
Luisi, Paulina, 210
Lutz, Bertha, 210

McGrath, Mark, 25
Madero, Francisco I., 161, 166
Madrid, Treaty of, 50
Magdalena River, 5
Magellan, Ferdinand, 16
Mahan, Alfred T., 145
Maranhao, State of, 47, 48
Mariátegui, José Carlos, 169

Marmol, José, 95, 138
Martí, José, 170, 173
Masonic lodges, 71, 122
Matos, Gregório de, 39
Mauá, Viscount, 127
Maximilian, 99, 107, 124
Mayas, 7, 11
    civilization, 7–8
Mazombos, 49, 67, 75, 76, 83, 89, 91, 101, 115, 140, 141, 142
Mendoza, Antonio de, 52
Mendoza, Pedro de, 18
Mercantilism, 39–41, 72–73, 192
    reaction to by new nations, 111
    vestiges in early twentieth-century Mexico, 160, 166
Mestizo, 19, 51, 74, 78, 79, 82, 140, 141, 162, 175
    in early twentieth-century Mexico, 160
Mexico, 5, 7, 8, 16, 17, 31, 32, 39, 68, 81, 92, 95, 97, 98, 99, 100, 112, 127, 130, 131, 132, 133, 134, 135, 142, 144, 146, 152, 170, 188, 189, 190, 191, 197, 198, 199, 200, 204, 205, 207, 214, 228, 229
    Cárdenas government, 201–2
    the Church question in the nineteenth century, 103, 105–7
    consequences of early economic liberalism, 111
    early evidences of nativism, 68
    lack of preparation for independence, 87–88
    landowning structure, 36
    land reform, 194–95
    Mexican Revolution, 159–68, 170, 210, 215
    Mexican Revolution and the Indian, 176
    military budgets prior to 1850, 96
    movement for independence, 78–80
    political development in the nineteenth century, 124–25
    size of urban middle sector at end of nineteenth century, 140
    Spanish conquest of, 16–17
    Spanish recognition of, 99
    steel industry, 197–98
    unions in, 200
    women, 209, 210
Mexico City, 5, 10, 18, 21, 52, 55, 56, 68, 78, 79, 100, 198
    description of a slum in, 206
Middle class, 188, 203, 205, 208, 213, 227, 229
    increasing identification with the elites, 203–4

Middle sectors, 126, 139, 141, 160, 167
    contribution of immigrants to, 140–41
    description and definition of in late nineteenth-century, 139–40
    in politics, 152–59
    size of, 140
Military, 187, 208
    in Argentine politics, 156
    and Bolivian Revolution, 223–24
    in Chilean politics, 157
    and democratization process, 212, 213
    description of, 213–14
    diminishing role in Mexico, 165
    key to power in nineteenth century, 125
    and middle sectors in Brazil, 1889–1930, 152–55
    military governments in 1960s, 230
    as a national institution, 96, 115
    and the overthrow of Brazilian democracy, 213
    role in overthrow of Brazilian monarchy, 123
    as source of power for caudillos, 95
    as source of power for Iturbide, 92
    subordination to civilian government in Chile, 123
Militia, 49–50, 54, 73, 74, 76, 223
Minifundia, 190, 191, 195
Mining, 38, 110, 112, 134
Miranda, Francisco de, 69
Missionaries, 58, 59, 60
Missions, 60
    description of 59–60
Mistral, Gabriela, 209
Mita, 33
Mitre, Bartolomé, 71, 124, 139
Moderative power, 90
Modernization, 123, 125–31, 141, 142, 155, 188, 194, 227, 228, 232
    caudillos as modernizers, 93–94
    contrasting modern and traditional societies, 188–90
    failures of, 189–90
    as a goal of nationalism, 168
    importance of industrialization to, 196–97
Molina, Maria Dolores Bedoya de, 209
Monarchy, 153
    adopted in Brazil, 89–90
    debated in Spanish America, 91–92
    Mexico adopts monarchy, 91
    as a reason for Brazilian unity, 101–2, 121
    role in colonial empires, 42
Monoculture, 37, 38
Monroe, James, 98, 143

Monroe Doctrine, 98, 143
Monte Caseros, Battle of, 95
Montt, Manuel, 124
Mora, José Maria Luis, 95
Morelos, José María, 79, 80, 159
Moret Law, 176–77
Morrow, Dwight W., , 166, 167
Mosquera, Tomás Cipriano, 92
Mulatto, 22, 74, 77, 140
Municipal government:
  in colonial Brazil, 48–49
  in colonial Spanish America, 52–53
  source of power for Americans, 76, 81

Napoleon, 76, 77
Napoleon III, 99, 107, 144
Nationalism, 67, 83, 119, 155, 156, 213, 228
  in the Caribbean, 181
  and change, 168–74
  in Cuba, 226
  cultural, 164, 169–70
  definition, 168
  economic, 166, 171–74, 216
  in Guatemala, 216, 218
  and the racial heritage of Latin America,
    175, 176
Nationalization:
  bauxite in Guyana, 182
  copper in Chile, 174
  oil and sugar estates in Peru, 174
  oil in Bolivia, 172, 174, 221, 225
  oil in Mexico, 166, 172, 221
  railroads in Mexico, 166
  tin in Bolivia, 222–23
  of U.S. property in Cuba, 226
National Renovation Party (RN), 215, 216
National Revolutionary Movement
    (MNR), 222, 223, 224
Nativism, 67, 70, 73, 75, 76, 80
  manifestations of, 68, 168
New Christians, 61
New Laws of 1542, 32
New Spain, 52, 68, 78, 80, 103
Newspapers, 70–71, 138
Nicaragua, 121, 125, 146, 210
Nixon, Richard, 214, 230
Nóbrega, Manuel da, 33, 59

Obregón, Alvaro, 161, 162, 163–64, 165, 167
O'Higgins, Bernardo, 70, 81, 92
Oil, 156, 162, 166, 197
  as a cause of Chaco War, 221
  as a nationalist issue, 172
Oligarchy, 152, 154, 155, 156, 230

Olney, Richard, 146
Orellana, Francisco de, 17
Orinoco River, 5, 210
Orozco, José, 164
Ortiz, Fernando, 178
Ortiz, Josefa, 210
Overseas Council, 45

Pacific Mail Company, 110
Pacific Steam Navigation Company, 109
Palma, Ricardo, 138–39
Pampas, 6, 57
  exploitation of Argentine pampas in
    late nineteenth century, 132–33
Panama, 15, 17, 56, 57, 156–57, 204, 214
Panama Canal, 146, 147
Paraguay, 81, 94, 101, 103, 188, 204, 214,
    221
  important role of the woman, 210
  landowning structure, 190
Paraguay River, 6
Paraná River, 6
Parliamentary government, 91, 97, 122, 157
Party of Revolutionary Institutions (PRI),
    164–65, 167
Passarinho, Jarbas, 232
Patriarchy, 142
  caudillismo as an inheritance of, 93
  in colonial Brazil, 50, 51
  in nineteenth century, 112–113
Patrimonialism, 37, 39
Patrocínio, José Carlos do, 177
Paul III, Pope, 32
Peasants, 18, 35, 108, 136, 153, 154–55, 163,
    188, 190, 194, 196, 215, 220, 222, 223,
    227
  and land reform, 194–95
  misery of, 192–94
  participation in Mexican Revolution,
    159, 160, 162, 165
  Peasant Leagues, 196
Pedro I, 83, 89, 90, 91, 92, 110, 121
Pedro II, 91, 121, 122, 123, 129
  description of, 121–22
Peña, Roque Saenz, 155
Peninsular, 75, 78, 79, 80
Pérez, José Joaquín, 124
Perón, Eva Duarte de, 202
Perón, Juan D., 198, 200, 202–3
Pershing, John, 167
Peru, 7, 17, 18, 32, 39, 52, 55, 57, 82, 98,
    101, 102, 112, 144, 168, 172, 174, 176,
    198, 204, 206, 207, 209, 214
Peurifoy, John, 219
Philip III, 34

Philip V, 53
Physiocrat doctrine, 71
Picchia, Menotti del, 179
Pita, Sebastião da Rocha, 68
Pizarro, Francisco, 17
Pizarro, Gonzalo, 17
Plan of Ayala, 161
Plan of Ayutla, 106
Plan of San Luis Potosí, 161
Plantation economy, 37, 50, 114–15
  description of slave labor on nineteenth-century Brazilian coffee plantation, 132
Plaza, Galo, 174
Political parties, 120–21, 211, 215
Polk, James, 143
Pombal, Marquis of, 48, 62
Population:
  of Brazil at end of eighteenth century, 50–51
  of Brazil in nineteenth century, 152–53
  of cities, 137
  distribution, 5
  of Latin America, 1900, 136
  of Latin America, 1971, 3
  overpopulation, 3–4
  Spanish America at end of eighteenth century, 55
Populist government, 200, 212–213
Portales, Diego, 123, 124, 157
Porto Bello, 40
  description at mid-eighteenth century, 56
Portugal, 11–13, 14, 39, 40, 41, 43, 45, 49, 50, 51, 76, 91, 98
  early trade with Brazil, 15
  and the independence of Brazil, 83, 89
  recognition of Brazil, 99
Positivism, 129–30
Potosí, 33, 57
Prado, Eduardo, 147
Presidencia, 52
Price-Mars, Jean, 178
Proletariat, see Working class (urban)
Puerto Rico, 60, 146
  abolition of slavery, 176
Punta del Este, 194

Querino, Manuel Raimundo, 179
Quesada, Gonzalo Jiménez, 17
Quito, 5, 18

Racial attitudes, 179, 183
  changing of toward blacks, 176–78, 180

circulation of specious European racial doctrines, 175–76
Racial discrimination, 179, 180, 181, 182, 183
Racial mixture, 3, 19, 22, 50, 77, 169
Railroad, 127–28, 134, 157, 169
Ramírez, José Antonio Alzate, 69
Ramos, Graciliano, 192–93
Rebouças, André, 176
Recognition of new states, 99–100
Recopilación de Leyes de las Indias, 43
Reducción, 59
Reform, 160, 211, 235
  and the Church, 212
  definition of, 155
  desire for reform in early twentieth century, 151
  general failure of, 214, 215
  and middle sectors, 152
  and military, 155
  political parties advocating reform, 211
  in Uruguay, 158–59
Refrigerator ship, 132, 133
Regionalism, 101, 102, 169
Reinóis, 49, 75
Repartimiento, 32–33, 35
Residencia, 43
Revolution, 187, 215, 228, 235
  the Bolivian Revolution, 220–25
  comparison of Mexican, Guatemalan, Bolivian, and Cuban revolutions, 228
  the Cuban Revolution, 225–30
  definition of, 160
  the Guatemalan Revolution, 215–20
  the Mexican Revolution, 159–68
Río, José Mora y del, 164
Rio-Branco, Visconde do, 176
Rio de Janeiro, 5, 44, 46, 47, 76, 82, 137
  Rio Conference, 1942, 207
Rio Grande, 3
Rivera, Diego, 164, 168
Roads, early travel by, 100–101, 130
Rodó, José Enrique, 147, 169
Rodrigues, Raimundo Nina, 178
Rojas, Ricardo, 169, 170
Romanticism, 138
Roosevelt, Franklin D., 166, 167
Rosas, Juan Manuel de, 94–95, 99, 124, 169
Royal Mail Steam Packet Company, 109, 110
Royal Patronage, 58–59, 90, 104, 107
Russia, 98

Sabugosa, Conde de, 46

Salas, Manuel de, 72
Salvador da Bahia, 5, 21, 22, 46, 47
Sá, Mem de, 45
San Martín, Grau, 226
San Martín, José de, 70, 81, 82, 92
Santa Anna, Antonio López de, 95, 106, 124
Santiago (Chile), 18
    description of, 138
    population growth, 137
São Carlos, Francisco de, 68
São Paulo, 5, 198
    growth and description of the city, 137
Sarmiento, Domingo Faustino, 139
Senado da Câmara, 48–49
Sepúlveda, Juan Ginés de, 32
Sertão, 51
Sesmarias, 35, 36
Seville, 16
Siles, Hernán, 224
Silver, 16, 18, 27, 33, 57
Slave revolts, 22, 178
    fear of in Brazil, 101
    Haiti, 77–78
    praise of resistance of blacks to slavery in Brazil, 178
Slavery, 21, 134, 153
    abolition after independence, 82, 111–12 123, 176
    abolition of slavery in Brazil, 176–78
    abolition of slavery in Cuba, 176–77
    beginning of black slavery in New World, 21
    beginning of black slavery in Portugal, 21
    description of slave labor on a nineteenth-century Brazilian coffee plantation, 132
    slavery of Indians, 30, 33, 34, 35
Slums, 205–7
Smith, Adam, 111
Social welfare, 156, 157, 158, 159, 163, 200–204, 216
Society for Afro-Cuban Studies, 178
Solís, Juan Díaz, 15
Sousa, Luís de Vasconcelos e, 46
Sousa, Tomé de, 58
Soviet Union, 223, 226; *see also* Russia
Spain, 13–14, 16, 39, 40, 50, 51, 52, 57, 70, 72, 76, 78, 98, 144, 146
    Constitution of 1812, 97
    pressure applied to abolish slavery in Caribbean, 176–77
    search for westward passage, 15, 16
    Spanish intervention in nineteenth-century Latin America, 98–99

Stability, search for in the newly independent countries, 89–94
Steam engine, 126
Steamship, 109, 129, 147, 169
Steel, 197–98
Strong, Josiah, 145
Sucre, José de, 81, 82, 92
Sugar, 16, 27, 37, 38, 44, 46, 50, 51, 71, 77, 225
Surinam, 181
Sutherland, Elizabeth, 182–83

Taxes, 38–39, 47, 82
    in Guatemala in the 1940s, 215, 217
    protests against, 71, 73–74
Telegraph, 128–29, 147, 169
Tenentes, 155
Tenochtitlán, 8, 9
Terry, Fernando Belaúnde, 172
Texas, 101, 143, 144
Textiles, 15, 135, 197
Tierra del Fuego, 6
Tin, 221, 222, 225
Todos os Santos Bay, 5
Toledo, Francisco de, 52
Tordesillas, Treaty of, 13–14, 50
Toro, David, 221–22
Torres, Camilo, 233
Torres, Juan José, 224
Torres, Ramón Casaus y, 105
Trade:
    growing U.S.–Latin American trade, 145
    growth of, in first half of nineteenth century, 108–9
    growth of, in last half of nineteenth century, 131–32
Transandine Telegraph Company, 129
Transportation:
    consequences of improving international transportation, 109
    physical difficulties of, 100–101
Treasury Council, 45
Trinidad and Tobago, 181
Trujillo, Rafael, 233
Tupac Amaru Revolt, 74
Tupí, 7, 10–11
Tyler, John, 143

Ubico, Jorge, 33, 207, 215, 216, 219
Ugarte, Manuel, 147
Underdevelopment:
    improper economic theories adopted, 111
    paradox of poverty in plenty, 107–8
Unión Cívica Radical, 155, 156

Unions, 156, 158, 163, 200–204, 216, 223
United Fruit Company, 216, 217, 218, 219
United Nations Economic Commission for
    Latin America, 173
United States of America, 69, 72, 82, 91,
    95, 98, 101, 102, 109, 129, 133, 142,
    207, 212, 214
  and Alliance for Progress, 230, 231
  compared, 224–25
  and Cuba, 225–26
  and the Dominican Republic, 233
  emergence as principal consumer of
    Latin American exports, 131
  extent of business penetration in Latin
    America, 173
  and Guatemala, 217–20
  as a model for modernization, 126
  nationalists attack, 173–74
  reactions to Bolivian and Guatemalan
    revolutions
  reaction to Mexican Revolution, 166–67
  reaction to revolution, 228
  and the recognition of new Latin
    American states, 99–100
  relations with Latin America,
    1823–1914, 143–47
  rise in investments after World War II,
    199
  U.S. investment by 1914, 134
Unity, difficulties in maintaining, 100–102
Universities, 61–62, 70, 138
Urban interests, 123, 205
  opposed to rural interests in Brazil, 153
Urbanization, 18, 136, 141, 204–7
  definition of urban, 136
  effect of railroads on, 128
  urban growth and conditions, 136–38,
    204–7
Uruguay, 5, 6, 94, 95, 101, 102, 103, 125,
    140, 152, 171, 198, 204, 214, 229
  education in nineteenth century, 139
  role of the middle sectors, 157–59
  women, 210
Uruguay River, 6, 127

Valdes, Gabriel, 173
Valdivia, Pedro de, 17
Valparaiso, description of, 137
Varela, José Pedro, 139
Vargas, Getúlio, 172, 197, 200, 201, 207, 208
Vasconcelos, José, 163, 164, 169
Vasconcelos, Zacharias de Góis e, 122
Venezuela, 17, 54, 72–73, 81, 82, 97, 101,
    127, 189, 191, 198, 204, 206, 207, 214

Vera Cruz, 40
Vial, Manuel Camilo, 134
Viceroy, 44, 45, 46, 47, 48, 52, 54, 75
Viceroyalty, 45, 46, 52, 54, 83, 101
Vieira, Antonio, 33
Vilhena, Luís dos Santos, 107
Villa, Francisco, 161, 162, 166–167
Villegas, Daniel Cosío, 87–88, 168
Violence:
  as the path to power in nineteenth-
    century Latin America, 93
  violent protest in Brazil, 1922–1930,
    154–55
Visita, 43
Visitador, 13, 75

War:
  influenced role of women in Latin
    American society, 210
  in the nineteenth century, 102–3
War of the Pacific, 102, 210
War of the Reform, 107
War of the Spanish Succession, 53
War of the Triple Alliance, 103, 210
West Indies, 46
Wilson, Henry Lane, 166
Wilson, Woodrow, 166
Women:
  in Brazil in mid-nineteenth century,
    115
  in Chile at end of nineteenth century,
    137–38
  in the conquest, 19
  in development of Latin America,
    209–11
  as plantation manager, 114–15, 210
  role of Eva Perón, 202
  and voting, 208, 210
Working class (urban), 152, 156, 159, 160,
    163, 165, 171, 188, 200–204, 205, 208,
    215, 227
World War I, 134
World War II, 207

Yoruba, 178
Yriart, Juan Felipe, 231
Yucatan, 8, 15, 17

Zapata, Emiliano, 161, 162, 176
Zumárraga, Juan de, 59

copy 1

LATIN AMERICA: A CONCISE INTERPRETIVE HISTORY
E. Bradford Burns

"Latin America is a huge region in the process of change from a traditional to a more modern society. At some times and in some places the pace of that change has been nearly imperceptible. Yet, at other times and in other places the change has taken place at a dizzying speed. Though change has been erratic, sometimes ineffectual, often spotty, and occasionally reversed, it is nonetheless the most salient characteristic of Latin America in the twentieth century."

— from the *Preface*

It is of critical importance that the tension, stress, and change that characterize present day Latin America be viewed in a broader perspective than the current preoccupation with its immediate effect on the international scene. The forces that shaped the current Latin American crises can best be understood against the panoramic background of Latin American history and culture. This outstanding book presents such a multidimensional and interpretive view.

HIGHLIGHTS INCLUDE:

THE ORIGINS OF A MULTIRACIAL SOCIETY
CONFRONTATION AND CONQUEST
THE INSTITUTIONS OF EMPIRE
INDEPENDENCE: A CHANGING MENTALITY
 BEGETS NEW ATTITUDES AND ACTION
THE TRANSFER AND LEGITIMIZATION OF POWER
THE EMERGENCE OF THE MODERN STATE
THE PRESENCE OF THE UNITED STATES
MEXICO'S VIOLENT RESPONSE TO THE PAST
NATIONALISM AS A FORCE FOR CHANGE
DEVELOPMENT, DEMOCRACY, AND DISILLUSIONMENT
CHANGING RACIAL ATTITUDES
THE REVOLUTIONARY OPTION

Prentice-Hall, Inc., Englewood Cliffs, New Jersey

0-13-52429

DATE DUE